The Unabridged Vegetable Cookbook

Nika Hazelton

The Unabridged Vegetable Cookbook

Drawings by Shelly Sacks

M. EVANS AND COMPANY, INC.
New York, New York 10017

M. Evans and Company titles are distributed in
the United States by the J. B. Lippincott Company,
East Washington Square, Philadelphia, Pa. 19105;
and in Canada by McClelland & Stewart Ltd.,
25 Hollinger Road, Toronto M4B 3G2, Ontario

Library of Congress Cataloging in Publication Data

Hazelton, Nika Standen.
  The unabridged vegetable cookbook.

  Bibliography: p.
  Includes index.
  1. Cookery (Vegetables) 2. Vegetables.
I. Title.
TX801.H37   641.5'636   76-23451
ISBN 0-87131-213-1

Design by Joel Schick

Manufactured in the United States of America

9 8 7 6 5 4 3 2 1

For my son, Julian

ACKNOWLEDGMENTS

My special thanks go to two people who have helped me greatly with this book: Martha Durham, a researcher, and R. A. Seelig, of the United Fresh Fruit and Vegetable Association of Washington, D.C.

I am also indebted to Messrs. Theodore Torrey, Manager of Vegetable Research, W. Atlee Burpee Co.; Pete Bonucci, Garden Seed Coordinator at Northrup, King & Co.; Dr. Alan Stoner, Research Horticulturist for USDA, Vegetable Laboratory of the Agricultural Research Center; and to Derek Fell, Director of the National Garden Bureau and Director of All-America Selections.

Preface

This book is about fresh vegetables, their history, nutrition, and ways of keeping and preparing them. Any plant eaten as a vegetable rather than as a fruit has been included, regardless of its botanical classification.* For instance, the tomato is a fruit, which we eat as a vegetable, whereas rhubarb is a vegetable we eat as a fruit. I have only discussed vegetables that are available in the United States, omitting many tropical, exotic and rare vegetables which would be hard to find in our country.

As in all but standard cookbooks, the recipes reflect my personal preferences. I have tried not to repeat the excellent, basic recipes found in standard cookbooks. I have chosen dishes which feature a specific vegetable, rather than the many soups, stews and casseroles in which vegetables play a secondary part. I have omitted recipes that struck me as uncommonly exotic, such as some Latin American, African and Oriental dishes.

My basic usage instructions reflect my own experiences: I think vegetables should be eaten as fresh as possible, and I consider overcooking the death of almost any vegetable. I also think that, in general, vegetables should be cooked simply to let their own flavor dominate without confusing it with too many herbs, seasonings and other ingredients. Vegetable cookery is mostly a matter of timing;

* Sources used for botanical information include Webster's Second International Dictionary and Webster's Third New International Dictionary.

and the successful cook tends to rely on judgment rather than careful measurement.

The nutritional statements and caloric figures are based upon the definitive source on the subject, *Composition of Foods, Hand Book No. 8*, Agricultural Research Service of the United States Department of Agriculture.* The caloric values are based upon 100 grams, which translates to about 3½ ounces. This amount is close enough to 4 ounces, or ½ cup (liquid) measure, an average vegetable helping. Generally speaking, there is little difference in the number of calories in cooked, unseasoned vegetables whether fresh, canned or frozen.

Finally, I may add that this book is based upon a lifetime preference for vegetables over other foods.

* For sale by the Superintendent of Documents, U.S. Government Printing Office, Washington, D.C.

Vegetables Then and Now

Primitive man initially gathered the edible parts of wild plants for food, an interesting and admirable effort, though not quite as brave as trying the first oyster or lobster. From this first step, the realization followed that the seeds of some food plants, notably the grasses, could be sown, harvested and stored. Wheat and barley, two of our oldest crops, were apparently cultivated in the Middle East between 8000 and 5000 BC, and rice was a staple crop in China as early as 2800 BC. Whether this early crop cultivation occurred by accident or purpose we cannot know, but we do know that it was the essential step towards civilization. Agriculture enabled man to develop a settled, stable way of life without which civilization could not have developed.

Man's transition from food-collector to food-cultivator was a slow one, taking thousands of years during which many plants evolved from their original wild state. It is difficult to retrace the paths of evolution: by natural variation, human selection of seeds, and natural or man-made hybridization, many food plants have changed considerably. This especially holds true for the cucumber, onion, sweet corn, white and sweet potato and squash, to mention a few, whose wild ancestors are impossible to identify.

The presence of a wide variety of food plants in different parts of the world is largely due to the activities of man. In very early times, these plants traveled to parts of the world that were easily reached by land. Later the seafaring and empire-building nations of antiquity, such as the Phoenicians, the Persians, the Romans and the Arabs,

9

introduced their native food plants to places that were not familiar with them.

The great, all-important interchange of crops took place after 1492, when Columbus, returning from his first voyage, took back to Spain the first corn ever to reach Europe, and on his second voyage, brought European seeds back to America. Among the crops introduced to America from the Old World were citrus, sugar cane and rice, as well as all the European crops familiar to the settlers of the temperate zones. But the exchange of food plants was not limited to America and Europe. The ships of the slave traders, along with their infamous cargoes, brought to America the food crops of West Africa such as yams and pigeon peas, and brought back to Africa American crops such as corn and cassava. Within a short time, these New World plants were being widely cultivated in Africa, supplementing the limited crops native to the regions south of the Sahara. Other trading between continents brought bananas and rice to Africa via Portuguese ships coming from Asia; chiles from America were brought to Asia and enabled the Indians to make hotter curries. In Australia, food crops date back to the first European settlements at the end of the 18th century, since the native aborigines did not cultivate plants. Coffee, which originated in Ethiopia, traveled first from Mocha and then Java to Latin America where it became a primary cash crop, and pineapple, from Brazil, became equally important to Hawaii and some Caribbean islands.

It is unfortunately beyond the scope of this book to treat the history of food plants more fully than it is in the following pages. Suffice it to say that the improvement of food plants is by no means a new practice. Seed selection was a fine art in the 18th century, and the emergence of the science of genetics in the 19th century enabled plant breeders to select suitable parent plants, or hybridize them or produce new genetic variations by treating plants with chemicals or even x-rays. The sight of plants treated with controlled radiation, which I saw years ago at the atomic labs in Brookhaven, was bizarre. Yet experiments in radiation genetics by the Atomic Energy Commission have also produced rust-resistant oats and peanuts with a 30 per cent higher yield. And science did double the yield of many crops during the last century, as well as improving greatly on their quality.

All of this brings us to the future of vegetables.

Vegetables, A Brave New World

Scientific plant breeding has other purposes besides the obvious ones of producing larger yields, better quality, and greater ease of growing and handling. It is also concerned with the plants' increased tolerance to heat and frost, with their suitability for various soils and climates and their resistance to diseases and pests, with more uniform sizes, shapes and maturing times, and of course, with better looks. Breeding objectives often differ for commercial shippers and processors and for the home gardener and roadside stand. Commercial growers and shippers labor under the external pressures of mass merchandising demands. Supermarket chains, which sell practically all of the nation's food, require carrots and potatoes of a size and quality that can be uniformly graded and packaged. The supermarket green bean must have a high fiber content so that it can remain on the shelves for a week before wilting, whereas the home gardener's tender, low-fiber bean goes into the pot soon after it is picked. Commercial shippers must produce tomatoes for specific uses; the 1975 catalog of the Ferry-Morse Seed Company, one of the nation's most important, lists some 40 varieties of commercial tomatoes. Eating tomatoes are different from tomato-paste tomatoes, and tomatoes to be canned whole must be able to retain their shape. The commercial producer needs tomatoes that do not crack, that stand up to mechanical harvesting, that come off the plant easily, that mature uniformly and that ship well. Some growers say that to transport a fully ripened tomato would be either impossible or prohibitively expensive. Consequently, commercially grown tomatoes have to be harvested when immature and then allowed to ripen in transit and after reaching their destination. Locally grown tomatoes can be ripened fully on the vine, and there is no need for me to go into the flavor difference. The reason many supermarkets, even at the height of the local tomato season, sell their anemic-looking imitations of the real thing is that many supermarkets find it simpler to order from growers thousands of miles away because local tomatoes are too tender (is this an euphemism for being really ripe, I wonder?) and therefore bruisable and wasteful in the distribution to the supermarket chain's branch stores.

Besides meeting the demands of mass merchandising, the plant breeder has many other objectives. One is working on smaller sized vegetables, since families tend to be smaller nowadays. An over-sized, 5-pound head of cabbage for a family of three sits around in the refrigerator for two weeks; a 2- or 2½-pound size would be more practical. A small watermelon weighing 5 pounds, designed for a small family, has already proved to be popular. Carrots, too, are bred for different purposes: the small Nantes variety is of high eating quality which also cans well whole or in slices whereas the Chantenay is a big triangular carrot, grown for dicing, and the Imperator, long and slim, has a shape that ships well. Pumpkins vary according to their use; the canner wants flesh of more specific gravity and a less watery texture, but for the jack-o'-lantern trade the big aim is a stem that will stay on the plant.

The most spectacular results of scientific breeding are the plants that could help combat malnutrition in some parts of the world if social and physical obstacles could be overcome. There are new rice varieties that have increased yields from the world average of 1300 pounds of milled rice an acre to between 1700 and 2100 pounds, that are more pest-resistant, that are adapted to new growing conditions and that need far less fertilizer. We know of the production miracle of hybrid corn, but going even further, a new type of corn has been developed which has nearly doubled the effective protein content of normal corn, surpassing that of milk.

The genetic breeding of new, improved plant varieties has not solely transformed the commercial production of vegetables. Closely linked to it is the advent of the mechanical harvester, which has already taken over the work of tens of thousands of agricultural workers in the endless vegetable fields of California, Arizona, Texas and other states. Lettuce, celery, spinach, cauliflower, tomatoes, corn, onions and peas are among the mechanized vegetable crops, and more and more mechanical harvesting is being done for fruits. To illustrate the machine's usefulness: in the early Sixties in California, 125,000 acres of tomatoes had to be picked by a labor force of 40,000, and while an average bean picker can pick 1.06 bushels per hour by hand, a single operator can pick 95.8 bushels per hour by machine. Yet harvesters are harder on plants than skilled human hands; with beans, for instance, a greater quantity of immature and broken beans and leaves are left which have to be removed from the fields.

Mechanical harvesters are cleverly designed and constantly improved upon. Harvester celery, for instance, is packed in the field on a mobile packing house called a mule train. Workers preceding the mule train cut the roots off the celery with a knife and break off unwanted parts from the stalk, which is popularly called a bunch. These are then placed on a wing conveyer and transported to the center of the mule train where they are cut to standard length, spray washed, packed into wire-bound crates and then loaded on trucks bound for pre-cooling in the plant to keep fresh. Meanwhile, the machine returns stalk tops and other unwanted parts to the ground, to be turned over later.

After harvesting, there is the costly job of getting vegetables to the packing plant in good condition, cooling them before and after packing, providing proper moisture, ventilation and so on, which are all problems of a technical complexity stunning to the layman. A leaf of lettuce, besides being one of nature's wonders, is also a wonder of scientific ingenuity by the time it reaches our table; and lettuce marketing costs in 1969 amounted to 63 per cent of the price the consumer paid for it.

The parties involved in plant breeding work are the commercial seed companies which do it for profit, the United States Department of Agriculture which frequently works with state research stations which are usually connected with a university, and some amateurs. One of the ways by which their efforts are judged each year are the All-American Selections (National Seed Trials). New vegetables are grown in 25 separate trial gardens in the United States, Canada and Mexico under every possible climatic condition and successful new varieties are given an award. Research for the award has given us sweet corn with a very small cob, peas with pods that stay tender even when the peas are large, and cauliflower with the remarkable characteristic of growing a full head with the leaves already tightly curled over the head to keep it white (previously the leaves had to be hand-tied). From the Orient new vegetables are also in the offing. The industrious breeders of Taiwan are working on heat-resistant potatoes, soybeans and Chinese cabbages; and the Japanese are working on an edible mushroom which can be grown indoors on a dish of sawdust within two weeks of sowing the spores.

What About the Flavor?

Given the plant breeder's relentless search for brave new vegetables, one might well ask what has happened to the flavor of those beauties bred for commerce. For years, breeders were mainly concerned with factors such as disease resistance, size and yield; but within the last five years, according to one expert, there has been a renewed emphasis on what are charmingly called quality factors. Technical questions, such as the ones mentioned above, have so nearly been answered that breeders can now take a second look at qualities like flavor, and there is also public demand for better tasting vegetables, thanks to the boom in home gardening and the general awareness of natural foods. At Northrup King, a major seed company, they are working on a more beany taste in bush beans, by putting the very beany Blue Lake pole bean into a bush plant. The "bitter principle" is being bred out of cucumbers, and we may also anticipate sweeter corn. The acidity in tomatoes is another concern since the flavor in a tomato, to a large extent, depends on the ratio of sugar and acid. The fashionable sweet and mild yellow tomatoes, for example, which have been advertised as low-acid or acid-free, merely taste less acid because of their higher amounts of sugar.

According to the experts, it is flavor rather than nutrition that people now demand in vegetables. However nutritious, if it doesn't taste good no one will eat it. An example of this is a new orange-red tomato, developed at Purdue University, which has been proven to have ten times the vitamin C content of most other tomatoes—but it tastes terrible.

Concerning the flavor of vegetables, we shall see what we shall see. But looking back at the meager choice of fresh produce of a few years back, and to what is available now, I think that fresh vegetables are here to stay.

Canning and Freezing

The home canning and freezing of vegetables has once more become a matter of great public interest, and it would seem natural to find instructions for both in these pages. The reason that there are none is that after consulting experts in both fields, I have been assured by them that it would not be possible, in the space of this book, to tell how to do both properly and safely; it is enough to mention that deadly botulism may be caused by improperly home-canned goods.

Since neither canning nor freezing improves the quality of food, it is essential to start with high quality raw materials. It is not worthwhile to preserve anything that is not absolutely fresh, selected at the stage of maturity best for table use, remembering that vegetable varieties differ when grown in different soil and climatic conditions and that some varieties also can freeze better than others. Immature vegetables will lack flavor and may shrivel; starchy, overmature ones may lose flavor and develop a fibrous texture. In other words, vegetables must be processed at their peak, or as the saying goes, "Two hours from the garden to the freezer." Obviously this is not possible without a home garden or access to a reliable farm stand with the varieties best suited for preservation. As I know from experience, store-bought city vegetables are seldom worth preserving. Proper freezers are essential for successful freezing and not many city apartments have them; the freezing compartments of refrigerators do not have the necessary, constant low temperatures that are necessary to preserve food safely. And with all preserving, costs must be considered: it is one thing to buy one's vegetables and another, to grow them oneself. There are also the cost of canning equipment, the cost of the freezer itself and the cost of operating it.

The general freezing directions found in many books are most inadequate, frequently for lack of space. Thus canning and/or freezing vegetables deserve books of their own, and for those interested, there are up-to-date sources. I stress the importance of being up-to-date, since research in food preservation continues and technology changes. Here are three recommended sources of information:

1. *Home Freezing of Fruits and Vegetables*, published by the Agricultural Research Service, a consumer service of USDA. For a *free* copy, write to Office of Communication, United States Department of Agriculture, Washington, D.C., 20250, and request Home Garden Bulletin No. 10: Home Freezing of Fruit and Vegetables.

2. *Putting Food By*, by Ruth Hertzberg, Beatrice Vaughan and Janet Greene, The Stephen Greene Press, Brattleboro, Vermont, soft cover, $4.95.

3. *Handbook for Freezing Foods*, by Mable Doremus and Ruth Klippstein, Cornell Extension Bulletin 1179, Cornell University, Ithaca, New York, 50¢. However, the vegetables mentioned are for New York State which does not necessarily help people in other parts of the country.

I recommend getting in touch with the Agricultural Extension Services and County Agents of the different states for pertinent local information. I am also told that the accurate material is put out by the makers of canning jars, such as Ball or Mason.

The Unabridged Vegetable Cookbook

AKEE
Ackee

Blighia sapida

The fruit of a tropical evergreen tree of West African origin which is now grown in the West Indies, whose edible part looks like a small heap of solidified scrambled eggs. Thanks to its appearance and rather oily consistency, akee is known as "the poor man's scrambled eggs" in Jamaica, where together with salt codfish, it becomes the island's national dish. However, akee, which is rather bland, is also used with meats, cheese and in au gratin dishes, or boiled or fried.

The akee fruit is about three inches long and red when ripe. The ripe fruit opens naturally, usually displaying three black seeds in each fruit. These seeds are surrounded by a flesh-colored aril which is the edible part of the akee; some people have compared its appearance to a tiny creased brain. Great care must be taken to avoid the pink tissue joining the aril to the seed since it is highly poisonous, as are the underripe or overripe fruit. Only ripe, naturally opened fruit should be used. In spite of these inherent dangers, akee is widely used and canned for export—it is perfectly safe in this form, as I, with all the Jamaican expatriates sighing for akee the world over, can testify.

AKEES AND CHEESE

4 servings

Serve on hot boiled rice or toast.

2 tablespoons butter
1 small onion, minced
1 16- or 18-ounce can akees,
   drained

1 cup grated Swiss or Cheddar
   cheese
freshly ground pepper
2 tablespoons minced parsley

Heat the butter in a frying pan. Cook the onion until it is soft and golden. Add the akees. Cook, stirring with a fork as you would cook scrambled eggs, for 3 or 4 minutes or until thoroughly heated through. Stir in the cheese. Cook, stirring all the time, until the cheese is melted. Remove from heat and season with pepper. Sprinkle with the parsley before serving.

JAMAICAN SALT COD AND AKEE

4-6 servings

Serve with rice and beans.

1 pound salt cod
1 pound fresh akees or 1 16- or
  18-ounce can akees, drained
4 slices lean bacon, diced, or 4
  ounces blanched salt pork,
  diced
1 onion, cut into thin rings
2 medium onions, minced
1 garlic clove, mashed

2 medium tomatoes, peeled and
  chopped
¼ teaspoon dried thyme
½ teaspoon minced seeded hot
  pepper or to taste or hot
  pepper sauce to taste
2 tablespoons melted butter
freshly ground pepper

Soak the cod in water to cover overnight. Drain. Cook in fresh water to cover until flaky and tender. Drain and remove any skin and bones. Flake the fish. While the fish is cooking, cook the fresh akees over low heat in water to cover for 15 minutes. Drain and add to the fish. In a large frying pan, cook the bacon or the salt pork until crisp. Remove the cooked bacon or pork bits with a slotted spoon and add them to the fish and the akees. Pour off half of the fat. Cook the sliced onion in the remaining fat until crisp. Remove with a slotted spoon and set aside. Cook the minced onion and garlic in the fat until the onions are tender and golden brown. Add the tomatoes, the thyme and the hot pepper. Cook, stirring constantly, for about 5 minutes. Add the flaked fish, the akees and the bacon or pork bits. Stir carefully with a fork. Cook over low heat, stirring frequently, for about 5 minutes. The dish must be thoroughly blended and heated through. Stir the melted butter into the dish. Turn into a heated serving dish and garnish with the onion slices and freshly ground black pepper.

ANNATTO

Bixa orellana

The common-usage name for the seeds of the tree, native to the West Indies and the South American tropics. Annatto seeds, after treatment, yield an orangy-reddish powder used as a dye both for foodstuffs and for industrial uses. Cheddar cheese and butter are two outstanding examples of annatto-dyeing, which is legal and harmless to health. Annatto is also widely used as a seasoning in Latin American and Philippine cooking, especially as an inexpensive saffron substitute. It makes food look a glorious, radiant orange-yellow.

ANNATTO OIL OR LARD

1 cup

Some West Indian, especially Puerto Rican, cooking uses this colorful flavored oil or lard as a basic fat.

1 cup salad oil or lard   ½ cup annatto seeds

Heat the oil or lard in a small saucepan. Add the annatto seeds. Cook over low heat, stirring frequently, until the fat colors a rich orange. Remove from heat immediately when the color starts to lighten. Strain into a jar. Cover and refrigerate. The fat will keep for months.

ARROWHEAD
Duck Potato
Sagittaria latifolia

One of the American varieties of a worldwide family of freshwater plants whose fleshy underground tubers were eaten by the Indians as a potato substitute. The hard tubers are about the size of a walnut; they grow at the ends of long subterranean runners, so far from the parent plant that it is said the Indians relied on stores which they found already assembled by muskrats. The tubers, practically all starch, are white on the inside and have a milky juice which is rather nasty when raw. After cooking, however, it becomes sweetish; the cooked tuber has a kind of diminished sweet-potato taste. The Indians boiled or roasted them in hot ashes. An authority recommends the tubers be baked or boiled in a little salted water until tender but firm, peeled and mashed or quartered and eaten with butter, pepper and salt, or chilled, sliced and served with a vinaigrette dressing.

Other arrowhead varieties are grown in the Orient, notably China (Chee-koo), Japan (kuwai) and Korea; they are found in Hawaiian and some Oriental markets in the United States.

ARROWROOT
Maranta arundinacea

The edible starch obtained from the tubers of a tropical shrub widely grown in the West Indies which is used as a thickener in cooking. The processed starch is familiar to us as the extremely fine powder we buy in small jars or packages in gourmet markets. However, the tubers themselves are also occasionally found under their Chinese name of "chok-wo" in Oriental markets. The ivory colored tubers are generally four to eight inches long (they can be longer) and about one inch thick. They are served boiled and scraped and seasoned with butter, as innocuously bland when eaten as a vegetable as in their powdered form. It may also be comforting to know that the mashed tubers are useful in dealing with wounds from poisoned arrows and scorpion and black spider bites.

Arrowroot is cultivated commercially in the West Indies, especially in St. Vincent, which provides almost all of the world's export supply. *Maranta arundinacea,* although the true arrowroot, is but one of several tropical tubers used in making arrowroot starch: cassava (see page 110) and taro (see page 336) being others, along with an English variety (Portland arrowroot) made from the common cuckoo-pint *(Arum maculatum).*

Arrowroot is an almost pure starch, neutral in flavor, containing only 0.2% protein and no vitamins. It produces soups, sauces, pie fillings and puddings which are clear and sparkling with none of the heaviness of other thickeners. It is also remarkably easily digested and therefore suited for baby and invalid food. The starch is more popular in England than in the United States. Its greatest vogue was in Victorian cookery, with its passion for jellies and puddings of all kinds.

Arrowroot must be cooked at a lower temperature than other starches, because high heat and prolonged cooking make it break down. As such, it is very good for sauces and egg dishes which must not boil. Some useful proportions:

1½ teaspoons arrowroot equals 1 tablespoon flour

To thicken, allow 2½ teaspoons for each cup liquid.

ARTICHOKE, GLOBE
Common or French
(Cynara scolymus)

Chinese or Japanese Artichoke, see page 193.
Jerusalem Artichoke, see page 194.

Globe artichokes are the fleshy, leafy buds of a three- to five-foot formidable-looking plant that resembles a thistle in size and habit. Though some varieties are tender enough to be eaten raw, as in Southern Europe, globe artichokes are generally cooked. Since only a very small part of the vegetable is edible, artichokes present a unique and astonishing sight: after being eaten whole, there is more of them, in volume, than before, whole platefuls of laboriously nibbled leaves and castoff fuzz.

The ancients used its earlier form, the cardoon (see page 103), of which the tender stalks were eaten. In the second century after Christ it fetched the highest price on the vegetable markets of Rome, though Pliny the Elder considered it monstrous. The globe artichoke as we know it was first recorded in Naples around 1400. From Italy it went to France and England where Henry VIII fancied it greatly, possibly because of its alleged virtues as an aphrodisiac. But its greatest use was in Spain, Italy and other Mediterranean and Near Eastern countries. The name itself is of Arabic origin, "al-khurshuf," which became artichaut in French, carciofo in Italian, alcachofa in Spanish and artichoke in English.

Today, most American artichokes are grown in mid-coastal California where they find the soil and mild, humid climate they need to thrive. Castroville, an indifferent little California town, calls itself the Artichoke Capital of the World and it might well be, to judge from the endless, orderly artichoke fields around it.

Globe artichokes are not to be confused with Chinese or with Jerusalem artichokes which are totally different plants in every respect. Globe artichokes have only recently become known to the general American public rather than being limited to European immigrants. Many people still don't know any alternative to eating them boiled whole. Yet French cookery does wonders with the bottoms, and Italians quarter and slice the vegetable to be braised or deep fried. Unfortunately, the varieties of artichokes found in Europe are not available here where the big globe reigns. Occasionally it is possible to find in Italian markets small artichokes, which can be deep-fried and eaten *in toto,* or the tiny Italian carciofini, which are pickled for antipasto. None, however, are as small and tender as the violet-hued artichokes of Venice and the deep green French ones.

How to Buy

Artichokes are available all year, a minimum supply July and August, peak April and May. Buy uniformly solid heads which are heavy in relation to size with thick, fresh-looking compact leaves without a blemish. Avoid soft artichokes with loose, spreading leaves and discolorations. However, early in November, for about three months, "winter-kissed" artichokes come into the market with bronze markings on the outer leaves which are caused by the first frosts. The frost matures the plant slowly and enhances the flavor. Size has little if anything to do with flavor. Choose large artichokes for stuffing and for making artichoke bottoms and hearts.

Artichoke hearts and bottoms are available canned, ready for eating, or pickled; these are usually French or Italian imports. Artichoke hearts are also available frozen, needing only minimum cooking. There is even an Italian aperitif made from artichokes, called Cynar.

Allow one artichoke for each serving.

How to Keep

Refrigerate in a plastic bag or closed container to prevent them from drying out.

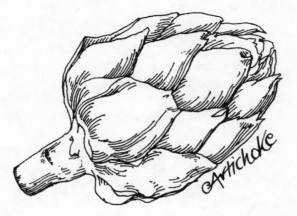

Nutritive Values

Artichokes contain small amounts of vitamins and minerals.

3½ ounces cooked—50 to 60 calories depending on maturity.

How to Use

Important! Once they are cut, artichokes discolor rapidly on contact with air. To prevent this, before starting work on them prepare a bowl of acidulated water, that is, water mixed with lemon juice. Use about 3 tablespoons of lemon juice to 1 quart of water. Work as fast as you can and drop the prepared artichoke pieces into the water as soon as you've finished with them. Keep them there until cooking time, but dry thoroughly on kitchen paper before using in the recipe. Finicky cooks are advised that contact with carbon knives, iron, steel or aluminum also darkens artichokes and gives them a slightly harsh flavor. They are best cut up with stainless steel knives and if boiled, this should be done in stainless steel or enameled cookware. If at all possible, artichokes should be sautéed in non-aluminum or non-iron frying pans, such as tinned copper or earthenware.

Some recipes, notably fancy French or professional ones, advocate cooking artichokes *au blanc,* that is, after being rubbed with lemon, they are poached in acidulated water with a sprinkle of flour and a little oil. This does keep them white, but also removes quite a lot of their flavor. I do not think it necessary to do this in home cooking.

Whole Artichokes

Since they are laborious eating, they are best served as a separate course. The usual manner is with the fingers tearing off leaf after leaf, dipping them into sauce, then scraping off the bottom of the vegetable with the teeth until the "choke"—the core of inedible light, thin fuzz—is reached. The fuzz is then scraped or cut off, leaving bare the heart, the most delectable part of the vegetable, to be eaten with the knife and fork.

Wash the artichoke and carefully break off the stem if you can, or cut it off with a knife either flush with the base or leave a ½- to 1-inch stub. Pull off and throw away the small leaves at the base and any tough and discolored leaves. Trim the base by paring from the base (and if necessary, the stubs of the stem) spirally, cutting off all the dark green, uneven and tough parts. Dip the artichoke quickly in acidulated water. Then lay it on its side and cut off about one-third of the top evenly with a sharp knife. Or else with kitchen scissors cut off the spiny top of each leaf. Cook in boiling acidulated and salted water (add 1 tablespoon olive oil to each quart water) until tender, from 15 to 30 minutes, depending on size and variety. Drain and stand artichokes bottom-side-up on a plate to drain off any excess liquid. *Or else:* Prepare the artichokes as above. Stand artichokes upright in a deep saucepan large enough to hold them snugly. Add ¼ teaspoon salt for each artichoke and 2 to 3 inches of boiling water and 1 to 2 tablespoons olive oil. Cover and boil gently for 15 to 30 minutes or until tender, or until the base can be pierced with a fork. Lift out the cooked artichokes and turn them upside down to drain. If the artichokes are to be stuffed, gently spread the leaves to make room for the stuffing and scrape out the center fuzz, or choke, with a spoon.

Artichokes can be cooked in plain boiling salted water, but the lemon juice and olive oil make them tastier and better looking.

Artichoke Hearts and Bottoms

There is a difference between artichoke hearts and bottoms, though the terms are often used interchangeably. Artichoke hearts have leaves or parts of leaves that are tender and chokes that are infantile enough to be ignored. Artichoke bottoms, the French *fonds d'artichaut,* are the fuzzless bottoms of more mature vegetables.

To make artichoke hearts, have acidulated water ready before starting. Prepare the stem and outer leaves as in Whole Artichokes. Proceed removing leaves until only the very tender, greenish-white ones remain. Lay the artichoke on its side and cut off the top third of the remaining leaves. To make artichoke bottoms, do the same but cut off two-thirds to four-fifths of the remaining leaves. In both cases, starting from the bottom, peel in a spiral motion until the whole base is smooth and rounded. Remove the fuzz if the artichoke bottom is to be braised or sautéed; if blanched or boiled, remove the fuzz after boiling. Drop the finished hearts and bottoms into acidulated water. Drain, dry and cook according to recipe. Depending on the recipe, the hearts and bottoms may or may not be blanched (to blanch, plunge into boiling water for 3 minutes; drain) before using. Or cook uncovered in a little boiling salted water until just tender; cooking time depends on size, but ranges, generally speaking, from 5 to 15 minutes. Do not overcook. You may add a little olive oil to the water and a sprinkling of herbs, such as sprigs of fresh rosemary or thyme or their equivalent in dried herbs.

Quartered and Sliced Artichokes

Prepare the artichokes as above, leaving only the tender, greenish-white leaves. Then lay each artichoke on its side. Cut off the green top part of the leaves in one stroke. Dip artichoke in acidulated water and shake dry. Cut the artichoke into four parts as you would quarter an apple. Drop three parts into the acidulated water and work on one part after the other. Working quickly, core each part, removing the fuzz or choke, as you would core a quartered apple. Drop immediately back into acidulated water.

Small tender artichokes may be quartered. But American artichokes are seldom small and tender, so that the prepared quarters must be thinly sliced; the tougher the artichoke, the thinner the slice.

Fats to Use in Artichoke Cookery

Artichokes are robust vegetables which usually seem to need the heartiness of olive oil. The hearts and bottoms only are delicate enough to be cooked with butter. However, using only olive oil in braising artichokes would make for too rich a dish; it is better to use equal parts of olive oil, water and consommé.

FRIED ARTICHOKES

4 servings

4 medium artichokes, trimmed
  and thinly sliced
acidulated water (1 quart water
  to 3 tablespoons lemon juice)
olive oil

flour
2 eggs, beaten with 1
  tablespoon olive oil
salt

Drop the artichoke slices into the acidulated water. In a deep frying pan, heat about 2 inches of olive or peanut oil to the smoking point. As the oil heats, drain the artichokes and dry them thoroughly between paper towels. Dip a few slices at a time first into the flour and then into the beaten egg. Fry in the hot oil until crisp and golden. Remove with a slotted spoon and drain in a serving dish lined with a triple layer of paper towels. Keep the fried artichokes warm in a low oven as you fry the remaining slices. When all the slices are fried, blot the top layers in the dish with paper towels to drain them thoroughly. Pull the paper which lines the dish out from under the artichokes, sprinkle with salt and serve very hot.

BASIC BRAISED ARTICHOKE HEARTS OR BOTTOMS

4 servings

3 tablespoons butter
1 tablespoon olive oil
juice of 1 lemon
½ teaspoon salt

8 medium artichoke hearts or
  bottoms
chicken consommé or water

Heat together the butter, olive oil, lemon juice and salt, preferably in an enameled saucepan. Add the artichoke bottoms. Simmer covered over low heat about 10 to 15 minutes or until tender. Shake the pan frequently to prevent sticking. If necessary, add 1 or 2 tablespoons of consommé at a time to keep the pan moist.

RAGOUT OF ARTICHOKE HEARTS

4 servings

8 medium raw artichoke hearts
   or bottoms
2 tablespoons butter
1 tablespoon olive oil
1 medium onion, minced
1 garlic clove, mashed
4 small to medium ripe
   tomatoes, peeled, seeded and
   chopped fine

4 tablespoons minced parsley
salt
freshly ground pepper
2 tablespoons drained capers or
   ½ cup pitted chopped black
   olives

Cut the artichoke hearts into quarters. Heat the butter and the olive oil in a deep frying pan. Cook the onion and the garlic, stirring constantly, until the onion is soft. Add the artichoke quarters. Cook over low heat, stirring frequently and carefully, for about 7 to 10 minutes or until half tender. Add the tomatoes and the parsley. Season with salt and pepper. Simmer covered for 10 more minutes or until tender. Stir in the capers or the olives. Serve very hot.

PURÉE OF ARTICHOKE HEARTS

4 servings

Serve with fillets of sole or lamb chops.

8 large braised artichoke hearts
   or bottoms (see page 28)
¼ cup heavy cream
3 tablespoons butter

salt
freshly ground white pepper
2 tablespoons minced parsley

Cut the artichoke hearts into pieces. Purée half with 2 tablespoons of cream in the blender. Purée the remaining artichokes with the remaining cream and combine the two. Heat the butter and add the artichoke purée. Season with salt and pepper. Mix well and heat through thoroughly. If too thick, add a little more cream, 1 tablespoon at a time. Serve in a heated serving dish, sprinkled with parsley.

STUFFED HORS D'OEUVRE ARTICHOKES

6 servings

6 medium artichokes
acidulated water (1 quart water
   to 3 tablespoons lemon juice)
3 cups minced parsley
3 anchovies, minced
1 tablespoon capers, drained
2 tablespoons minced fresh
   basil or 2 teaspoons dried
   basil, crumbled

1 teaspoon salt
¼ teaspoon freshly ground
   pepper
1 lemon, sliced
3 tablespoons olive oil
boiling water
3 cups French dressing made
   with lemon juice

Cut off the artichoke stems at the base and pull off tough outer
leaves. Trim the artichoke base. Cut off the top third of each artichoke to remove the spiny tips. Put the artichokes upside down on a
chopping board and press stem ends to open them. Drop the artichokes into the acidulated water to prevent discoloring. Taking out
one artichoke at a time, dig out the fuzzy chokes with the point of a
knife, a grapefruit knife or a spoon. Drop back into water. Combine
the parsley, the anchovies, the capers, the basil and the salt and
pepper and mix well. Drain one artichoke at a time and stuff it with
some of the parsley mixture. Tie each artichoke with a string to
prevent its opening during cooking. Place the artichokes side by side
in a deep frying pan or saucepan just large enough to hold them
tightly. Top each with a lemon slice. Pour the olive oil into the frying
pan and add about 1 inch boiling water. Cook without a cover for 3
minutes. Turn heat to low, cover and simmer for about 20 to 30
minutes or until the artichokes are tender. Check for moisture; if
necessary, add a little more water and olive oil to keep the 1-inch
level. When cooked, transfer to serving dish. Cool. Pour about ½
cup French dressing into small, individual bowls. Place a bowl and
one artichoke on each plate. Use the French dressing as a dunk for
the artichoke.

ARTICHOKES AND PEAS

4-6 servings

Serve with a cheese soufflé.

2 or 3 slices lean bacon, minced
½ small onion, minced
¼ cup minced parsley
1 small garlic clove, minced
2 tablespoons butter
2 tablespoons olive oil
6 medium artichokes, trimmed, and thinly sliced
2 tablespoons minced fresh basil or 1 teaspoon dried basil, crumbled

salt
freshly ground pepper
⅓ to ½ cup hot chicken consommé
2 pounds peas, shelled (about 2 cups) or frozen peas, barely thawed

Combine the bacon, the onion, the parsley and the garlic clove on a chopping board and mince together to a paste. Heat the butter and the olive oil in a heavy casserole. Add the bacon mixture. Cook, stirring constantly, for 3 to 4 minutes. Add the artichokes, the basil, salt and pepper and ⅓ cup of the consommé. Simmer covered over low heat for 10 minutes, stirring frequently. Add the peas and, if necessary to prevent scorching, more consommé. Simmer covered for about 5 to 10 more minutes, or until the vegetables are tender.

ARUGALA
Rucola, Rocket, Roquette
(See page 296)

ASPARAGUS
Asparagus officinalis

The edible shoots or spears rising from the rootstock of a vegetable believed to be a native of the Eastern Mediterranean and Asia Minor. Its taste is delicate yet distinctive, its shape, whether svelte or plump, always elegant and its color, ranging from bright green to snow-white (depending on the variety and the way it is grown), decorative on whatever kind of china it is served. Furthermore, asparagus takes well to fancy sauces, which may be one reason why it is considered a symbol of epicurean eating.

Asparagus always has been a popular vegetable, whether wild or cultivated. The Greeks ate it wild, the Romans both wild and cultivated. As early as 200 BC Cato gave excellent growing instructions and Pliny deplored a species that grew near Ravenna, of which three heads would weigh one pound. Generally speaking, the Ancients preferred wild asparagus, a taste for which there is a lot to say. This wild asparagus can still be bought in Italy, and sometimes in the United States. Anybody who has tasted its superlative flavor, a kind of essence of asparagus, will feel somewhat let down by the tamer flavor of cultivated asparagus.

As for cultivated asparagus, there are different national tastes. The Americans like green asparagus, the thicker the better (though the thinner tastes better), possibly because it looks richer. Opposite is the French, Belgian, German and other Central European preference for colossal snow-white stalks, which are milder in flavor though somehow more voluptuous.

This difference is achieved by different cultivation methods. Green asparagus is cut after the shoots have risen from the earth into the open air. White asparagus is grown buried in mounds where the soil, ridged high over the roots, hides the shoots from the light that would make them green; Belgian endives are similarly grown in the dark to keep them white. These luscious white asparagus have brought fame to Argenteuil in France and Malines in Belgium and to some towns in Southern Germany where at asparagus time the local restaurants prepare the vegetable in dozens of ways, attracting visitors from far away to wallow in asparagus orgies. There are other varieties too, such as the purple-tipped asparagus favored in Italy.

Americans and Europeans eat asparagus differently. In America, people cut off the tip of the stalk (with a fork and not with a knife) and eat it with the fork, ignoring what goodness there is in the stalk. In Europe asparagus is eaten with the fingers down to its last tender moment, which is considered unrefined by Americans, just as their way is considered insensitive by the Europeans. This difference may also be the reason why asparagus in Europe is invariably peeled up to its tip (a swivel vegetable parer is best) whereas it is not in American homes. I personally always peel asparagus and eat it down, using my fingers, since I can't bear to waste half an inch of this vegetable delight.

Asparagus has long been valued for its medicinal properties. It is a diuretic and a laxative and said to be good for people who suffer from dropsy. Others have advocated its use to restore eyesight and ease toothache.

How to Buy

Available from March through June, peak supplies from April to June. *Buy* fresh asparagus that is a rich green color, with closed, compact tips, round spears and a fresh look. The stalks should be tender but firm.

Avoid asparagus that has ridged spears, open and spread out tips, or moldy or rotting tips. This kind of tired old asparagus is not worth cooking since it is tough, stringy and poor in flavor.

Though some white American asparagus is canned, white asparagus in thick stalks is usually imported from France, Belgium, Germany and other European countries in tins or glass jars. It is tender all the way through, beautiful to look at and disappointingly bland in flavor. It is entirely a luxury for show.

How to Keep

Refrigerate in a plastic bag or in the vegetable drawer in the refrigerator. Do not wash before storing. If the stalks seem a little limp, cut a thin diagonal slice from the ends and stand them in cold water for 5 or 10 minutes. But cook asparagus as soon as possible.

Raw, refrigerator shelf—3 days.

Cooked and covered, refrigerator shelf—2 days.

Nutritive Values

A good source of vitamin A and a fair one for vitamins B and C and iron.

3½ ounces raw—26 calories.

3½ ounces cooked—20 calories.

How to Use

When ready to cook, lay the asparagus on a cutting board. Cut off the tough white part at the bottom of the stalks. Or snap it off, though it is impossible to snap evenly. Cut all the stalks the same length for better cooking and prettier serving. If the asparagus is very thin, it need not be peeled. But since most is not, it is better peeled with a swivel vegetable parer up to the tip, beginning at the bottom and leaving only the tender scales at the head. You have to judge where it starts to be tender. Peeled asparagus is almost totally, if not totally, edible. Then place the asparagus, tips down, into a deep bowl. Quickly run cold water over them. Shake the stalks to loosen any sand in the tips. Lift out and if sandy repeat the quick washing under running cold water until the water is clean. **Never soak asparagus.** The stalks may be used whole, tips only, cut into 1½-inch pieces or diagonally. Asparagus can be steamed, boiled or cooked in a pan. Most important: do not overcook it. It should be firm and almost tender. The best way to find out is to stick the point of a knife into the thickest stalk; it should meet some resistance. It's been my experience that most recipes give you far too long a cooking time. You can always cook asparagus longer, but you can't un-cook it from mush.

To steam

Using soft kitchen string, tie the asparagus into serving-size bundles, or if it is a small amount, in one bundle. Stand the bundles into the bottom of a double boiler. Add enough boiling water to cover about 2 inches of the stem, more if the stalks are very long. Add about ½ teaspoon salt. Cover with the inverted top part of the double boiler. Cook for about 5 to 15 minutes, depending on size and age. Remove from pan with tongs or 2 forks. Drain, cut and remove string, arrange on serving plate and season. Serve at once with buttter or sauce.

To boil

Place the stalks (tied or untied) in a deep frying or other wide-bottomed pan. Pour in from ½ to 1 inch boiling water. Add about ½ teaspoon salt. Cover the pan. Bring quickly to the boiling point, lower heat to medium and cook for 5 to 10 minutes. Lift from pan with tongs or 2 forks, drain, arrange on serving plate and season. Serve at once with butter or sauce. The tips and stalks of cut-up asparagus should be cooked separately in a minimum of water. Cook the stalk pieces covered for about 2 to 3 minutes, then add the tips and cook 5 to 7 minutes longer or until barely tender.

To cook in a pan

This is the Oriental way of cooking the vegetable. Cut the stalks on the diagonal into about ¼-inch slices; leave the tips whole. Heat just enough butter or oil in a frying pan to cover the bottom. Do not brown the butter. Add the slices and the tips and season lightly with salt and pepper. Cover the pan and bring it to steaming. Then lower the heat to low and cook for about 3 to 5 minutes or until barely tender, shaking the pan frequently to prevent sticking.

Seasoning Asparagus

Hot or cold, asparagus is a natural for plain and fancy sauces. Melted butter or French dressing are the most common ones, Hollandaise the great favorite. I prefer to eat asparagus lightly seasoned with salt and pepper, with a sprinkle of fresh lemon juice. Try it this way at least once.

ASPARAGUS IN CREAM

2-4 servings

The simpler the recipe the finer the asparagus taste.

2 pounds asparagus, trimmed
   and peeled
2 tablespoons butter
asparagus cooking water
salt

freshly ground white pepper
⅛ teaspoon ground nutmeg
4 tablespoons heavy cream,
   heated

Cook the asparagus in boiling salted water for 5 minutes only; it should be only half tender. Drain it carefully, reserving the cooking water. Place it in a casserole that can go to the table. Add the butter and 2 tablespoons of the cooking water. Simmer covered over very low heat for about 10 minutes, or until the asparagus is tender. Shake the casserole frequently to prevent sticking, and if necessary, add a little more water, 1 tablespoon at a time. Stir a little salt and pepper and the nutmeg into the hot cream. Pour over the asparagus. Cook for 2 or 3 more minutes, or until thoroughly heated through. Serve very hot.

ASPARAGUS MILANAISE

4 servings

The eggs make this a main course.

2 pounds asparagus, trimmed
   and peeled
¾ cup grated Parmesan or
   Swiss cheese

⅓ cup hot browned butter
4 or 8 butter-fried eggs
   (optional)

Cook the asparagus until just tender. Drain it carefully. Butter a shallow baking dish generously and heat it in a low oven. Lay half of the asparagus in the dish. Sprinkle the tips with half of the grated cheese. Repeat with the remaining asparagus and the remaining cheese. Drizzle the butter over the asparagus tips. Lay the fried eggs on top of the asparagus and serve very hot.

FLEMISH ASPARAGUS

4 servings

This may be a luncheon main dish, followed by salad, cheese and fruit. Allow 1 pound asparagus for each serving.

4 hard-cooked eggs, mashed	2 tablespoons fresh lemon juice
1 cup butter, melted	2 tablespoons minced parsley
salt	4 pounds asparagus, trimmed
freshly ground pepper	and peeled

Combine the mashed eggs, butter, salt and pepper in a small saucepan. Cook over low heat long enough to heat through thoroughly. Remove from heat and stir in the lemon juice and parsley; keep hot while the asparagus is cooking. Turn into a sauce dish and serve as soon as the asparagus is ready. Cook and drain the asparagus and place the spears side by side on a clean kitchen towel. Line a serving platter with a large napkin in a way that half of the napkin overlaps. Place the asparagus on the napkin and cover with the overlapping part of the napkin. This will absorb any moisture remaining in the asparagus.

PIQUANT GREEN SAUCE FOR COLD ASPARAGUS

about 1⅓ cups   6 servings

This sauce takes the place of the usual vinaigrette and may be used for any cooked cold vegetables as well as for seafood.

¾ cup olive oil
2 cups parsley heads
1 hard-cooked egg, chopped
2 tablespoons drained capers
1 tablespoon minced onion
1 garlic clove, minced
2 anchovies, chopped, or 1
   tablespoon anchovy paste

1 or 2 tablespoons chopped
   fresh basil or 1 teaspoon
   dried basil
1 teaspoon salt
¼ teaspoon freshly ground
   pepper
juice of 2 lemons
3 pounds cooked cold asparagus

Combine all the ingredients except the asparagus in a blender top. Blend to a purée. Pour the sauce into 6 individual little bowls (such as little white soufflé bowls) and chill. At serving time, divide the asparagus into 6 servings and place each on a plate. Set the bowls with the sauce on the plate for dunking.

AVOCADO
Alligator Pear
genus *Persea*

The avocado is the pear-shaped fruit of a handsome, glossy-leafed shade tree native to tropical America. It is prized for its appetizing flesh which is yellowish-green in color. The fruit can weigh as much as three to four pounds, be roundish rather than pear-shaped, and have a skin as thin as that of an apple or one that is coarse and pebbly, greenish or russet in color. The buttery flesh, which is easy to eat, surrounds a large, inedible pit from which a plant may be grown. Home gardeners do this with more enthusiasm than success, producing sad, tall, spindly stems with a few top leaves, which they cannot bear to throw away because they are living green things. Though a fruit, avocados are treated generally as a vegetable in appetizers, salads, soups and on the half shell since the pit cavity makes a natural container for all sorts of fillings.

The name is apparently an attempt to reproduce phonetically the Aztec name of "ahuacatl" though the Aztecs also had a picture character to describe the fruit. Describing it as a pear is obvious because of its shape though it is anybody's speculation as to where the "alligator" part comes in—possibly from a vague resemblance of the avocado's pebbly skin and that of the repulsive reptile. Avocados are also known as poor man's or subaltern's butter, or vegetable butter.

The three generally recognized races—the Mexican, Guatemalan and West Indian avocados—have flesh that varies from green to yellowish white, but the flavor is invariably bland, vaguely nutty, buttery and very soothing. In appearance, the Mexican is a small, smooth-skinned fruit, usually purple or black in color. The Guatemalan is a medium-sized fruit, green, purple or black in color with a more or less pebbly or rough skin. The West Indian is a large, smooth-skinned fruit, green to red or purplish in color. In between these races are about two dozen varieties that are grown commercially.

How to Buy

Available throughout the year, peak season from December to May. Calavo is the brand name of a California grower. *Buy* fruit that is heavy with a skin that is uniform in color and without cracks or bruises. *Avoid* fruit with dark sunken spots and damaged skin surfaces. Generally, the seeds fit tightly in the cavity, but in some varieties, the seeds are often loose and rattling at maturity.

How to Keep

To be good eating, avocados must be properly ripened, that is, they must be slightly soft. For *immediate use,* choose fruit that yields to gentle pressure. Whole ripened avocados may be stored in the warmest part of the refrigerator for about eight to ten days, depending on ripeness. For *later use,* choose firm avocados. Keep them at room temperature where they will ripen from about three days to a week and even longer. Never store unripe avocados in the refrigerator.

If half an avocado is to be stored, rub the cut surfaces with half a lemon to prevent discoloration. Keep the pit in its cavity since it also prevents discoloration. Wrap the fruit tightly in plastic wrap and refrigerate.

Nutritive Values

Depending on their variety and size, avocados offer a fair amount of vitamins A and B_1, thiamine, riboflavin and ascorbic acid as well as iron, calcium and phosphorus. The oil content ranges from 5 to 25 per cent and even 30 per cent in some varieties. The low carbohydrate content makes the avocado useful in diabetic diets. It is easily digestible.

3½ ounces raw—167 calories.

How to Use

Important: Cut avocados discolor rapidly in contact with the air. When preparing the fruit, immediately rub the cut parts with half a lemon or dip in lemon juice.

To cut or to peel an avocado, use a stainless steel knife which retards darkening. Cut the fruit into halves lengthwise, twist halves a little to separate them and remove the pit. Scrape off any peel of the pit which may have clung to the cavity. To peel, lay the avocado, cut side down, on a counter and pry off the skin with a paring knife or with the back of a teaspoon. Peeled avocados can be sliced, diced, mashed or puréed, and used raw or baked. Avocados are best combined raw with cooked foods; mixing should be done at the last moment, away from the heat. Apart from their use in salads, the best known avocado dish is the Mexican salad Guacamole, also used as a dip.

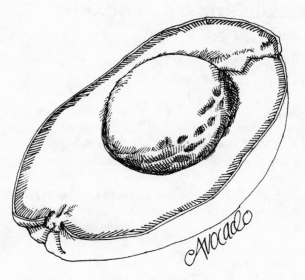

COLD AVOCADO SOUP

4-6 servings

The soup should be well seasoned.

2 medium avocados
2 tablespoons lime or lemon
    juice
4 cups cold chicken consommé,
    fat free
salt

freshly ground pepper
dash of Tabasco
1 cup light cream or ½ cup sour
    cream and ½ cup light cream
paprika

Cut the avocados, remove the pit and scoop out the flesh. Place in a blender with all the other ingredients except the paprika. Blend until smooth. Chill covered for 1 hour or longer. Serve with a sprinkling of paprika.

COLD SHRIMP-STUFFED AVOCADOS

6 servings

Serve with a salad of new potatoes dressed only with sour cream, a little mustard and salt and pepper.

3 large avocados
juice of 1 lemon
1 pound cooked shelled shrimp
   (reserve 6 whole shrimp),
   coarsely chopped
1 hot chili pepper, peeled if
   fresh, seeded, washed and
   chopped fine

1 hard-cooked egg, chopped
2 dozen pitted green or black
   olives, chopped
mayonnaise
salt
freshly ground pepper
3 tablespoons minced fresh
   coriander leaves or parsley

Cut the avocados into halves lengthwise. Remove the pit. Carefully scoop out the flesh without damaging the shells. Put the flesh into a bowl. Sprinkle each shell with a little lemon juice to prevent darkening. Mash the avocado flesh with a fork. Add the shrimp, hot pepper, egg, and olives. Mix well. Add enough mayonnaise, beginning with ⅓ cup, to bind the ingredients together. Taste and season with salt and pepper. Stuff the avocado shells with this mixture. Top each shell with one of the reserved shrimp and sprinkle with a little coriander.

GUACAMOLE

about 4 cups

This is the true Mexican version of this popular avocado sauce, from *The Complete Book of Mexican Cooking* by Elisabeth Lambert Ortiz. If possible, make guacamole just before serving since avocado darkens. Or cover *tightly* with plastic wrap or aluminum foil and use soon. Putting the pit in with the guacamole is supposed to retard darkening, but I have not found this to work well.

2 large, very ripe avocados
1 medium tomato, peeled, seeded and chopped
½ small white onion, minced
2 or more canned serrano chiles, chopped

several sprigs of fresh coriander, finely chopped
salt
freshly ground pepper
pinch of sugar

Peel and mash the avocados with a fork. Mix well with the other ingredients. Pile into a serving dish.

Note: I stir 1 or 2 tablespoons fresh lemon juice into my Guacamole because I think this freshens the dish. I also use whatever canned chili peppers I have at hand, drained, seeded and rinsed before chopping. Last, I frequently serve Guacamole in hollowed-out tomatoes, with a sprig of coriander or parsley on top.

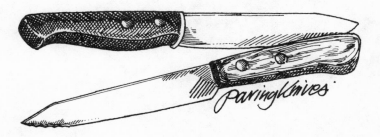

paring knives

BAMBOO SHOOTS
Bambusa vulgaris, Phyllostachys pubescens and other species

The ivory-colored little young sprouts we eat come from the thick pointed shoots that emerge from under the ground under a bamboo, a tropical plant. Left to grow, they would form new stems and end up as adult bamboos, often enormously tall plants, used for construction and in many other ways in tropical and subtropical Asia. Bamboo shoots are a staple of Chinese, Japanese, Korean and other Asian cooking and they are becoming popular among non-Orientals in the United States. Afficionados say that their taste is reminiscent of artichokes, but more realistically, it is bland and pleasantly crunchy; basically in cooking, bamboo shoots are fillers, added for texture contrast. The shoots are usually eaten freshly boiled; Oriental cooks take great care to add them to a dish for the least possible cooking time, so as not to rob them of their crispness. They can also be pickled, deep fried or used much as mushrooms are used, or for texture contrast in seafood, meat or vegetable dishes.

Bamboo shoots reach us canned, imported from the Far East in a lightly salted liquid. They are readily available in supermarkets. If not all the bamboo shoots in a can are used in a recipe, they should be put into a clean glass jar filled with cold water and sealed with a tight lid. The jar should be placed in the warmest part of the refrigerator and the water changed daily. Bamboo shoots should always be used up as soon as possible, however, or they lose what flavor they have and, more importantly, their crunchiness which after all is their raison d'être.

3½ ounces, raw—27 calories.

BAMBOO SHOOTS AND PORK SOUP

4-6 servings

Far Eastern cookery frequently combines pork and bamboo shoots.

2 tablespoons butter
1 garlic clove, mashed
½ teaspoon ground coriander
¼ teaspoon cayenne pepper
2 tablespoons soy sauce
1 cup thinly sliced cooked pork
   or ¼ pound lean boneless
   pork, thinly sliced

1 teaspoon sugar
6 cups chicken consommé
salt
1 cup thinly sliced canned
   drained bamboo shoots or
   fresh bamboo shoots
½ cup chopped watercress or
   green onion tops

Heat the butter in a large saucepan. Stir in the garlic, coriander, cayenne and soy sauce. Cook, stirring constantly, for 2 minutes. Add the pork. Cook, stirring all the time, until the pork is browned on all sides. Add the sugar and the consommé. Taste and if necessary add a little salt. Simmer covered for 10 to 15 minutes or until the pork is thoroughly cooked. Add the bamboo shoots and cook 3 minutes longer. Remove from heat and stir in the watercress. Serve very hot.

BAMBOO SHOOTS AND SPINACH

3 servings

⅓ cup peanut oil or salad oil
½ cup finely shredded bamboo
   shoots
1 pound spinach, trimmed,
   washed and torn into bite-
   sized pieces

2 teaspoons soy sauce
salt

Heat the oil in a frying pan or in a wok. Add the bamboo shoots. Cook, stirring constantly, for 2 minutes. Add the spinach and cook for 1 more minute. Stir in the soy sauce and a little salt. Transfer to a hot serving dish and keep hot. Over high heat, reduce the pan juices to 2 or 3 tablespoons. Pour over the vegetables and serve.

BANANA
genus *Musa*

Bananas are the seedless fruit of a tropical plant of which there are more than 100 cultivated varieties. This most familiar of all tropical fruits is best known as a dessert fruit, with a yellowish-white soft pulp and a zip-off skin, but it can also be used as a vegetable. Furthermore, there are a number of strictly cooking bananas, less sweet and with a higher starch content, of which the Plantain is the best known, see page 270.

Bananas grow on trees which look vaguely like palms but which are really gigantic herbs that can grow up to 12 feet tall with enormous, oblong droopy leaves. The wild varieties have seeds, but in the cultivated ones grown for commerce, the seedless fruit grows from the female flower (the male flower is sterile). Half spirals of clearly separated bananas, called hands, each carry 12 to 16 individual fruit. The whole bunch may have 200 single bananas and weigh up to 80 pounds. It looks to the layman's eye as if bananas grow upside down. Each plant bears a single crop, then it is cut down and resurrects from its own suckers arising from the underground. Thus the life of a banana plant can last for scores of years.

Among the many varieties of bananas, the Gros Michel (*Musa sapientum*) is the principal one to reach the United States because it travels best in the refrigerated ships especially constructed for the purpose. Sometimes other varieties can be found in our markets, such as the small, thinner-skinned ladyfinger bananas and red bananas, a small choice considering the enormous variety of flavors in different types of bananas. Personally, I remember the ''apple'' and ''peach'' bananas of Brazil which really did taste like the fruit they were named for, and friends have told me of a Malaya variety called locally ''crocodile's fingers.''

A nonedible use of the plant involves production of fiber from special species (the banana is related to the fibrous Manila hemp): the leaves are used for wrapping food for cooking (as we use aluminum foil), for thatching and umbrellas. In various parts of the globe, bananas are also made into beer, liqueurs and a powerful wine. Other banana products include flour used for baby and invalid food because of the fruit's easy digestibility, and banana chips as cocktail tidbits, as well as spreads, chutneys, candies and the like.

How to Buy

Bananas are available all year round. They come from Central and South America.

Banana flakes, flour and chips are available in specialty stores.

Buy firm unblemished fruit, regardless of size, without bruises. Fully ripe bananas are yellow with brown flecks; use these first. Buy bananas by the bunch as single bananas deteriorate quicker.

Avoid bruised, discolored, overly soft fruit. Mold on the darkened skins means decay.

For keeping, buy bananas with green tips and an all-over greenish-yellow skin and let them ripen at room temperature.

Totally brown bananas need not always be rotten. Touch them *gently* to see if the flesh is still firm and not mushy and use them immediately.

For cooking, bananas should be still slightly green and firm, or they will cook into mush.

How to Keep

Let bananas ripen at room temperature, in a cooler room if you want to slow the process. But never keep them in the refrigerator. Chill only just before using.

Room temperature—1 week.

Nutritive Values

Bananas provide good quantities of vitamin C and some vitamins A and B_1. They are low in protein and fat, high in carbohydrates, and when truly ripe, very easily digested.

1 medium banana—85 to 100 calories.

How to Use

Cut bananas darken rapidly when exposed to the air. To prevent discoloration, rub or dip immediately in lemon juice. Use a stainless steel rather than a carbon knife to slice them. When tearing a single banana from a bunch, be careful not to tear off any part of the skin of the adjoining fruit or it will darken where exposed to the air.

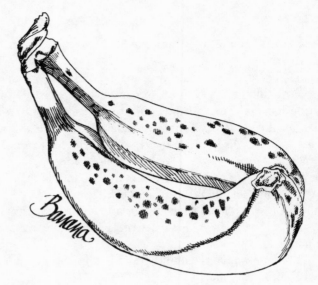

CURRIED BANANAS

4 servings

Choose unripe, firm bananas or make the dish with plantains. Serve with a meat curry.

3 tablespoons butter
½ teaspoon turmeric
1 teaspoon curry powder or to taste

4 large bananas, peeled and cut into halves lengthwise
1 teaspoon salt
⅓ cup plain yoghurt

Heat the butter in a frying pan large enough to hold the banana halves side by side. Stir in the turmeric and the curry powder. Cook over medium heat, stirring constantly, for about 3 minutes. Add the bananas, lower the heat and sprinkle with salt. Cook for about 5 to 7 minutes or until heated through. Shake the pan frequently to prevent sticking, or stir gently with a wooden spoon. Turn over once using two wooden spoons in order not to break the bananas. Spoon the yoghurt over the bananas. Turn the heat to medium. Cook for 3 to 5 more minutes, or until the yoghurt is heated through, shaking the pan frequently.

BANANA AND MANGO CHUTNEY

about 5 cups

It is important to cook the mixture slowly, for a long time.

3 mangoes, each weighing
   about 1 pound
1 medium onion, minced
1 large garlic clove, minced
1 cup golden raisins
5 large ripe bananas, sliced
2 or 3 tablespoons finely
   chopped fresh ginger or 1
   tablespoon ground ginger

1 cup sugar
1 tablespoon salt
1 cup cider vinegar
1 tablespoon Tabasco or hot
   pepper sauce to taste

Peel the mangoes. Cut the flesh from the pit and cut into pieces. Put the mangoes into a large saucepan and add the onion, garlic, raisins, bananas and ginger. Stir the sugar and the salt into the vinegar until dissolved. Stir in the Tabasco, beginning with 1 teaspoon. Pour the mixture over the fruit and mix well. Bring to the boiling point and lower the heat to very low. Simmer uncovered, stirring frequently, for about 2 hours, or until thick and cooked down. Cool and spoon into sterilized jars, or refrigerate. The chutney will keep for 2 months or more in the refrigerator.

BASELLA
Basella rubra

A slender, annual vine with picturesque green or purplish leaves that is grown as an ornamental garden plant or eaten as a spinachlike vegetable in the Far East, such as in Hawaii, India, China and Japan. In the United States, basella occurs occasionally as a decorative plant and there have been attempts to popularize it as a vegetable. In short, it is one of those greens eaten because they are there. Basella can be treated like spinach, but it is best in Oriental recipes using greens.

BEAN

The general name of some species of the large and varied Leguminosae family whose fruit is a pod which opens along two sutures when the seeds are ripe. Depending on the varieties, either the pod and seeds (as in green beans) or the seeds alone (as in kidney beans) are eaten.

Next to cereals, beans are the most important human food. The protein content of some varieties is higher than that of any other vegetable and substitutes for animal proteins in human nutrition. Beans, which also have the advantage of being easily grown, dried and stored (this last of great importance), are the basic food in many parts of the world where animal proteins are scarce. Apart from their high protein content (the soybean has the highest), beans are rich in vitamin B, minerals and carbohydrates. Best of all, beans provide an easy-to-cook, palatable food which lends itself to an enormous variety of dishes and stretches other foods.

Different kinds of beans originated in different parts of the world, in the Far East, Africa, Europe and the Americas. Broad beans were cultivated in the Old World for over 4000 years; in the New World, kidney beans go back more than 2000 years. Beans not only played an important part in the diet of the Egyptians, the Greeks and the Romans, but also in their ritual offerings of food for the dead and to the powers of the underworld, in divinations and other cult activities. Chinese documents tell us how in the first century AD, merchants made their fortunes with a popular bean relish. Beans were a major food for the Indians of all the Americas. Our own Indian tribes believed the bean to be a god-given gift; the Hopi made their Bean Festival a major one of their religion. Beans are part of world folklore; magic beans, jumping beans, ghostly beans, laughing beans still enchant us. Beans have even been mentioned as aphrodisiacs, but alas, I could find no research nor witness to tell if this is really so.

Though botanically inaccurate, for the cook, beans are divided into two categories: those which are eaten fresh and whole, like green beans, and those which are shelled and eaten fresh or dried, like lima or kidney beans. I've grouped them accordingly, both in basic information and recipes. In bean cookery it should be remembered that fresh beans, such as green and wax beans, may be substituted for each other, as may dried beans, such as white beans or red beans. Naturally, the flavor, texture and the appearance of the finished dish will vary according to the beans used.

ADZUKI BEAN
Phaseolus angularis

MUNG BEAN
Phaseolus aureus

RICE BEAN
Phaseolus calcaratus

These highly nutritious beans play an important part in the diet of Southern and Eastern Asia. The small *adzuki beans* have been cultivated in many varieties for thousands of years in China, Japan and Korea. They are imported into the United States dried or in cans, made into a meal, or used for making cakes and candies in Oriental cookery. *Mung beans* are ancient Indian food, of which the small seeds and the green pods are eaten. Over a hundred varieties are grown in Asia; in the United States they serve as a forage plant or for sprouting. The small *rice beans* are extensively cultivated in Southern Asia as a food plant.

   All these beans may be used in the usual way in soups and stews or with rice. Kidney and other red beans may serve as a substitute.

GREEN or WAX (YELLOW) SNAP BEAN
Phaseolus vulgaris

Green beans are the most popular of fresh beans, though they are bought, stored, and cooked in the same manner as wax or yellow beans. Green beans were and still are known as string beans, though the first so-called stringless bean appeared in 1894. The name brings excruciating pain to bean growers who have spent a great deal of time and money to make them as stringless as possible. The most exquisite of all green beans is the little sliverlike, dark green bean found in France and Italy, as different from its grown-up American cousins as a ballerina from a hospital matron.

How to Buy

Snap beans are available all the year round, peak season May to October.

Buy smooth, crisp pods that snap easily and which are free from blemishes and spots. The pods should be well filled but with immature seeds.

Avoid flabby or wilted pods, discolored, blemished pods and thick, fibrous pods which are too mature.

Allow about ¼ pound for each serving; one pound cooked gives approximately 3 cups.

Dried green beans, a Pennsylvania Dutch specialty, are available in limited quantities.

How to Keep

Put unwashed beans into plastic bags and refrigerate. Plan to use as soon as possible, because time toughens and discolors the beans.

Raw, refrigerator shelf—3 to 4 days.

Cooked and covered, refrigerator shelf—1 to 3 days.

Nutritive Values

Cooked for a short time in a small amount of water, snap beans are a fair source of vitamins A and B.

Snap beans, 3½ ounces cooked—25 calories.

How to Use

The way beans are cut affects their flavor and their cooking time. When ready to use, wash beans well in cold water. Snip off stems and tops. Beans may be left whole; snapped or cut straight across in

1- or 2-inch pieces; Chinese-style in long slanting slices; or French style in thin slivers, for which there is also an inexpensive kitchen gadget. Snap beans may be cooked in quantities of boiling salted water (the French way), drained, rapidly rinsed in cold water and drained again before being finished as the recipe directs. Or cook small or cut beans in about 1 to 2 inches water with about ½ teaspoon salt per pound of beans. Bring to the boiling point, cook vigorously without a cover for 2 to 4 minutes to retain the color, then cover tightly and cook until barely tender. Young, cut beans may take as little as 3 minutes, large mature ones as much as 15 or more minutes. Cooking time depends on the variety, the age and the size of the beans.

Cook beans for the shortest possible time, only until just tender and crisp; cooked green beans should be bright green. Overcooked snap beans are mushy, flavorless and dingy.

Cook *frozen* beans according to package directions; in many cases the assigned cooking time is too long and overcooks the beans. Re-heat *canned* beans quickly in a little of their own liquid, just enough to prevent scorching.

JACK BEAN
Canavalia ensiformis

A shrub bean grown in warm parts of the Old and New Worlds mostly as a forage plant. The pods may grow to a length of a foot but when they are small and tender they are eaten as a green vegetable and cooked like green beans. The large white seeds, each with a dark eye, are also cooked and eaten the way broad beans are, though their tough skin should be peeled off and they should be thoroughly cooked in a change of waters before consumption.

POLE BEAN
Phaseolus coccineus

Pole beans, as opposed to bush beans, are any of several varieties so called because their vines need the support of poles as they climb. Their pods can grow twice the length and diameter of an ordinary green bean, which they otherwise closely resemble. Kentucky Wonder is one of the best known varieties.

Pole beans cook tender in a shorter time than other green beans. Cook in the same manner, but watch closely and cook only until just tender crisp.

SCARLET RUNNER BEAN
Phaseolus coccineus or multiflorus

A variety that is the most popular green bean in Great Britain. This pole bean comes originally from Mexico and the Southwest, where variants of this bean have been grown since prehistoric times.

When young and tender, the pods of scarlet runner beans are cooked and eaten like other green beans. Dried scarlet (colored from pink, spotted to black) runner beans are occasionally available in Southwestern markets and are cooked like other dried beans.

YARD-LONG BEAN
Chinese Long Beans
Vigna sesquipedalis

A vine originating in tropical Asia, with slender edible seed pods which may grow to a length of three or four inches while only one half inch or so wide. Yard-long beans belong mainly to tropical East Asian cookery, but they are also occasionally found in California or other Southern markets, mainly as a curiosity.

Use only when small and tender. Cook as other green beans, but for a shorter time.

GREEN BEANS LYONNAISE

4 servings

1½ pounds green or wax beans, trimmed and washed	½ teaspoon dried thyme
	salt
3 tablespoons butter	freshly ground pepper
1 large onion, minced	2 tablespoons minced parsley

Cook the beans in boiling salted water until tender but still crisp. While the beans are cooking, heat the butter in a deep frying pan. Add the onion. Cook, stirring constantly, for 3 to 5 minutes or until the onion is tender and golden. Drain the beans and add them to the frying pan. Stir in the thyme and salt and pepper. Cook over medium heat for 3 or 4 minutes stirring with a fork to coat the beans with the onion. Sprinkle with parsley and serve hot.

SOUTHERN POLE BEANS AND NEW POTATOES

4-6 servings

2 pounds pole beans, trimmed and washed

2 pounds very small peeled new potatoes or peeled new potatoes cut into quarters

½ pound ham hock or bacon in 1 piece

⅓ cup water

salt

freshly ground pepper

freshly baked corn bread

If desired, snap the beans into pieces. Place in a heavy saucepan. Add the potatoes, the ham and the water. Simmer covered over low heat until the potatoes are tender. Season with salt and pepper. Serve with freshly baked corn bread.

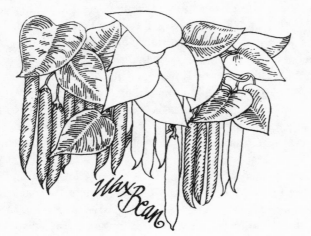

Wax Bean

GREEN BEANS PROVENÇALE

4 servings

1½ pounds green or wax beans, trimmed and washed	2 large tomatoes, peeled, seeded and chopped
2 tablespoons olive oil	salt
1 tablespoon butter	freshly ground pepper
1 medium onion, very thinly sliced	¼ cup minced fresh basil or 1 or 2 tablespoons dried basil
1 garlic clove, mashed	¼ cup minced parsley

Cook the beans in boiling salted water for 5 minutes. Drain and plunge into a bowl of cold water. Drain again. Heat the olive oil and butter in a deep frying pan. Add the onion and garlic and cook for 5 minutes, until the onion is soft. Add the tomatoes, salt, pepper, the basil and the parsley. Cook, stirring frequently, for about 5 minutes. Add the beans and mix well. Cook covered for 3 to 5 minutes or until the beans are just tender.

BROAD BEAN
Fava Bean
Vicia faba

Broad beans are one of the most ancient vegetables cultivated in the Western World, and for centuries they were the only readily available beans in Europe. The Mediterranean people of old had many curious beliefs about them; Egyptian priests thought them unclean, Pythagoras the Greek loathed them and the Roman pontifex was not allowed even to mention them since they were a funeral plant—bean feasts traditionally ended funerals. But the common Romans ate them, so much so that candidates for public office distributed broad beans at election time, when they were also used as counters in voting.

Broad beans have always been a staple of European and Mediterranean countries: in England, in Germany where they are called pig beans (Saubohnen), in France (fèves), in Italy (fave), and in the Arab countries (fool). In the United States, broad beans (also known as shell beans, Windsor beans, or horse beans) are becoming more common in our markets, especially those catering to ethnic groups.

Broad beans have large, rich green pods which can grow to over a dozen inches in length. They are heavy and their seeds are big and flat, resembling lima beans. Beans and their pods are eaten together occasionally; more usually the beans are shelled, to be eaten fresh or dried. When mature, broad beans have a tough skin which is better peeled off before cooking. Since they are a rather coarse vegetable, they are best cooked with bacon, ham or pork, the traditional ways, or served with these meats. If young and tender, or when peeled, fresh broad beans may be cooked like lima beans. Dried broad beans are cooked like other dried beans.

Broad beans are high in proteins, carbohydrates, and minerals, and when fresh, vitamins.

Allow about ¾ to 1 pound unshelled beans for each serving.

3½ ounces, raw, immature seeds, fresh—105 calories.

3½ ounces raw, mature seeds, dried—338 calories.

FAVA BEAN PURÉE

4 servings

Serve with thick tomato slices sautéed in butter as an accompaniment to any lamb or veal dishes or with roast chicken. Sprinkle the de-fatted meat juices over the purée.

5 pounds fava beans in the pod	salt
boiling water	freshly ground pepper
6 tablespoons butter	⅛ teaspoon ground nutmeg

Shell the beans. If they are very large, remove the tough skin with the tip of a sharp knife. Cook covered in enough boiling water to cover the beans generously for about 10 minutes or until the beans are very tender. Drain and reserve the cooking water. Purée in a blender with 1 or 2 tablespoons of the cooking water or mash through a sieve. Return the bean purée to the heat and add the butter. Cook over very low heat, stirring constantly, for 5 minutes or until the beans are very hot. Season with salt and pepper and nutmeg.

ROMAN FAVA BEANS

4 servings

The Romans make this dish with *guanciale*, pork jowl, which is hard to find in this country. In its stead, pancetta may be used, a tightly rolled cut of pork (it is the same cut as bacon) which is not smoked, but cured in salt and spices. Pancetta, found in Italian food stores, is used as a flavoring in the way we use bacon. It has a definite, pleasing flavor. When none is available, use prosciutto, or bacon, though the flavor of the dish will be different. Serve with roast pork or lamb.

4 pounds fava beans in the pod
1 tablespoon lard or olive oil
1 small onion, minced
4 ounces pancetta or bacon, cut
   into ¼-inch strips

¼ cup water or beef consommé
salt
freshly ground pepper

Shell the fava beans. If they are very large, remove the tough skin with the tip of a sharp knife. Heat the lard in a heavy saucepan. Cook the onion in it until golden. Add the pancetta and cook 1 minute longer. Add the fava beans, water and salt and pepper. Mix well. Simmer covered over low heat for 5 to 15 minutes, depending on the size and toughness of the beans. Stir frequently and check the moisture and seasoning.

LIMA BEAN
Phaseolus limensis

Lima beans are New World beans, natives of South America where different varieties have been cultivated for centuries. In this country, they grow as tall vines or as bushes, with large dark green pods which contain a few flat, smooth big or small seeds, varying in color from the palest green to buff and mottled buff. The pods are shelled and the beans eaten fresh or dried. Their taste is delicate and mealy.

Lima beans are among the most popular American beans and considered finer than other beans; in Europe, they are unknown to all but botanists though nobody knows why this is so. In our South, they are sometimes called "butter beans," a term also used by New Englanders to describe yellow "wax" beans. Though different varieties are marketed, for consumers lima beans fall into two basic categories: the large, so-called Fordhook beans, and small baby limas, which are whitish-green in color. These are the lima beans canned or frozen.

How to Buy

Available the year round, though scarce from January through June. Peak season from July through September. However, practically the whole crop is frozen or canned. *Buy* limas whose pods are clean, bright, fresh, dark green and properly filled. The shelled bean should be plump with tender skin, and the color of the skin should be a good green or greenish white. *Avoid* flabby pods or pods that are dry, shriveled, spotted, yellowed or with decayed sunken areas. *Shelled limas,* occasionally sold thus for convenience, should be tested for blemishes and for tenderness by puncturing the skin. Beans with hard tough skin are overmature and lacking in flavor.

Allow ¾ to 1 pound unshelled beans per serving. Two pounds unshelled give about 2½ cups shelled.

How to Keep

Shell only when ready to cook. Store unshelled limas in a moisture-proof container and refrigerate. Though unshelled lima beans will keep for about three days, it is best to use them as soon as possible. Shelled limas are very perishable and should be used as soon as shelled.

Unshelled, refrigerator shelf—3 to 4 days.

Cooked and covered, refrigerator shelf—2 to 4 days.

Nutritive Values

A fair source of proteins, carbohydrates and vitamins A and C.
Young beans, 3½ ounces, cooked and drained—99 calories.

How to Use

When ready snap pod open or use scissors to cut a thin strip lengthwise from the inner edge to make shelling easier. Remove beans.
Cook beans, covered, in a minimum of boiling salted water until just
tender; cooking time depends on age and size of the beans, varying
from 5 to 15 minutes.

Cook *frozen* lima beans according to package directions; frequently
the cooking time is too long and overcooks the beans. Reheat *canned*
lima beans quickly in a little of their own liquid, just enough to
prevent scorching.

Dried lima beans are cooked like other dried beans.

SUCCOTASH

4 servings

I find that the addition of a little hot pepper or hot sauce improves the
dish.

2 pounds lima beans in the pod
boiling water
4 large ears corn
1 tablespoon butter
¼ teaspoon hot pepper flakes or
    dash of Tabasco (optional)

½ cup heavy cream
salt
freshly ground pepper

Shell the beans. Cook them in boiling water to cover for about 5
minutes or until half tender. Cut off the corn kernels and scrape the
liquid from the cob with the dull edge of a knife. Add corn and liquid
to the beans. Mix well. Stir in butter and hot pepper flakes or Tabasco and cook for 5 minutes. Stir in the cream and heat through
thoroughly. Do not boil. Season with salt and pepper.

LIMA BEANS IN CREAM

4 servings

To my mind, the best of all lima bean recipes.

4 pounds lima beans in the pod
boiling water
2 tablespoons butter, cut into
  pieces
¾ cup heavy cream

salt
freshly ground pepper
⅛ teaspoon ground nutmeg
2 tablespoons minced parsley
  and chives, mixed

Shell the beans. Cook them in boiling water to cover for about 5 to
7 minutes or until almost tender. Drain. Stir in the butter and cook
for 1 minute, stirring to coat the beans. Stir in the cream and season
with salt and pepper and nutmeg. Cook over low heat for about 3
minutes or until the cream is hot and slightly thickened. Do not boil.
Sprinkle with the parsley and serve very hot.

DRIED BEANS
Phaseolus vulgaris

Dried beans, in many varieties, have been and still are a staple food
of a large part of mankind. Apart from their high protein content and
their tastiness, another advantage is their easy storage and long shelf
life. Many dried beans are ground into flours and used as diet supple-
ments or in allergy diets. These bean flours are often important in Far
Eastern diets.

In Europe, especially in Mediterranean countries like Italy, some
varieties of kidney and other beans are eaten fresh as well as dried.
These fresh beans, characterized by a somewhat wilted yellowish
pod, are beginning to find their way into our markets (especially
Italian ones) during the summer. Shelled, they are prepared like any
dried beans that have been soaked prior to cooking, though they take
less time. Their flavor is excellent and far superior to that of dried
beans.

A list of the most popular dried beans in the United States follows, although of course different regions have different favorites. There are different varieties of each kind of bean and they are grown in all the farming areas of the country.

BLACK OR TURTLE BEANS

Black beans are small, oval in shape, with a black skin hiding a whitish inside. They are largely used for soups such as the famous Black Bean Soup, and are Southern favorites. Black beans are the staple of South American countries such as Brazil, invariably served with rice.

BLACK-EYE AND YELLOW-EYE "PEASE," "COWPEAS" (See page 256)

CRANBERRY BEANS

These small beans are pink with pink markings. A traditional New England dish made with them is Cranberry Succotash.

FLAGEOLETS

Small, oval green beans with a delicate flavor used widely in France, especially with lamb dishes. Available in the United States either canned or dried, imported from France.

LIMA BEANS

(See page 58)

PINTO AND PINK BEANS

Though related, these beans look different. Pintos are pale pink mottled with brown, pinks are more brownish red than their name implies. Both varieties turn red-brown in cooking. Pinto and pink beans are much used in Mexican cooking.

RED BEANS, CHILE BEANS

Their color is darker than that of red kidney beans. They are used in Mexico and in the Southwest for Spanish dishes and chile con carne.

RED KIDNEY BEANS

Red in color with a purple hue, these beans have a distinctive flavor suited to soups, casseroles, chile con carne and salads. They are probably the most widely used American bean, and equally popular in France, Scandinavia and other European countries.

SOYBEANS
(See page 313)

MARROW BEANS

These beans are the largest and roundest of the white beans, grown chiefly in the East.

GREAT NORTHERN BEANS

They are large, with a distinctive flavor.

NAVY BEANS

Smaller than Great Northerns, they are used extensively by canners of pork and beans. These are the Italian "cannellini" beans available here in cans.

LUPINI BEANS

These are seeds of the lupin and though botanically they belong to the pea family, they resemble beans because of their flat, round, penny-like shape. The yellow variety has been used in Southern Europe cooked as any bean, or boiled and pickled in brine, and sold outside taverns to stimulate thirst. The shell is tough and must be slipped off before eating, and the flavor is bland, thoroughly uninteresting and on the somewhat acrid side. Pickled Lupini Beans in jars are found in American supermarkets and Italian groceries. For centuries, roasted Lupini Beans have served as a coffee substitute in the poorer countries of the Mediterranean.

PEA BEANS

The smallest of the white beans used widely in New England for "Boston Baked Beans."

Haricot is the French word for all beans. The name is qualified by the kind of bean, such as *haricots verts*, or *haricots rouges, secs,* respectively green beans, or dried red beans. In France, many of the beans which we only know as dried, such as navy or kidney beans, also appear on the market as fresh beans. When French recipes call for *haricots blancs* they usually refer to our navy beans or Great Northern beans. In England, *haricot* is the word used for various dried white beans, though there is also a brown variety.

How to Buy

Dried beans are available all the year round. *Buy* beans that are clean, uniform in size (for even cooking) and in quality with a bright, uniform color. If the color is dull, the beans have lost their freshness. *Avoid* beans which are shriveled, cracked, blemished or which have insect pinholes.

1 pound raw—approximately 2 cups.
1 pound cooked—approximately 6 cups.
1 cup, raw—approximately 2 to 2½ cups cooked.

How to Keep

Keep beans in or transfer unused beans from a package to a clean, covered container in a dry place.

Dried, kitchen shelf—1 year or more.
Cooked and covered, refrigerator shelf—1 to 4 days.

Nutritive Values

Dried beans are the highest source of proteins after animal proteins, though their protein quality is inferior to that of meats and dairy foods. They contain a fair amount of thiamine and are a very good source of iron.

3½ ounces cooked—120 calories.

How to Use

Packaged dried beans should be rinsed under running cold water before using. Bulk beans should be sorted over carefully; discard broken or defective beans and wash in several changes of cold water until the water is clear. Most recipes call for dried beans to be soaked before cooking. There are two methods.

For the overnight, old-fashioned method, measure the beans in a cup measure and place them in a deep bowl. Add 2½ to 3 cups water for each cup of beans. Soak overnight. If at all possible, use the nutritious, flavorful soaking water for cooking the beans or in the recipe. For the quick method, measure beans in a cup measure and place in a deep pot. Add 2½ to 3 cups water for each cup of beans. Bring to the boiling point and boil for 2 minutes. Remove from heat, cover pot and let stand at room temperature for 1 to 2 hours. Cooking time varies considerably for the different kinds of beans, ranging from approximately 45 minutes for small limas to 1½ to 2 hours for Great Northern, pinto and kidney beans. Beans may be cooked on top heat or in the oven.

Cover beans when cooking.

Do not cook beans quickly or over high heat because this breaks their skins. Simmer over low heat to keep them whole and flavorful.

Do not overcook beans.

Salt beans only when cooked; salt slows their cooking because it toughens them.

Acids, like wine, vinegar, tomatoes or lemon juice also slow down the softening process. Add them only when the beans are almost cooked.

A ham bone, sliced or cut-up bacon, chopped onion, garlic, celery, green pepper, carrots, and herbs, in reasonable quantities, added to the beans when cooking will add flavor to them.

When making a salad of cooked dried beans, add the dressing to the drained, *hot* beans. This step adds greatly to the flavor of the salad.

Cooked beans and bean dishes freeze well.

FLAGEOLETS BRETONNE

6 servings

This dish may be made with flageolet beans or navy or any small white beans. It is an excellent accompaniment for lamb and pork dishes.

2 cups dried flageolets, soaked
   and ready to cook
1 onion, stuck with 1 clove
1 medium carrot, scraped
½ celery stalk
½ teaspoon dried thyme
3 sprigs parsley
1 bay leaf
water

2 tablespoons butter
½ cup minced onion
½ cup minced shallots
1 cup peeled chopped tomatoes
½ teaspoon dried thyme
salt
freshly ground pepper
2 tablespoons minced parsley

Put the beans into a large saucepan. Add the onion, carrot, celery and bouquet garni (made with the thyme, parsley and bay leaf tied together in a small piece of cheesecloth). Add water to cover plus 3 inches. Bring to the boiling point. Lower the heat and simmer covered for 45 minutes to 1 hour or until the beans are tender. Remove the onion, carrot, celery and bouquet garni. Drain and reserve the cooking liquid. Heat the butter in a casserole. Add the onion and shallots and cook, stirring constantly, until they are golden; do not brown. Add the tomatoes and the thyme. Cook for 5 more minutes, stirring frequently. Add the beans and a little of their cooking liquid, beginning with 2 tablespoons. Season with salt and pepper. Stir gently with a fork to mix well. Simmer covered over low heat for 10 to 15 minutes. Check for moisture; if necessary, add a little more bean liquid. Sprinkle with the parsley and serve very hot.

BLACK BEANS

12 servings

Long, slow cooking in the oven makes the best beans; it is also painless. Reheat leftover beans or make into soup.

2 pounds dried black beans
12 cups water
2 medium onions, chopped
2 garlic cloves, chopped
1 or 2 teaspoons ground cumin
 (optional)
1 teaspoon ground thyme

2 pounds ham or prosciutto
 hocks or 1-pound slab bacon,
 in 1 piece
salt
freshly ground pepper
sour cream

Wash and drain the beans. Put them and the water into a large casserole of a size that will go into the oven. Add the onions, garlic, cumin, thyme and the ham. Cover and cook in a slow oven (275° F) for about 8 hours or until the beans are tender. At serving time, remove the meat and discard. Skim off as much fat as possible. Or chill, skim off fat and reheat slowly in the oven. Season with salt and pepper. Serve with sour cream on the side.

CRANBERRY BEAN SUCCOTASH

4-6 servings

1 cup dried cranberry beans,
 soaked and ready to cook
boiling water
4 large ears corn

5 tablespoons butter or to taste
salt
freshly ground pepper
¼ teaspoon dried thyme

Cook the beans in boiling water to cover plus 3 inches in a covered saucepan for about 1 hour or until tender. Drain and return to saucepan. Cut off the corn kernels and scrape the liquid from the cob with the dull edge of a knife. Add the corn and liquid to the beans. Stir in 4 tablespoons of the butter, salt and pepper and thyme. Cook covered over low heat for about 5 minutes or until the corn is tender. Shake the pan frequently to prevent sticking. Remove from heat and stir in the remaining tablespoon of butter.

RANCH-STYLE PINTO BEANS

4-6 servings

2 cups dried pinto beans,
    soaked and ready to cook
2 large tomatoes, peeled and
    chopped
1 medium onion, chopped
2 garlic cloves, minced
½ hot chile pepper, peeled,
    seeded and chopped, or to
    taste

½ teaspoon ground cumin
2 tablespoons olive oil
juice of 1 lemon
salt
freshly ground pepper
toasted tortillas

Put the beans into a large saucepan. Add water to cover plus 3 inches. Bring to the boiling point. Lower the heat and simmer covered for about 1 hour or until the beans are almost tender. Drain and reserve the cooking liquid. Return the beans to the saucepan and add the tomatoes, onion, garlic, chile pepper, cumin, olive oil and lemon juice. Simmer covered over low heat, stirring frequently, until the beans are tender. Check for moisture; if necessary, add a little of the cooking liquid to prevent scorching. Season with salt and pepper. Serve very hot with toasted tortillas.

KIDNEY BEANS IN RED WINE

6 servings

You may use 2 pounds fresh kidney beans in the pod, shelled.

2 cups dried kidney beans,
    soaked and ready to cook
1 onion stuck with 1 clove
1 garlic clove, mashed
1 teaspoon dried thyme
3 sprigs parsley
1 bay leaf

¼ pound lean bacon, in one
    piece or tied together if sliced
3 cups dry red wine
3 cups water
salt
freshly ground pepper
2 tablespoons butter

Put the beans into a large casserole. Add the onion, garlic, bouquet garni (made with the thyme, parsley and bay leaf tied together in a small piece of cheesecloth), bacon, the wine and the water. Bring to the boiling point and lower the heat to very low. Simmer covered for 1 to 2 hours or until the beans are tender. Remove the onion and the bouquet garni and throw away. Remove the bacon. Drain the beans and season with salt and pepper. Turn into a heated serving dish and keep hot. Cut the bacon into small dice. Heat the butter in a small frying pan and cook the diced bacon for 2 or 3 minutes. Add the bacon to the beans and mix well. Serve very hot.

TUSCAN BEANS

4-6 servings

The dish should be well flavored with sage.

1½ cups dried white beans,
  soaked and ready to cook
2 tablespoons butter
3 tablespoons olive oil
2 or 3 tablespoons minced fresh
  sage or 1 to 1½ teaspoons
  dried sage or ground sage

salt
freshly ground pepper
⅓ cup fresh tomato sauce

Cook beans in boiling water to cover plus 3 inches for 45 minutes to 1 hour or until the beans are tender. This must be done over very low heat to prevent the beans from bursting open. Do not salt or the beans will be tough. Drain the beans. Heat together the butter and the olive oil. Add the beans, sage and salt and pepper to taste. Cook over medium heat for about 3 minutes, stirring with a fork so as not to break the beans. Add the tomato sauce and cook for 3 minutes longer or until sauce and beans are very hot.

BEAN SPROUTS

Bean sprouts are the seeds of grains or legumes that have germinated and, in doing so, converted their fats and starches into easily digestible vitamins, sugars and proteins. The taste of the pale tender shoots, depending on the variety of bean sprouted, is crisp, usually pleasant and somewhat nutlike, bland enough to be added to salads and main dishes. The ease with which sprouts can be produced at home or their inexpensiveness when bought in Oriental stores have made them a valuable addition to American nutrition. Of course they have been popular for thousands of years in China.

The most commonly sprouted beans are the small round green or golden *mung beans (Phaseolus aureus),* natives of tropical Asia which have been cultivated in China for thousands of years. They are an essential of Chinese cookery. Mung beans are made into another basic Chinese and Japanese food; thin, colorless transparent spaghettilike threads known as cellophane noodles. Bean sprouts are produced from other beans as well, such as soybeans. But the kind sold fresh or canned in Oriental stores and supermarkets are sprouted mung beans.

Bean sprouts are available the year round. Buy fresh looking, crisp sprouts with moist tips. Short sprouts mean young, tender ones. Refrigerate in a plastic bag and use as soon as possible.

Bean sprouts are a good source of proteins, vitamins A and C and minerals.

Mung bean sprouts, 3½ ounces raw—35 calories.

Mung bean sprouts, 3½ ounces, cooked, drained—28 calories.

To use

Wash thoroughly and drain well. Chill in ice water for about 30 minutes if they are to be served raw in a salad. Do not remove the loose hulls or little roots from sprouted beans since they contain most of the vitamins and the flavor. Cook in boiling salted water to cover for 2 to 3 minutes. Do not overcook—bean sprouts must be crisp.

EGG FU YUNG

4 servings

2 cups bean sprouts
boiling water
6 eggs, beaten
2 tablespoons grated onion
2 green onions, white and green
   parts, thinly sliced
salt

freshly ground pepper
1 cup cooked, peeled chopped
   shrimp or 1 cup cooked
   shredded pork
salad oil
soy sauce

Cook the bean sprouts in boiling water to cover for 3 minutes. Drain.
Combine the bean sprouts, eggs, grated onion, green onions, salt and
pepper and the shrimp or pork. Heat about 1 teaspoon oil in a small
frying pan. Add about ⅓ cup of the egg mixture and cook until set,
as you would a pancake. Turn over with a spatula and cook on the
other side. Transfer to a serving dish and keep warm in a low oven.
Repeat until all the egg mixture is used.

BEAN SPROUTS AU GRATIN

4 servings

2 tablespoons butter	freshly ground pepper
2 tablespoons flour	⅛ teaspoon ground nutmeg
1 cup milk or light cream	6 cups (about 1 pound) cooked
1¼ cups grated Swiss cheese	bean sprouts
salt	

Heat the butter and stir in the flour. Cook, stirring constantly, for 1 minute. Stir in the milk and cook until the mixture is smooth and thickened. Remove from heat and stir in 1 cup of the Swiss cheese. Stir until the cheese is melted. Taste and season lightly with salt and pepper and nutmeg. Add the bean sprouts to the sauce. Turn into a buttered 1-quart baking dish and sprinkle with the remaining ¼ cup of cheese. Bake in a preheated hot oven (400° F) for 10 minutes or until golden.

BEET
Beetroot, Red Beet
Beta vulgaris

Beets are vegetables that provide both edible bulbous red roots and leafy green stalks. Of the two, the roots are far more universally used because they stay fresh longer, are easily stored and are used in canning.

There are four different varieties of beets that are commonly cultivated:

1. The garden beet, the vegetable that we mean when talking of beets.
2. The leaf beet, or Swiss chard, of which only the leaves and stalks are eaten.
3. The sugar beet, one of the world's major sources of sugar.
4. The mangold, or mangel-wurzel, a major livestock feed.

Swiss Chard is the more anciently used form of *Beta vulgaris*. Since it is used as a vegetable of its own, details and recipes will be found on pages 333-336.

Sugar beets, derived from mangolds, are a relatively modern development as a source of sugar. Sugar beets are long white roots (as distinct from the bulbous red roots of the garden beet). It is easier and cheaper to make sugar from them than from sugar cane and it is impossible to distinguish between raw beet sugar and raw cane sugar since they are identical in appearance and chemical composition.

Mangolds as a cattle feed or for silage are derived from chard and are more extensively grown for these uses in Europe than in the United States.

How to Buy

Available the year round, peak season from June through October. They are marketed with or without the green tops, the fall crop which is stored being usually the one sold without them. *Buy* beets with a good round shape, smooth, firm flesh and a rich, deep red color. Choose small or medium beets which are tender whereas large ones may be tough. If the green tops are on, they should be fresh looking; however, somewhat wilted tops do not affect the quality of the root. *Avoid* spotted, pitted beets or beets with scales. Avoid also very large beets, or beets that are flabby and wilted.

Beet tops
Frequently beet tops are taken from young plants and sold in bunches as salad greens or potherbs. *Buy* beet tops which are thin-ribbed, fresh and clean. *Avoid* wilted tops or tops with even a touch of slime.

1 pound medium-sized, roots only—2 to 3 servings.

How to Keep

If the beets have tops, cut them off about 1 to 2 inches above the crown; leave root ends intact. If the beet tops are fresh, save them and store in refrigerator, using as soon as possible. Place the beets into a plastic bag or the vegetable drawer of the refrigerator.

Uncooked, refrigerator shelf or vegetable drawer—3 weeks.

Cooked or canned, covered, refrigerator shelf—1 week.

Nutritive Value

Beet roots are a good source of vitamins A and C and they contain small amounts of minerals. Beet tops are an excellent source of vitamins A and C as well as calcium.

3½ ounces beet roots, cooked and drained—32 calories.

3½ ounces beet tops, cooked and drained—18 calories.

How to Use

To preserve their color, beets are almost always cooked or baked whole until tender and then peeled. The exception is very small young beets which are scrubbed and cooked with their green tops. Since beets bleed easily, cut off any tops about 1 to 2 inches from the crown; this keeps the color loss during cooking at a minimum. Wash the beets and if large, scrub with a vegetable brush. Cook whole and unpeeled in boiling salted water to cover until tender. Cooking time varies from about 15 minutes to an hour depending on the age and size of the beets. Drain and cool quickly under running cold water. Trim crown and root ends and rub off the skin. Use as directed in recipe. If the beets are not used at the time of cooking, do not trim or peel them but store covered in the refrigerator. Or bake the beets until tender, as is done in France and Italy where ready cooked beets are sold at the greengrocer's. Baked beets are more flavorful than boiled ones. To bake, place the trimmed beets on a shallow baking sheet. Brush with a little oil and bake in a preheated moderate oven (350° F) until tender. Cool before peeling.

To Cook Beet Tops

Wash and trim the leaves, discarding any that are damaged. If the tops are big, cut them and any very big leaves into pieces. Cook covered in just enough boiling salted water to prevent scorching. Do not overcook. Drain and use as in recipe, or serve with butter and lemon juice.

PICKLED BEETS

4 servings

The universal Scandinavian relish. The cooked dressing improves the flavor greatly.

½ cup cider or white vinegar
½ cup water
¼ cup sugar
1 teaspoon salt
¼ teaspoon freshly ground
pepper

2 or 3 cups cooked beets,
peeled and thinly sliced
1 tablespoon caraway seeds

Combine the vinegar, water, sugar, salt and pepper in a saucepan. Bring to the boiling point. Cook for 5 minutes. Cool. Put the beets into a deep bowl and pour the dressing over them. Sprinkle with the caraway seeds. Cover the bowl. Let stand at room temperature for about 4 hours or refrigerate overnight. Drain before serving.

BEETS PARMESAN

4-6 servings

16 tiny cooked, peeled beets ⅔ cup heavy cream
salt ⅓ cup grated Parmesan cheese
freshly ground pepper

Put the beets into a saucepan. Season with salt and pepper. Add the
cream. Cook over low heat, stirring carefully, until the beets and the
cream are heated through. Stir in the Parmesan cheese and cook until
the cheese is melted and the cream thickened. Serve very hot.

STEAMED BEETS AND TOPS

4 servings

Delicious when the beets are small and very fresh.

2 bunches small beets with   salt
  fresh green tops   freshly ground pepper
3 tablespoons butter or more to
  taste

Cut the beets from the tops. Trim and wash the beets. Peel with a
vegetable peeler. Cut into slices. Cut the stems from the leaves and
wash the leaves in several changes of water. Shake dry. Put the cut
beets into a saucepan. Add 2 tablespoons butter and a little salt and
pepper. Top with the leaves. Add the remaining tablespoon of butter
and a little salt and pepper. Cook covered over medium heat for 5 to
10 minutes, tossing occasionally. The dish is ready when the beets
are tender and the pan juices have cooked down to a few tablespoon-
fuls.

BELGIAN ENDIVE
Witloof, Chicon
Cichorium intybus

Belgian endives are the large, tender sprouts produced by the roots of a variant of the chicory tribe (see Chicory page 132). They are shaped like pointed cylinders about four to six inches long and one inch across with tightly packed creamy white leaves ending in pale yellowish-green tips. Their flavor is slightly bitter and their texture very crisp. They are used in salads and, less frequently, as a cooked vegetable. A very popular winter vegetable, it is almost entirely imported from Belgium.

Witloof, in Flemish, or *chicon,* in French, belongs to a variety of chicory from whose root comes the ersatz coffee used in Europe, especially in France and Italy, to stretch the costly product of the coffee bean. The vegetable was first discovered by chance around the middle of the last century, when some coffee chicory roots that had been lying around in the dark were found to have sprouted some whitish leaves. An enterprising head horticulturist of the Brussels Botanical Gardens, M. Brezier, took up the challenge and grew the first Belgian endives, as we know them, in the cellars of the Botanical Gardens along with mushrooms. In 1872 the first witloof went to Paris, and from there it conquered the world.

In the United States the popularity of witloof is on the increase, since, among its other virtues, it is so extremely low in calories that they barely count. Imports into the United States are rising, and prices have come down considerably since the first shipment of fifty boxes came in 1911, when the endives sold for one and a half good, solid, pre-World War dollars a pound retail.

How to Buy

Available September through May. Peak November through April.

Buy crisp, firm, tightly closed endives which should be creamy white with pale yellowish-green tips, free from stains and blemishes. *Avoid* endives with loose leaves, or leaves that are browning at the ends or have brown stems or that are soft and wilted.

Allow 1 medium endive for 1 salad serving.

1 pound—approximately 12 endives.

How to Keep

Refrigerate in a plastic bag or in vegetable drawer.
   Raw, refrigerator shelf or vegetable drawer—2 to 3 days.
   Cooked and covered, refrigerator shelf—1 day.

Nutritive Values

There is not much nutrition in Belgian endives, but since they are very low in calories, taste good and are filling, they are valuable diet food.
   3½ ounces raw—12 calories.

How to Use

Remove any wilted leaves and trim off stem. *For salads,* either separate leaves or cut into ¼-inch rounds. Wash, drain and dry with a kitchen towel. Place in plastic bag or dry towel and refrigerate to crisp further. *To cook,* prepare as above but leave whole or cut into halves lengthwise. See following recipes.

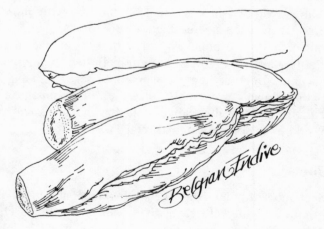
Belgian Endive

BELGIAN ENDIVE LOW-CALORIE APPETIZERS

Separate the leaves of several large, firm Belgian endives. Wash and dry them between paper towels. Wrap in a kitchen towel and chill in the refrigerator for added crispness. Use for any preferred dips. Or spread the stem-end of the leaves with a herbed cottage or cream cheese.

BRAISED BELGIAN ENDIVES

4 servings

Serve with roast pork or fowl.

4 tablespoons butter
1½ pounds small Belgian
  endives, trimmed and washed
½ cup chicken consommé or
  water

¼ teaspoon salt
freshly ground pepper
2 tablespoons fresh lemon juice

Butter a shallow casserole or baking dish with 1 tablespoon of the butter. Lay the endives in it in a single or double layer. Combine the water, salt, pepper and lemon juice and pour over the endives. Dot with 2 tablespoons of the butter. Cover tightly with a lid or with tied-on aluminum foil. Cook over low heat for about 10 minutes. Uncover and cook for 5 to 10 minutes longer or until the endives are tender but keeping their shape. The pan juices should be reduced to 2 or 3 tablespoons. For a golden effect, dot with the remaining tablespoon of the butter and run quickly under the broiler.

BELGIAN ENDIVES AND HAM AU GRATIN

4 servings

Serve as a luncheon dish with a tossed green salad.

8 large Belgian endives,
　trimmed and washed
2 tablespoons fresh lemon juice
½ teaspoon salt
water
2 tablespoons butter
2 tablespoons flour
1¼ cups milk

½ cup plus 2 tablespoons grated
　Swiss or Parmesan cheese
1 egg yolk
salt
freshly ground pepper
8 slices boiled ham or
　prosciutto

Put the endives into a saucepan with the lemon juice, the salt and just enough water to barely cover them. Simmer covered over low heat for about 10 minutes or until the endives are just tender; cooking time depends on the size. Drain the endives and dry them well between paper towels or they will make the final dish watery. Heat the butter in a saucepan and stir the flour into it. Cook, stirring constantly, for about 2 minutes. Stir in the milk. Cook, stirring all the time, until the sauce is smooth and thickened. Stir in the ½ cup of grated Swiss cheese. Remove from the heat and stir until the cheese is melted. Beat in the egg yolk. Season with salt and pepper. Wrap 1 ham slice around each endive. Place seam side down side by side in a shallow buttered baking dish. Pour the cheese sauce over the vegetables and sprinkle with the remaining 2 tablespoons of cheese. Bake in a pre-heated moderate oven (350° F) for about 15 minutes or until browned and bubbly.

Note: This dish may be made ahead of time, refrigerated and browned in the oven before serving. Do not leave too long in the oven or the dish will be watery.

BELGIAN ENDIVE AND BEETROOT SALAD

4-6 servings

One of the best winter salads. Combine the vegetables just before serving or the beets will color the endives red.

4 large, firm Belgian endives, trimmed and washed
2 medium beets, cooked and peeled
⅓ cup French dressing, made with the addition of 2 teaspoons Dijon mustard

lettuce
2 tablespoons minced parsley

With a sharp knife, cut the endives into long, thin strips. Cut the beets into julienne strips. Combine the vegetables in a kitchen bowl and toss carefully with the French dressing. Transfer the salad to a bowl lined with lettuce and sprinkle with parsley.

BREADFRUIT

Artocarpus

The fruit of a very beautiful large tropical tree originally found in the Pacific and Southeast Asia, which is part of the staple diet of millions of people in tropical countries such as Polynesia, the West Indies and Brazil. Breadfruit grow to up to eight inches in diameter and are roundish in shape with thick, warty rind and off-white flesh. Some have seeds, some not, but all are totally inedible until cooked, that is boiled, steamed or baked. Since breadfruit are high in carbohydrates, they serve as potato, rice or pasta substitutes. This starchy tropical vegetable is also a good source of thiamine and vitamin C. The flavor and texture as well as the color of the cooked breadfruit resemble somewhat grainy bread.

Breadfruit is associated with the famous mutiny of the *Bounty* crew in 1787; you may recall that the notorious Captain Bligh had been commissioned to introduce breadfruit plants into the West Indies from Tahiti.

Breadfruit, as common as it is in Puerto Rico and Hawaii, is not too frequently found in continental United States markets; it appears occasionally in Latin markets.

3½ ounces raw—approximately 103 calories.

BREADROOT
Pomme Blanche
Psoralea esculenta

These turnip- or spindle-shaped roots, also called prairie apple or prairie turnip, were used by the Great Plains and Western Indians as we use potatoes. They dug them, roasted them in ashes or dried and stored them for the winter. When needed, they were mashed, mixed with water and baked into cakes over the coals, as the early explorers and settlers who also used them tell us in their chronicles.

BROCCOLI
Brassica oleracea italica

When we speak of broccoli (the name comes from the Italian *brocco* meaning arm or branch), we mean sprouting broccoli, a cluster of green flowerbuds branching from a thick green stem with additional, smaller, clusters sprouting from the stem at the attachment of the leaves. There is another variety, with a dense white head, which is so like cauliflower that it is virtually indistinguishable and generally considered a cauliflower. Broccoli is a close relative of cauliflower, which is *Brassica oleracea botrytis,* and is less closely related to other *oleracea* such as cabbage, Brussels sprouts and kale.

Like other cabbages, broccoli is a native of the Mediterranean and Asia Minor. The Romans, according to Pliny, grew and ate it in the first century after Christ. The vegetable has remained popular in Italy, especially in Rome, during the centuries, in different varieties that tend to be purple in color and are especially flavorful. Hence the fact that broccoli is also called Italian broccoli or Calabrese, the variety common in the United States. In England, broccoli was introduced in the first part of the 18th century as "Italian asparagus," a touching conceit, though generally speaking, to this day the English remain cool to it. The French likewise treat it gingerly in their few broccoli recipes.

Today broccoli is a very popular American vegetable. Its popularity appears to have started with Italian immigrants who brought seeds, but broccoli only became better known in the 1920's, when D'Arrigo Brothers, Italian vegetable growers in San Jose, California, planted trial fields and shipped a few crates by express to Boston. The firm even supported an Italian radio program and ads for broccoli. From then on, the broccoli industry took off with a bang, both for the fresh and later, the frozen vegetable.

How to Buy

Available the year round, peak season October through April. *Buy* broccoli with heads with tightly closed and compact bud clusters which have not opened to show the yellow flowers. The color, depending on the variety, should be dark green, deep sage green or purplish green. Stalks and stem branches should be tender and firm with fresh leaves. *Avoid* bruised, wilted and flabby broccoli, or broccoli with open bud clusters showing the yellow flower and wooden looking stalks.

Allow ½ pound per serving. One medium bunch will make 3 to 4 servings.

How to Keep

Place unwashed broccoli in a plastic bag and refrigerate. Broccoli is very perishable, so use as soon as possible.

Uncooked, refrigerator shelf or vegetable drawer—3 days.

Cooked and covered, refrigerator shelf—1 to 3 days.

Nutritive Values

An excellent source of vitamins A and C if the vegetable is cooked quickly in a minimum of water. A good source of riboflavin, iron and calcium.

3½ ounces cooked spears, boiled and drained—28 calories.

How to Use

Only wash broccoli thoroughly when ready to use, but do not soak. Trim off only the toughest part of the stem. If the stalks are tough and more than 1 inch in diameter, peel them; this makes the whole stem edible and insures quicker cooking. If the peeled stems are larger than 1 inch in diameter, make 4 to 6 slashes through them up to the flowerets. This allows them to cook in the same time as the flowerets. Place in a saucepan with about 1 inch boiling water or stand up in the bottom part of a double boiler. Cover with a lid or with the top part of the double boiler and cook for about 7 to 10 minutes or until barely tender. During cooking remove the cover several times to let the steam escape; this keeps the broccoli green.

Or else divide the head into individual flowerets by slicing lengthwise from floweret to the bottom of the stem. If the flowerets are large, slice them into halves or quarters. Cook in the smallest possible amount of boiling salted water to prevent scorching for about 4 to 5 minutes or until just tender and crisp.

Broccoli may also be cut into thin diagonal slices (after peeling the stem) and sautéed quickly in hot shortening until just crisp.

Broccoli cooks quickly and is easily overcooked and mushy. Cook until just tender and very crisp.

BROCCOLI ROMAN STYLE

3-4 servings

1 bunch broccoli
3 tablespoons olive oil
1 garlic clove, whole
salt
freshly ground pepper

2 or 3 anchovies, mashed, or 1 or 2 tablespoons anchovy paste
1½ cups dry red or white wine

Trim the broccoli and cut into flowerets. Peel the stalks and cut them into 2-inch pieces. Wash and drain. Heat the oil in a deep frying pan. Cook the garlic in it until it turns brown. Remove and throw away. Add the broccoli and season with salt and pepper. Cook, stirring constantly, for 2 or 3 minutes. Add the anchovies and the wine. Cook over low heat for about 5 to 10 minutes or until the broccoli is tender but still firm. Stir occasionally with a fork, being careful not to break the flowerets.

PURÉED BROCCOLI

4-6 servings

Puréed vegetables don't wilt while waiting, which is the reason so many restaurants serve vegetables this way. Keep warm in the top of a double boiler, over hot water.

2 bunches broccoli, washed and ready for cooking

4 tablespoons butter, cut into pieces

salt

freshly ground pepper

2 to 4 tablespoons heavy cream

⅛ teaspoon ground nutmeg

Cook the broccoli until very tender and mushy. Drain and reserve the cooking liquid. Cut into pieces or mash with a fork. Strain through a sieve. Or purée in a blender, adding a little of the cooking liquid for easier blending. Return the broccoli purée to the saucepan and stir in the butter. Season with salt and pepper. Cook over medium heat, stirring constantly, until the broccoli purée is on the dry side. Stir in 2 tablespoons of the cream. The purée should be creamy but not soupy; if necessary for the proper consistency, add a little more cream. Stir in the nutmeg and serve very hot.

HOT OR COLD BROCCOLI SALAD
WITH CAPER SAUCE

4 servings

1 bunch broccoli	⅓ cup drained small capers
½ cup olive oil	freshly ground pepper
juice of 1 large lemon	

Trim the broccoli and cut into flowerets. Peel the stalks and cut them into 2-inch pieces. Wash and drain. Cook in boiling salted water to cover for 4 to 5 minutes or until barely tender. Drain and turn into a serving dish. Combine the remaining ingredients and mix well. Pour over the flowerets while they are still hot. Check the seasoning and toss gently with a fork. Serve at once or chill.

BRUSSELS SPROUTS
Brassica oleracea gemmifera

This plant, a member of the cabbage family, is a tall stemmed cabbage which forms many tiny heads called sprouts at the bases of the leaves. The lower leaves are pulled away allowing the sprouts to develop to an average size of one to one and one-half inches in diameter. Sprouts are one of the perennial English winter vegetables, though there, as in the United States, they are allowed to grow far too large, which coarsens their flavor and texture.

The history of Brussels sprouts is somewhat obscure. They are said to have been cultivated in Belgium in the 1500's but they don't appear to have been well known until their cultivation spread into France between 1800 and 1850. Sprouts have been known in America since the 1800's, but their cultivation was slow and they were not in general use as a vegetable. Their cultivation increased only after 1945, when frozen food industries started freezing them on a large scale. Thus, until recently, Brussels sprouts were a luxury vegetable, especially so in Europe, where tiny, fingernail-sized sprouts were prized for the delicacy of their taste.

How to Buy

Available unlimited quantities for ten months of the year, peak season October through February.

Buy the smallest available sprouts, with compact heads and bright green color; they should be free from all blemishes. *Avoid* soft, wilted, puffy heads or heads with loose or yellow leaves. Torn and smudgy leaves may hide insects.

Allow 1 pound per 3 to 4 servings. One pint box will serve 2 or 3.

How to Keep

Discard loose or yellowed leaves before storing. Place unwashed sprouts in a plastic bag and refrigerate. Use as soon as possible. Old sprouts acquire a strong flavor.

Raw, refrigerator shelf or vegetable drawer—1 to 2 days.

Cooked and covered, refrigerator shelf—1 to 2 days.

Nutritive value

Brussels sprouts are a good source of vitamins A and C and a fair source of iron.

3½ ounces, cooked and drained—36 calories.

How to Use

Wash thoroughly and trim off stem ends and loose leaves. If there are signs of insects, soak 10 minutes in cold salted water and rinse several times in changes of water. Cook in about 1 inch of boiling salted water without a cover for 4 minutes, then cover and cook 2 to 3 minutes longer, or until just tender. Drain. Do not overcook or sprouts will get mushy easily, acquire a strong flavor and lose vitamins.

BRUSSELS SPROUTS AND CHESTNUTS

4-6 servings

1 can (1 pound) whole
    chestnuts imported from
    France
1½ pounds Brussels sprouts,
    trimmed and washed
boiling salted water

4 tablespoons butter
salt
freshly ground pepper
¼ teaspoon ground nutmeg
¼ cup heavy cream
¼ cup minced parsley

Drain the chestnuts and wash them quickly under running cold water, taking care not to break them. Drain and dry between paper towels. Cook the Brussels sprouts in about 1 inch of boiling salted water until they are almost tender. Drain. Heat the butter and add the Brussels sprouts and the chestnuts. Season with salt and pepper and the nutmeg. Cover and cook over low heat, shaking the pan frequently, until the sprouts are tender. Add the cream, stir carefully with a fork and cook 1 minute longer. Turn into a heated serving dish and sprinkle with the parsley.

ITALIAN BRUSSELS SPROUTS

4 servings

1 pound Brussels sprouts,
    trimmed and washed
boiling salted water
4 tablespoons olive oil
2 garlic cloves, whole

salt
freshly ground pepper
2 tablespoons fresh lemon juice
¼ cup freshly grated Parmesan
    (optional)

Cook the Brussels sprouts in about 1 inch of boiling salted water until almost, but not quite, tender. Drain. While the sprouts are cooking, heat the oil in a large frying pan. Add the garlic. Cook over medium heat until the garlic is browned; remove the garlic and throw it away. Add the drained sprouts. Season with salt and pepper. Cook, stirring carefully with a fork so as not to break the sprouts, for 2 or 3 minutes. Add the lemon juice and cook for 1 minute longer. Turn into a heated serving dish and sprinkle with the Parmesan. Serve immediately.

BRUSSELS SPROUTS WITH LEMON SAUCE

3-4 servings

1 pound Brussels sprouts, trimmed and washed	salt
boiling salted water	freshly ground pepper
1 large or 2 small egg yolks	2 tablespoons fresh lemon juice or to taste

Cook the Brussels sprouts in about 1 inch of boiling salted water until tender but still firm. Drain the cooking liquid from the saucepan into a small bowl and reserve. Keep the sprouts warm in the saucepan in which they were cooked. Put the egg yolks into a heated serving dish and beat them well with a fork. Beat in 1 or 2 tablespoons of the reserved cooking liquid. Season with salt and pepper and beat in the lemon juice. Mix well. Turn the sprouts into the sauce and toss to coat them with the sauce. Serve immediately.

Note: This simple sauce is equally good with other vegetables, such as green beans, cauliflower, broccoli and chick peas.

BURDOCK
Arctium lappa

Burdock is a wild plant of which the leaves and the roots have been used both for medicine and food. It grows in the temperate parts of our country, and to most of us it is memorable for its wicked prickly burs that attach themselves to human beings with the greatest of ease and which are tiresome to pick off. The young tops with stems and leaves have been used as potherbs, and the roots, when young and thin, are eaten in Europe and by lovers of wild plants in the United States. In Hawaii and Japan, a large version of the roots is cultivated for their white (though coarse and fibrous) flesh beneath the grayish-brown exterior. Burdock appears in some Oriental markets of the United States, mostly known as *gobo* in Japanese. It is also imported canned from the Orient, as *gobo*. In the Middle Ages in Europe, burdock root was considered a good remedy against gall and kidney stones, skin disorders and as an antiscorbutic; applied externally, the leaves are said to relieve bruises and inflamed surfaces.

CABBAGE
Brassica oleracea

Cabbage is one of the members of the large *Brassica* family, cousin to kale and collards, broccoli, cauliflower, Brussels sprouts and kohlrabi. But when we speak of cabbage we mean the variety that has compact heads in many varieties and colors, the variety called *capitata*. There are cabbages with firm or loose heads, with flat or conical ones, plain or curly leaves, in shades of white, green or red. There are also exotic ones which don't look much like cabbages but still are true *Brassicas*. Cabbage is grown and eaten in most parts of the world. Almost any soil or climate will do, and in as little as three months growing time, an acre of cabbage plants will yield a greater amount of green vegetables than any other plant.

The origin of cabbage is ancient and obscure, though there is some evidence that the Eastern Mediterranean and Asia Minor may have been the place of origin of the species. The ancient Romans, as did the Greeks, thought highly of the vegetable, and the great Roman statesman, Marcus Porcius Cato, recommended it raw or cooked and as surpassing all other vegetables. He also suggested eating as much as possible with vinegar before a feast and still more afterwards. Raw cabbage with vinegar is still recommended by some as a fine hangover cure.

Cabbage has virtually become the national vegetable of Central and Northern Europe. Long considered the food of the masses, it is subject to national preferences for different kinds. Red varieties are most popular in Northern Europe and the savoyed varieties in the Southern parts. But most common is the smooth-leaved green or white variety.

American fondness for sauerkraut goes back to German settlers who brought it from their homeland where cabbage had been pickled for centuries, pickling being a basic method of food preservation before modern technology. But pickled cabbage is not limited to Germans and Americans: the Koreans have *kimchi,* a pickled cabbage dish which transcends in power anything found in the Western world.

As for cabbage lore: let us only remember that babies are found under cabbage leaves and that the Man on the Moon was sent there because he was caught stealing a cabbage from his neighbor on Christmas Eve. The Child in White who surprised him in this horrid deed said: "Since you will steal on this Holy Night, you and your cabbage must go to the moon."

How to Buy

Available the year round in 1- to 7-pound weights. There are 5 major market types:

Danish, also known as *Hollander,* solid-headed, late maturing, used for storage, with light, smooth leaves and either round, oval or somewhat flattened head.

Domestic, largely early season, with reasonably solid but not totally compact flat or round heads and crinkled or curled leaves. Does not keep well. Also used for sauerkraut.

Pointed, with pointed or conical heads, marketed in early spring as green cabbage. Mostly a Southwestern and a Western type.

Red, with a distinctive red or purplish color, largely used for pickling.

Savoy, loose heads with crinkly leaves throughout the head. This cabbage, a favorite of people of Latin descent, is becoming increasingly popular. The flavor is mellower than that of other cabbages.

Chinese cabbage, see page 138.

Buy firm heads that are heavy for their size. Outer leaves should be crisp and fresh looking, free of blemishes and with a fresh green or red color. Early cabbage and Savoy cabbage have softer, looser heads, but should have firm crisp leaves. *Avoid* heads that are too white, indicating overmaturity; blemished leaves with coarse discolored veins; or puffy heads. If leaf bases are separated from the stem, the cabbage may be strong in flavor and coarse in texture.

1 pound raw—2½ cups cooked, 3 servings.

1 pound raw—2½ cups raw shredded, 4 servings.

How to Keep

Refrigerate uncooked, unwashed and uncut in a plastic bag.

Firm hard cabbages will keep a week or more, soft-headed ones a few days.

Uncooked, refrigerator shelf—3 to 8 days.

Cooked and covered, refrigerator—1 to 4 days.

Nutritive Values

Raw cabbage is an excellent source of vitamin C, and of some vitamin A, provided it is cooked quickly and used soon after, as well as a fair source of minerals. Cabbage is ideal roughage to aid the digestion.

3½ ounces raw—24 calories

3½ ounces cooked and drained—20 calories.

How to Use

Wash head thoroughly and trim any wilted leaves or tough stem end. Cut into wedges and remove the center if the cabbage is old. Or shred cabbage on vegetable shredder or with a large wide knife, slicing across the head, or if the head is very large, after cutting it into halves or quarters. Savoy cabbage is either cooked whole or cut into serving-size wedges. Cook all green cabbage quickly to avoid odors. Cook wedges without a cover in about 1 inch of boiling salted water rapidly for about 2 to 3 minutes. Cover and cook a few more minutes, or until the cabbage is tender but still crisp. Drain and season.

Cook shredded cabbage without a cover in about ½ inch boiling salted water for 1 to 2 minutes; cover and cook for 1 to 2 minutes longer, depending on the size of the shreds. Do not overcook.

To braise cabbage, melt just enough butter or shortening to cover the bottom of a large saucepan or frying pan. Add cabbage wedges or shreds. Cook over low to medium heat for 2 to 3 minutes, turning the vegetable with a fork until it is coated with fat. Add a little water, cover the pan and steam for 5 to 10 minutes, depending on the size of the cabbage. Season when cooked and do not overcook. Red cabbage may be cooked by any of these methods, but add a little vinegar, lemon juice or a few pieces of a tart apple. These acids will hold the color. When combining red cabbage with another dish, cook it separately and add it later because otherwise it will discolor the dish.

Raw cabbage for salads may be either grated, shredded or cut into fine shreds.

FRENCH CABBAGE SOUP

8 servings

The soup can be made in advance and reheated.

3 cups potatoes, peeled and
  chopped
1 pound lean bacon or ham, in
  one piece
3 quarts water
1 medium cabbage weighing
  approximately 2 pounds,
  trimmed and chopped
6 whole crushed peppercorns
6 parsley sprigs
1 bay leaf

1 teaspoon thyme
½ teaspoon marjoram
2 garlic cloves, mashed
2 onions
2 carrots, quartered
2 stalks celery, sliced
2 peeled turnips, chopped
  (optional)
1 cup cooked red or white
  beans
salt

Place the potatoes and the bacon into a soup kettle. Add the water. Bring to the boiling point. Add all other ingredients except beans. Simmer, covered, for 2 hours or until meat is tender. Skim as needed. Remove meat and slice it into serving pieces. Skim off any excess fat from the soup. Return the meat to the soup. Add the beans. Season to taste with salt. Heat thoroughly. Serve with French bread.

NORTHERN ITALIAN SAVOY CABBAGE AND RICE SOUP

6-8 servings

If a thicker soup is wanted, increase the rice to 1 cup.

4 tablespoons minced salt pork, blanched
2 tablespoons butter
3 large, ripe tomatoes, peeled and chopped or 2 cups Italian-style canned tomatoes
2 garlic cloves, minced
¼ to ½ cup minced parsley
1 teaspoon dried thyme
1 small Savoy or other cabbage weighing approximately 1 to 1½ pounds, trimmed and shredded

8 cups beef consommé or water
salt
freshly ground pepper
⅓ cup rice
freshly grated Parmesan cheese

Combine the salt pork and the butter in a soup kettle. Cook over medium heat, stirring constantly, for about 3 minutes. Add the tomatoes, garlic, parsley and thyme. Cook covered, stirring frequently, for about 5 minutes. Add the cabbage and mix well. Cook over low heat, stirring frequently, for 10 to 15 minutes. Add the consommé, taste and season with salt and pepper. Reduce heat to low. Simmer covered for 30 to 45 minutes, stirring occasionally. Add the rice and cook for 15 to 20 more minutes or until the rice is tender. Serve with plenty of freshly grated Parmesan cheese.

STUFFED CABBAGE LEAVES WITH MUSHROOMS

6 servings

Serve with roast pork or veal.

6 large cabbage leaves
boiling water to cover
½ teaspoon salt
4 tablespoons butter or
  margarine, melted
2 cups (½ pound) chopped
  fresh mushrooms

1 cup soft bread crumbs
½ cup finely chopped celery
2 tablespoons grated onion
1 teaspoon salt
½ teaspoon ground thyme
ground black pepper

Cut out the coarse, heavy stems at the base of the cabbage leaves. Put the leaves in a deep frying pan. Add boiling water to cover and the salt. Cook over high heat for about 3 minutes or until the leaves are soft but not mushy; cooking time depends on their tenderness. Lift the leaves out of the water, drain and reserve the cooking liquid. Dry the leaves thoroughly between paper towels. Heat 1 tablespoon of the butter. Add the mushrooms and cook over high heat, stirring constantly, for 2 or 3 minutes. Remove from heat and stir in the bread crumbs, celery, onion, salt, thyme and pepper. Stir in the remaining butter and mix well. Cook over low heat, stirring constantly, until the mixture is well coated with the butter. Spread the cabbage leaves side by side on the kitchen counter. Place about ⅓ cup of the stuffing on each leaf. Roll tightly and fasten with toothpicks. Place the cabbage leaves, fastened side down and side by side, in a buttered shallow baking dish. Pour ½ cup of the reserved cabbage liquid around them. Bake in a preheated moderate oven (350° F) for about 20 minutes. Add more cabbage liquid if needed to prevent sticking.

CREAMED CABBAGE

4-6 servings

This is a lighter dish than the usual creamed cabbage. You may add 1 cup cooked peas to the cabbage.

1 medium cabbage weighing
    approximately 2 pounds,
    trimmed and thinly shredded
boiling salted water
2 to 4 tablespoons butter

1 cup milk or light cream
salt
freshly ground pepper
ground nutmeg to taste

Plunge the cabbage in a saucepan full of boiling salted water. Cook for 2 or 3 minutes. Drain and press out excess moisture. Put the cabbage into a saucepan. Add the butter, depending on taste, milk, salt, pepper and nutmeg. Simmer covered over low heat, stirring frequently, for about 5 minutes or until the cabbage is heated through.

CABBAGE AND TOMATOES

6 servings

3 tablespoons butter
1 small onion, minced
1 small cabbage weighing
    approximately 1 to 1½
    pounds, trimmed and
    shredded
½ cup boiling water
1 tablespoon flour
1 cup fresh tomato pulp (strain
    peeled tomatoes through a
    sieve or purée in a blender)

¼ cup minced parsley or fresh
    basil leaves
2 or 3 tablespoons sour cream
    or yoghurt
salt
freshly ground pepper

Heat 2 tablespoons of the butter. Cook the onion in it for 2 or 3 minutes, or until soft. Add the cabbage and the water. Cook over high heat, stirring constantly, for about 3 minutes or until the cabbage is quite tender but still crisp. Remove from heat. In a small saucepan, heat the remaining tablespoon of butter. Stir in the flour and cook for 1 minute. Add the tomato pulp and the parsley. Cook over medium heat, stirring constantly, for about 3 minutes or until the purée begins to thicken. Stir in the sour cream. Combine the tomatoes and the cabbage and mix well. Season with salt and pepper. Cover the saucepan and simmer over low heat for about 10 minutes, stirring frequently.

SWEET-SOUR RED CABBAGE

4-6 servings

Serve with roast pork, goose or duck, or braised beef.

1 medium red cabbage, weighing approximately 3 pounds	¼ cup water
	salt
	freshly ground pepper
3 tablespoons butter	2 medium tart apples, peeled, cored and chopped
1 tablespoon sugar or more, according to taste	½ cup red currant jelly
¼ cup cider vinegar	

Remove the tough outer leaves and the core from the cabbage. Cut into quarters. Shred the cabbage fine. Wash and drain. In a heavy saucepan, melt the butter. Stir in the sugar; do not let the sugar brown. Add the cabbage. Cook over medium heat, stirring constantly, for 3 or 4 minutes. Stir in vinegar, water and season with salt and pepper. Simmer covered over lowest possible heat or on an asbestos plate for about 1 hour, or until the cabbage is very tender. If necessary, add a little more water, 1 or 2 tablespoons at a time, to prevent scorching. Add the apples and the red currant jelly and mix well. Taste the cabbage. It should be sweet-sour; if necessary, adjust the taste with more sugar and vinegar, 1 tablespoon of each at a time. Simmer covered for 30 more minutes. Stir occasionally and check for moisture, adding more water if necessary.

SAUERKRAUT COOKED IN WINE *(Weinkraut)*

4-6 servings

Serve with fried meats or fish.

4 tablespoons lard, bacon fat or butter	1 cup dry white wine
2 medium onions, thinly sliced	salt
3 pounds sauerkraut	freshly ground pepper
	4 teaspoons sugar

Heat the lard in a heavy saucepan. Cook the onions in it until they are soft and golden; do not brown. Rinse the sauerkraut under running cold water and squeeze out all excess moisture. Add the sauerkraut and wine to the onions, mixing well. Do not press the sauerkraut down too hard, but keep it loose with a fork. Season with salt and pepper to taste and stir in the sugar. Simmer covered over low heat for about 1 hour. If necessary, add a little more wine to keep the sauerkraut moist, but it must not be soupy. This sauerkraut may be reheated.

CACTUS
Nopales, Nopalitos
genera Nopalea, Opuntia

The young padlike growths of some varieties of the nopal and opuntia cacti, which are popular vegetables in Mexico, Guatemala and other Latin American countries. Both cacti are known to Americans as ''prickly pears'' and sold under this name in many stores. Wrongly called leaves, these fleshy sections must be peeled cautiously, since they contain the cactus ''eyes'' with their vicious tiny thorns. The peeled vegetable is quite succulent, with a flavor and texture somewhat reminiscent of firm green beans. It is available the year round in Latin markets or canned and in jars.

To peel nopales, remove the eyes with the tip of a potato peeler or a sharp knife. Wash and cut, before or after cooking, into strips, ½-inch squares or chop. Cook covered in about an inch of boiling salted water for 5 to 10 minutes, depending on size. Cook until tender—the vegetable will remain firm. Drain and season to taste or add to a mixed meat and vegetable or vegetable dish.

CALABAZILLA
Calabaza, West Indian or Green Pumpkin
Cucurbita Foetid issina

This is one of the great family of squashes which include pumpkins, gourds, Hubbards, butternuts and others. It is a favorite of Latin American cookery which is now also found in Latin markets in the United States. Calabazas are mostly round in shape though some are long or pear shaped. Their heavy yellowish rind hides a vividly colored orange-yellow flesh with a flavor that is delicate and reminiscent of pumpkin. Large calabazas are generally not sold whole, but by the wedge. Use as any pumpkin or squash, in soups, as a vegetable, stuffed or in pudding or pie.

3½ ounces cooked—28 calories.

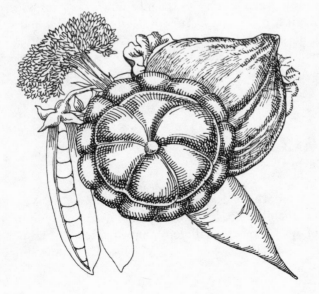

CALABAZA EN DAUBE

6 servings

In Martinique and Guadaloupe, this West Indian pumpkin dish is called a *Colombo de Giraumon*. You may substitute Hubbard squash, but the flavor will be different.

2 tablespoons butter
½ cup bacon, chopped fine
1 medium onion, minced
1 green bell pepper, minced
1 cup peeled chopped tomatoes
1 pound calabaza, peeled,
   seeded and cut into 1-inch
   pieces

⅛ teaspoon ground cloves
1 garlic clove, mashed
salt
freshly ground pepper
1 teaspoon curry powder
¼ cup water

Combine the butter and the bacon in a heavy saucepan. Cook, stirring constantly, for about 4 minutes. Add the onion and the green pepper and cook for 3 or 4 minutes, until the onion is soft. Add the tomatoes and cook for 5 minutes longer. Add the calabaza and mix well. Cook covered over low heat, stirring frequently, until the pumpkin is very tender and begins to fall apart. Stir in the cloves, garlic and salt and pepper. Simmer covered for 3 more minutes. Stir the curry powder into the water and add to the calabaza. Mix well and simmer for 5 more minutes, or until the vegetable is almost a purée.

CALLALOO
Callilu, Callau

A confusing term which describes the most famous of West Indian soups and the chardlike leaves of two plants used in the soup, which substitute for one another. Callaloo soup is found in Trinidad, Jamaica, Haiti, Guadaloupe and other islands. There are simple and elaborate versions, but all include the leaves of the two plants also called callaloo. One is the Taro (see page 336) with its succulent "elephant ear" foliage, and the other is the Chinese spinach (see page 317) with its smallish green leaves.

Lovers of the soup callaloo need not despair over the necessary leaves. Fresh spinach and Swiss chard have a very similar flavor and texture; either makes a good substitute for one of the most interesting dishes of Caribbean cooking.

CALLALOU

5-6 servings

". . . they sang callalou and away they flew, down to Demerara" (a children's song heard in St. Kitts, B.W.I.).

7 cups chicken consommé or
    water
1 medium onion, minced
1 garlic clove, mashed
½ teaspoon dried thyme
¼ pound (4 ounces) ham or
    lean bacon or salt pork, cut
    into small dice
1 pound callalou leaves, or
    Chinese spinach, or spinach
    or Swiss chard, shredded

½ pound small okra, trimmed
    (if large, cut into pieces)
½ pound fresh or frozen
    crabmeat, picked over and
    flaked
salt
freshly ground pepper
Tabasco or other hot pepper
    sauce

Combine the consommé, the onion, the garlic, the thyme, and the ham in a soup kettle. Bring to the boiling point. Lower the heat and simmer covered for 10 minutes. Add the greens and cook 10 minutes longer. Add the okra and the crabmeat and mix well. Turn heat to low and simmer covered for about 10 minutes. Season with salt and pepper and stir in Tabasco to taste.

CAPERS
Capparis spinosa

The unopened flower buds of a spiny shrub of Mediterranean origin, which pickled and spiced add zest to sauces, salads, creamed dishes, stews, seafoods and all dishes which can do with a bit of piquancy. The most desirable capers are the tiny, firm, perfectly round *nonpareil* which are mostly imported from France.

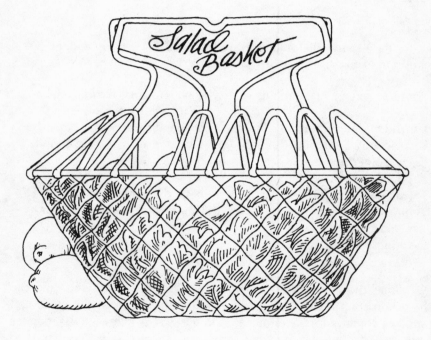

CARDOON
Cynara cardunculus

The cardoon is a whitish pale-green thistlelike plant which can grow to the height of three or more feet, looking rather like an overgrown bunch of celery with prickly leaves. Though a cousin of the artichoke, the edible parts of the cardoon are not the flower head but rather the tender and fleshy thickened stalks and leaf midribs. After removing the stringy parts, they are cut into pieces, blanched and eaten like celery in soups, salads and as a vegetable. Cardoons are a winter vegetable with a delicate flavor which resembles that of artichokes and oyster plants.

Cardoons are barely known in the United States, but they have been a favorite vegetable in their Mediterranean homeland since the days of the ancient Romans. Still a favorite and elegant French and Italian vegetable, the cardoon is used to a lesser extent in other European countries. In this country, it is grown in California and found in ethnic (especially Italian) markets. The pale color, like that of celery or endives, is achieved by blanching the plant under banked earth.

How to Use

Cardoons must be cooked before being used in a recipe. Since they discolor when cut and exposed to the air, like artichokes, have a bowl of acidulated water ready—that is, water and lemon juice or vinegar (2 tablespoons of either for each quart of water). Strip the leaves off the tender inner stalks. Remove the stringy parts as you would with celery. Cut them into 2- to 3-inch pieces. Trim the heart and cut it into pieces. Drop the pieces immediately into the acidulated water. Cook in boiling salted water to cover until tender but still crisp; cooking time depends on the size and age of the vegetable. An average cooking time is 5 to 10 minutes. Drain and dress with salt and pepper, melted butter and lemon juice, a white sauce, Hollandaise, tomato sauce or any sauce suited for vegetables. Cooked cardoons can also be sautéed or breaded and deep-fried.

CARDOONS IN CREAM

4 servings

This dish is delicious and delicate and must be prepared shortly before serving.

1½ pounds (approximately) edible parts of cardoon, cut into 2- or 3-inch pieces, cooked and drained

1 cup heavy cream
salt
freshly ground pepper
⅛ teaspoon ground nutmeg

Put the cardoons in a casserole that can go to the table. Add the cream, salt, pepper and nutmeg. Mix well. Bring to the boiling point. Simmer until the cream has thickened and is reduced by half. Serve immediately.

CARDOONS AU GRATIN

4 servings

1½ pounds (approximately) edible parts of cardoon, cut into 2- or 3-inch pieces, cooked and drained
salt

freshly ground pepper
4 tablespoons butter, cut into pieces
⅔ cup grated Swiss cheese
¼ cup fine dry bread crumbs

Generously butter a 1½-quart baking dish. Line it with half of the cardoons. Sprinkle very lightly with salt (the cheese will be salty) and pepper. Dot with half of the butter and sprinkle with ½ of the cheese. Top with the remaining cardoons, salt and pepper, the remaining butter and the remaining cheese. Sprinkle with bread crumbs. Cook in a preheated moderate oven (350° F) for 15 minutes or until golden.

CARROT
Daucus carota

Today's carrot—fleshy, orange, with varying shape—is a far cry from its wild ancestor, a small, tough pale-fleshed acrid taproot said to have originated in Middle Asia and the Near East. Carrot seeds from about 2000 or 3000 BC have been found in the remains of the lake dwellings of Central Switzerland, but there are no signs that the vegetable was cultivated. Most likely those ancients used it for medicinal purposes, as did the Greeks around the first century BC: they valued carrots as a stomach tonic. The wild vegetable was developed and improved in the Mediterranean countries, but how and when is unclear.

Carrots, which belong to the same botanical group as Queen Anne's lace, are one of the most popular vegetables in the United States. They are extremely nourishing; they store well and combine well with other foods such as with almonds in a superior cake. They are also one of the few vegetables that children will eat with pleasure. Though most American carrots are thick and large, the tiny baby carrots, two or three inches long, that are so popular in Europe are beginning to appear in our markets. Previously they were imported from Belgium and France.

How to Buy

Available the year round, the majority are sold sized, topped and prepackaged in plastic bags. Carrots with their tops are sold in bunches. They are fresher and preferable to the prepackaged kind.

Buy firm, smooth, clean, well-shaped bright orange-gold carrots with fresh green tops. Whether prepackaged or bunched, choose even sized carrots, the smaller the more tender and sweet. Young, sweet carrots have long rootlets. *Avoid* wilted, flabby, soft or shriveled carrots with a dim color. Avoid cracked, rough or forked carrots and carrots with wilted tops. Allow 1 pound or 1 medium bunch for 3 to 4 servings. One pound grated or shredded carrots yields approximately 3 cups.

How to Keep

Store prepackaged carrots in their bag in the refrigerator. Remove the green tops from bunch carrots and store the unwashed carrots in plastic bags in the refrigerator.
   Raw, refrigerator shelf—1 to 2 weeks.
   Cooked and covered, refrigerator shelf—2 to 3 days.

Nutritive Values

Carrots are one of the richest sources of vitamin A, necessary for good eyesight and bone formation, as well as some vitamin C. They also contain a good supply of minerals.
   3½ ounces raw—42 calories.
   3½ ounces cooked and drained—31 calories.

How to Use

Young or small tender carrots may be simply scrubbed with a vegetable brush and rinsed. Older, larger carrots may be scraped or peeled with a vegetable peeler. Cut carrots lengthwise into halves or quarters, sticks, thin or thick slices, or shred or grate them for salads. Cook carrots in an inch of boiling salted water (½ teaspoon per cup of water) in a covered saucepan until almost tender. Remove cover and cook a few minutes longer to reduce the cooking liquid. Season with salt and pepper and serve with butter and lemon juice, cream or according to recipe. Cooking time depends on age and size of the carrots. Whole mature carrots take from 10 to 15 minutes, whole baby carrots about 8 to 10 minutes, cut, sliced or shredded carrots 4 to 10 minutes. Large carrots may also be baked whole. Do not peel, only scrub them. Baking time is about 35 minutes. Or peel, boil until half tender and place in baking pan with roasting meat for 20 minutes.

To Make Carrot Curls

Scrape thick large carrots or peel them. Cut off a lengthwise strip that is about ¼ to ½ inch thick at the top to give a broad surface. With a vegetable parer, beginning at the tip end, cut thin strips from the flat surface. The strips may curl on their own; if not wrap them around a finger and fasten with toothpicks. Refrigerate in a bowl of ice water for an hour or more. Drain before using as a garnish.

MARINATED HORS D'OEUVRE CARROTS

4-6 servings

8 large carrots trimmed and cut
  into julienne strips
boiling water or chicken
  bouillon
½ cup olive oil
½ cup white vinegar
1 small onion, thinly sliced
2 whole peeled garlic cloves

1 teaspoon dried thyme
salt
freshly ground pepper
lettuce
juice of 1 large lemon
2 tablespoons minced parsley or
  dillweed

Put the carrots into a saucepan and cover with boiling water. Cook without a cover, stirring frequently, for about 3 minutes or until the carrots are barely tender. Drain. Combine oil, vinegar, onion, garlic, thyme and salt and pepper in a bowl (do not use aluminum). Add the carrots. Toss with 2 forks to coat the carrots with the dressing. Cover and refrigerate overnight. Drain the carrots and remove the garlic. Pile in a bowl lined with lettuce. Sprinkle with the lemon juice and the parsley or dill.

CARROTS COOKED IN ORANGE JUICE

4 servings

4 large or 6 medium carrots,
  trimmed
2 tablespoons butter
1 tablespoon light brown sugar
⅓ cup fresh orange juice

grated rind of ½ orange
grated rind of ½ lemon
⅛ teaspoon ground mace
salt

Cut the carrots into thin slices. Combine all the other ingredients and bring to the boiling point. Lower heat to low. Add the carrots. Simmer covered, stirring frequently, for about 5 minutes. If necessary to prevent scorching, add a little more orange juice, 1 tablespoon at a time. There should be just a little sauce in the finished dish.

SUGAR-BROWNED CARROTS

4 servings

A standard Danish recipe.

4 large or 6 medium carrots,
  trimmed
boiling water

3 tablespoons butter
2 tablespoons sugar
salt

Scrape the carrots. Cut them into thin 3- or 4-inch strips. Wash and drain. Put the carrots into a saucepan and add just enough boiling water to barely cover them. Cook covered for 3 or 4 minutes or until just tender; carrots must remain crisp. Drain. Heat the butter in a frying pan. Stir in the sugar. Cook over low heat, stirring constantly, until the sugar has melted and is golden. Add the carrots. Cook, stirring constantly with a fork, until the carrots are golden on all sides. Do not scorch. Sprinkle with salt. Serve very hot.

FLEMISH CARROTS

6 servings

This is a rich dish which can be served by itself as a first course or as the sole accompaniment to roast meats.

8 medium carrots cut into
   julienne strips
boiling water
½ cup boiling water
¼ cup butter
salt

freshly ground pepper
1 teaspoon sugar
2 egg yolks
½ cup heavy cream
2 tablespoons fresh lemon juice
2 tablespoons minced parsley

Plunge the carrots into a saucepan full of boiling water. Cook them for 2 or 3 minutes. Drain. Put the carrots into a buttered casserole, preferably one that can go to the table. Add the ½ cup boiling water, butter, salt, pepper and sugar. Bring to the boiling point and reduce to lowest possible heat. Cook covered for 5 to 10 minutes or until just tender and dry. Stir or shake the casserole every few minutes to prevent sticking; if necessary, add 1 tablespoon of water at a time to prevent scorching. But if the carrots are soupy, cook without a cover to reduce the cooking liquid. Remove from heat. Beat together the egg yolks and the cream. Add to the carrots and mix. Return to low heat and cook only long enough to heat through. Remove from heat and stir in lemon juice and parsley. Serve very hot.

CASSAVA
Manioc, Mandioca
Manihot utilissima

The root of an extremely important tropical plant which furnishes the basic starch in the diet of millions of people in certain warm countries where potatoes and grains do not thrive. The cassava root is also the source of commercial tapioca. The plant itself is a big handsome bushy one, grown also for ornamental purposes in tropical gardens. The hard, finger-shaped roots of the two major varieties, "bitter" and "sweet," are usually brought to market when they measure some ten inches in length and two or more inches across. The skin is pinkish-brown, covered with a hairy brown network of veins which hide a clean off-white flesh. Cassava must *never* be eaten raw since the juice of the root contains greater or lesser amounts of the deadly poison hydrocyanic or prussic acid, which however disappears completely with thorough cooking.

A flourlike meal called "farinha" or "farofa" is the form in which cassava appears on the tables of all classes of people in South and Central America. As I remember from the time I lived in Brazil, the bowl of farinha was as much a part of the table as salt and pepper, to be sprinkled generously over the basic black beans and rice or any other food, adding bland starch to flavorful starch. Farinha is prepared by peeling, washing and grating the roots into a cloth bag, which is then squeezed and pressed to release the milky, poisonous juices. The meal is then dried in the sun or over a fire, sifted and served as is or baked into thin cakes known as cassava bread. The milky juices from the cassava are boiled down and flavored with cinnamon and cloves and brown sugar to make cassareep, which is then used in many sauces and as the main ingredient in pepperpot, a West Indian stew. Cassereep is also sold bottled in West Indian markets.

Cassava is available the year round in Latin markets, where it is best known as yuca. Use as soon as possible after buying since the flesh discolors easily. Refrigerate until using.

Cassava may be used like any other starchy vegetable. It must be thoroughly cooked before serving as is or added to other dishes such as stews. To *cook* cassava, peel and wash the root thoroughly. Cut into 2- or 3-inch pieces. Cook in plenty of boiling salted water for a minimum of 1 hour. As they become tender, the cassava pieces also become somewhat fibrous. Drain, season with salt and pepper and butter, or mash like potatoes or add to recipe according to directions.

3½ ounces cassava flour, uncooked—350 calories.

CAULIFLOWER
Brassica oleracea botrytis

This member of the cabbage family is a cultivated low plant with a single stalk bearing a large round tightly packed mass of white or creamy flower buds. The cluster of buds is called "curd" because it looks like curd. There are a number of varieties of cauliflower including ones with green or purple heads which are prized in Italy and the Mediterranean countries for their superior flavor, but which are unknown in the United States.

Though cabbage has been used by man since antiquity, the origin of cauliflower and broccoli, its brother or sister vegetable depending on how you look at it, is rather vague. There are some intriguing 2nd century AD Roman writings but it is not quite clear whether cauliflower or broccoli is meant. We know that the French grew it in 1600, and that it was sold in London vegetable markets in 1619. In the United States, early and late varieties were known in the early 1800's, but it has become an important American crop only since 1920. The name comes from two Latin terms: *caulis* meaning stem or stalk or cabbage and *floris,* meaning flower.

How to Buy

Available the year round, peak supplies September through November, low from May through August. *Buy* clean, firm, creamy-white heads with compact curd and fresh, juicy green leaves. *Avoid* heads with spotted, speckled or bruised curd. Smudgy and speckled surfaces indicate aphids (plant lice). Avoid granular-looking heads, or heads with spreading clusters.

Allow 1 medium head cauliflower (about 1 pound) for 4 servings.

How to Keep

Refrigerate in the plastic bag in which it was bought or, unwashed, place in a plastic bag. Use as soon as possible; old cauliflower acquires a strong taste and odor.

Uncooked, refrigerator shelf—3 days.

Cooked and covered, refrigerator shelf—1 to 2 days.

Nutritive Values

Cauliflower is a good source of vitamins C and A, and a fair source of iron and other minerals.

3½ ounces raw—27 calories.

3½ ounces cooked—22 calories.

How to Use

Trim off the tough outer leaves and cut off the woody base. Fresh and tender leaves may be cooked with the cauliflower or trimmed off and cooked as a separate vegetable. The head may be left whole or separated into flowerets. The flowerets may be sliced lengthwise or chopped. Wash thoroughly and drain. Cook covered in 1 to 2 inches of boiling salted water (½ teaspoon salt per head). Cook only until just tender and still crisp. A whole head face down in the water takes 15 to 25 minutes, flowerets 5 to 9 minutes, sliced or chopped cauliflower 3 to 5 minutes. Cooking time also depends on the age and size of the vegetable. Drain.

One or 2 tablespoons of milk or 1 or 2 tablespoons of lemon juice added to cooking liquid helps preserve the white color.

Do not overcook cauliflower or it will become mushy, discolored and strong flavored. When cooking cauliflower for salad or later use, drain and then plunge immediately into ice water to stop the cooking. Drain again, cover with plastic wrap and chill in refrigerator.

Serve hot cauliflower with melted butter and lemon juice or herb butter or a creamy cheese or Hollandaise sauce. Or dress cooked cauliflower with French dressing for a cooked salad to be served at room temperature. Young, tender cauliflower may be separated into flowerets as an appetizer for dipping, or with or without French dressing or mayonnaise as a relish or a salad.

CAULIFLOWER MAYONNAISE

4 servings

1 medium cauliflower
½ cup French dressing
1 tablespoon Dijon mustard

½ cup mayonnaise
1 tablespoon drained capers

Trim the cauliflower and separate it into flowerets. Wash and drain. Cook in 1 to 2 inches boiling salted water for 5 minutes or until barely tender. Drain. While still warm, place in a serving dish and toss carefully with the French dressing. Cool. Stir the mustard into the mayonnaise. Coat the cauliflower thinly with the mayonnaise. Sprinkle with the capers and chill.

CAULIFLOWER IN CHEESE SAUCE

4 servings

Serve as a main dish, with a green vegetable.

CHEESE SAUCE

1 tablespoon butter
1 tablespoon flour
1¼ cups light cream or milk
½ cup grated Swiss cheese
1 teaspoon Dijon mustard

salt
freshly ground pepper
dash of Tabasco (optional)
1 medium cauliflower
paprika

In the top of a double boiler, heat the butter and stir in the flour. Cook for 1 minute. Stir in the milk. Cook over low heat, stirring constantly, for 3 or 4 minutes or until smooth and thickened. Stir in the cheese and the mustard. Taste and if necessary add a little salt and pepper. Stir in the Tabasco. Cook, stirring constantly, for 3 or 4 minutes or until the cheese is melted and the sauce is smooth. Keep warm over hot water in the bottom part of the double boiler. Trim the cauliflower and separate it into flowerets. Wash and drain. Cook in boiling salted water for 3 or 4 minutes or until almost tender. Drain. Place in a buttered shallow baking dish. Cover with the cheese sauce and sprinkle with the paprika. Cook in a preheated hot oven (400° F) for 5 minutes or until the top is golden brown.

CELERIAC
Celery Root, Celery Knob, Turnip-rooted Celery
Apium graveolens rapaceum

A variety of celery grown for its enlarged roots rather than for the stalks and leaves of ordinary celery. Only the root is eaten. This root is usually of an irregular globular shape, two to four inches across, with a rough brownish skin and whitish flesh. It is eaten raw in salads or cooked as a hot vegetable or in soups and stews. The flavor is an intensive celery one with smoky overtones.

Celeriac apparently originated in the Mediterranean. In the United States it was mentioned in the early 1800's, but it has never caught on as it did in Europe. There it is the most popular form of celery and very often the only one. However, in recent years celeriac, a flavorful winter crop, has been appearing in increasing quantities in our markets.

How to Buy

Available from September through April. *Buy* firm, clean roots. Press the top of the root to be sure it is firm since a soft spot on top means internal decay. Choose smaller rather than larger heads since the latter may be woody. *Avoid* soft, wilted looking roots with unduly large crevices and knobs on the skin.

Allow 1 pound for 2 to 3 servings.

How to Keep

Remove and throw away top leaves and root fibers. Wrap in plastic wrap and refrigerate. Use within a week of purchase.

Raw, refrigerator shelf—1 to 7 days.

Cooked and covered, refrigerator shelf—3 to 4 days.

Nutritive Values

Celeriac is a minor source of minerals.

3½ ounces raw—40 calories.

How to Use

Celeriac must be peeled before being eaten raw or cooked. Since it darkens when cut have a bowl of acidulated water ready (3 tablespoons lemon juice or vinegar for each quart of water) into which to drop the cut pieces to prevent discoloring. Or rub them with half a lemon. There are two ways of preparing celeriac. If the roots are small and not woody and are to be used for salad, peel quickly, preferably just before serving. Rub the cut surface with lemon. Remove woody core and cut into slices, sticks or dice, place in a bowl and toss with a little lemon juice. Then dress with French dressing, mayonnaise or rémoulade (a French way), check the seasoning and refrigerate.

If celeriac is to be used cooked, either cook it whole, unpeeled or peeled and prepared as above. To cook *whole,* scrub the root with a vegetable brush and cut off the leaves and rootlets. Cook covered in boiling salted water to cover for about 20 to 30 minutes, or until just tender. Do not overcook since celeriac tends to go mushy. Peel when cool enough to handle and cut as desired. Cook peeled slices, sticks or dice, or shredded celeriac in about an inch of boiling salted water (½ teaspoon salt for each cup of vegetable). A little lemon juice in the cooking liquid will help keep it white. Cover the pot and cook for 3 to 10 minutes, depending on the size of the pieces, or until just tender. Do not overcook or you will have mush. Drain and use in recipes. If the celeriac is to be cooked further in the recipe, cook it the first time only until half tender.

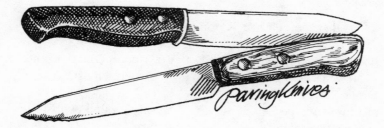

Paring Knives

PURÉE OF CELERIAC AND POTATOES

4 servings

Serve with pork or game. The purée should be of the consistency of mashed potatoes.

2 large celeriacs (knob celery)
2 very large potatoes
boiling salted water
4 tablespoons butter at room
  temperature

salt
freshly ground pepper
⅓ to ½ cup heavy cream.
2 tablespoons minced parsley
  (optional)

Trim and peel the celeriacs. Quarter and cut into eighths as you would an apple. Cut off any woody core. Peel the potatoes and cut them into pieces the same size as the celeriac pieces. Wash and drain the celeriac and the potatoes. Put into a saucepan and add boiling salted water to cover. Cook covered over medium heat until the vegetables are tender. Drain and reserve the cooking liquid for soups. Press the vegetables through a sieve or a food mill. Do not purée in a blender since this affects the texture. Beat in the butter. Season with salt and pepper. Beat in the cream. Return to heat and beat until hot and fluffy. Sprinkle with parsley and serve immediately.

DANISH CELERIAC SALAD

4 servings

In this salad the celeriac is not cooked.

a bowl of acidulated water (1
  quart water and 3 tablespoons
  lemon juice)
3 medium-to-large celeriacs
½ cup heavy cream
½ cup mayonnaise

1 teaspoon Dijon or other
  prepared mustard
salt
freshly ground pepper
lettuce
2 tablespoons minced parsley

Prepare the acidulated water into which to drop the cut celeriac in order to prevent discoloring. Peel the celeriacs until only the white part shows and drop into the acidulated water. Taking out one celeriac at a time, cut it into very thin slices (⅛ inch or less). Cut the slices into slivers the size of a kitchen match. As you've finished with them, drop all the pieces back into the acidulated water. In a salad bowl, whip the cream. Fold in the mayonnaise, mustard, salt and pepper and mix well. Drain the celeriac pieces and dry them between paper towels. Fold into the dressing and toss with two forks. Pile in a salad bowl lined with lettuce and sprinkle with the parsley.

CELERY

Apium graveolens dulce

Leaf celery or bunch celery, as we know it, is the cultivated version of a wild plant native to wet places in temperate Europe from Asia Minor to England. The wild version is inedible; it is tough and has rank, bitter juice, whereas our cultivated celery is a most useful vegetable, totally edible.

There are ancient Roman writings about a celerylike plant, but they do not identify it as a food plant; very likely it was used as medicine, as a blood purifier, nerve tonic and stimulant. This appears to have been celery's use into the 16th century, the time when it began to be cultivated in Italy for eating and became increasingly milder in flavor. The first definite notice of celery as a food plant comes from France, in 1623, when it began to be used to flavor soups, meats and stews. The leaves and stalks were also eaten with oil and pepper.

Though there are many celery varieties, basically two kinds are found in our markets, green and golden. Green celery, whatever the variety, is generally called "pascal." The general name "golden heart" covers the varieties of celery blanched to give its stalks their light, whitish-golden color and yellow-green leaves. Celery comes to the market in trimmed bunches with an average length of 12 to 16 inches.

As a vegetable, celery has many advantages. It is inexpensive, crisp, flavorful, good raw or cooked, and perhaps best of all, extremely low in calories: nine for a raw cupful.

How to Buy

Available the year round, sold in whole bunches with leaves or trimmed bunches. *Buy* celery with fresh leaves and firm, crisp, glossy stalks that snap easily. *Avoid* soft, spongy, wilted or loose stalks which have tired yellow leaves.

Allow 1 medium bunch for 4 to 6 servings.

Allow 1 heart for 2 servings.

How to Keep

Rinse the bunch under running cold water and shake dry. Do not separate the stalks from the root. Place in a plastic bag and close it firmly to keep in the moisture celery needs. Refrigerate.

Raw, refrigerator shelf—1 to 2 weeks.

Cooked and covered, refrigerator shelf—3 to 4 days.

Nutritive Values

An indifferent to fair source of vitamins and minerals.

3½ ounces raw—17 calories.

3½ ounces, cooked and drained—14 calories.

How to Use

When ready to use, separate the stalks from the bunch. Trim the leaves and base of the stalks. Remove any strings with a vegetable parer. Use the outer stalks for cooking and the tender, inner stalks for salads and for eating raw. To make celery hearts, trim off outer stalks and all but the smallest leaves and slice lengthwise into two parts. Wash and drain the trimmed celery. Do not waste the leaves; fresh or dried (see below) their concentrated flavor adds greatly to soups, stews and salads.

To *cook* celery, cut into thin, thick or slanted slices, cut into strips, or chop. Cook covered in an inch of boiling salted water (½ teaspoon per cup of celery) or bouillon (even better) for 3 to 8 minutes or until just tender and very crisp and dress with butter, herb butter, white or cheese or other sauce. Cooking time depends on the size of the pieces. Cook celery hearts in boiling salted water or bouillon to cover for about 10 minutes or until just tender and crisp.

To dry leaves cut them off neatly, wash and dry well between paper towels. Place the celery leaves on a shallow baking sheet. Dry in a very slow oven (225° F); the leaves must be very dry. Store in a covered container as is or rub through a sieve to make a powder and store.

BRAISED CELERY

3-4 servings

Serve with pork.

1 large bunch celery	2 cups peeled, chopped
boiling salted water	tomatoes
2 tablespoons olive oil	salt
4 slices prosciutto or ham,	freshly ground pepper
minced	dash of Tabasco (optional)
1 small onion, minced	1 tablespoon capers, drained, or
2 tablespoons minced parsley	¼ cup chopped pitted olives

Trim the celery and remove the tough outer stalks and the leaves and reserve for stews. String the other stalks with a vegetable peeler. Cut into 3-inch pieces. Cook in boiling salted water to cover for 3 minutes or until half tender. Drain. Heat the olive oil in a saucepan. Add the prosciutto, onion and parsley. Cook, stirring constantly, for about 3 minutes. Add the tomatoes and cook for 3 minutes longer. Add the celery. Season with salt and pepper and Tabasco. Simmer covered until the celery is tender. Check occasionally for moisture; if too dry add a little hot water. Stir in the capers or olives.

CELERY REMOULADE

4-6 servings

½ cup sour cream
½ cup mayonnaise
1 tablespoon chopped capers
2 tablespoons chopped scallions
1 garlic clove, crushed
1 tablespoon chopped fresh dill

1 teaspoon fresh lemon juice
1 tablespoon chopped parsley
¼ teaspoon salt
3 cups sliced celery
1 cup chicken consommé

In a medium bowl, combine sour cream, mayonnaise, capers, scallions, garlic, dill, lemon juice, parsley and salt. Mix well. Cover and let stand for at least 1 hour to blend the flavors. Cook the celery, covered, in the chicken consommé for 10 minutes or until tender but still firm. Drain and add to the sauce. Mix well. Chill for 1 hour before serving.

CHARD
(See page 333)

CHAYOTE
Sechium edule

A tropical squash, round or pear shaped, three to six inches long and several inches across, with a large, single seed. The rind of the chayote is like that of summer squash and, depending on the variety, it may be smooth or ribbed or even covered with smooth spines, varying in color from white to dark green. The flesh is light, fiberless, firm and crisp, looking and tasting vaguely like a bland honeydew melon. The cooked chayote can be used in as many ways as other squash. The plant also yields edible young spring shoots and tuberous roots. The first are eaten like asparagus and the second like potatoes. The whole plant also yields a valuable straw used for making baskets and hats.

Chayote is widely cultivated throughout the tropical regions of the world. It originated in Mexico, where the Mayas and Aztecs grew it long before the discovery of the New World. The varieties of names by which chayote is known testifies to its great popularity: chayotli in Mexico, xuxu in Brazil, christophene and chocho in the West Indies, vegetable pear and mirliton in Louisiana, pepinella and brionne in France (to which it came from North Africa).

How to Buy

Though grown for some time in the warm parts of the United States, chayote is now beginning to come into the market and is best found in Latin markets. *Buy* chayote like a vegetable, not a fruit. Choose very firm, young chayotes; when young enough, even the inner seed is edible after cooking. The harder the chayote, the better. *Avoid* chayotes which are wrinkled or soft.

Two pounds will make approximately 4 servings.

How to Keep

Store like summer squash in refrigerator.
Raw, refrigerator shelf—1 to 2 weeks.
Cooked and covered, refrigerator shelf—2 to 4 days.

Nutritive Values

Chayote has no great nutritional values; it is low in fats and proteins.
3½ ounces, raw—28 calories.

How to Use

Chayote is a bland vegetable and should be well seasoned. It may be used in all recipes calling for tender summer or winter squash. Young, tender chayotes need not be peeled; but older, tougher examples are better peeled. The vegetable may be cut into quarters and cooked, drained and dressed with butter, lemon juice, or herbs. Or it may be creamed or mashed like winter squash. It may also be fried or stuffed or combined in soups and casseroles with meat and other vegetables. Cook only until just tender.

CHAYOTES STUFFED WITH CHEESE

6 servings

Like any squash, chayotes may be stuffed with any favorite filling.

3 large chayotes, washed
2 quarts boiling salted water
3 tablespoons butter
1 cup grated Swiss or Cheddar
   cheese
salt

freshly ground pepper
dash Tabasco
2 tablespoons fine dry bread
   crumbs
boiling water

Cut the chayotes into halves lengthwise. Cook in the boiling salted water until the flesh is soft. Drain and cool. Remove the core. With a teaspoon, scoop out the flesh, taking care not to break the shells. Mash the flesh. Heat two tablespoons of the butter in a saucepan. Cook the chayote flesh, stirring constantly, for about 2 minutes. Stir in the cheese and cook only until the cheese is melted. Remove from heat. Taste and if necessary add a little salt and pepper and a dash of Tabasco. Stuff the chayote shells with the mixture. Place side by side in a shallow baking dish. Sprinkle each shell with about 1 teaspoon bread crumbs and dot with the remaining butter. Pour ½ inch boiling water around the chayotes. Cook in a preheated moderate oven (350° F) for 20 to 30 minutes or until golden. If necessary, add more boiling water to keep the ½-inch level.

CHESTNUT

genus *Castanea*

Chestnuts are the edible nuts of several varieties of a tree of the same name which is related to the oak family. They are an important food crop in many parts of the world, especially in China, Japan and southern Europe.

The American chestnut, *Castanea dentata,* once grew in large forests from Maine to Alabama. A fast-growing, tall tree, it was the most important hardwood of the East in the 19th century, greatly appreciated for its lumber which went into fences, masts, railroad ties and mine timbers, for its bright brown nuts, for the tanning properties of the bark and for its shade. Today only ghostly gray trunks with shoots that never mature remain in our forests. Practically all the trees were killed in 1904 by the great chestnut blight, an Asiatic parasitic fungus with particularly virulent properties. The chestnuts we eat today are imported from Europe and the Far East. Now, however, a good deal of scientific research is being done by the U. S. Department of Agriculture in an effort to rescue the American species with fungicides and by other means.

The European chestnut, *Castanea sativa,* has nuts larger than those of the American variety and dark mahogany-brown shells. This species and its varieties is variously known as the French, Italian and Spanish chestnut, and as the sweet chestnut of England. Chestnuts have long been a staple food in Europe, where they were cultivated for centuries to use fresh or dried as a fruit or made into a meal that often served for bread. Chestnuts are still used in these ways in Italy, France, Spain and other Mediterranean countries. The ancient Greek writer Theophrastus tells us that Mount Olympus, the home of the Gods, was thick with chestnut trees. In my Roman childhood, when autumn arrived we used to gather chestnuts that grew in profusion in the thick forests of the Roman hill towns. Now the constant forest fires of Italy have decimated the century-old trees.

There are many cultural varieties of the Japanese and Chinese chestnut, *Castanea crenata;* the nuts of the Japanese tree are less sweet and smaller than the Chinese. These varieties are either totally or nearly immune to the chestnut blight and, along with the resilient European varieties, are used in crossbreeding with American chestnuts to produce new, disease-resistant varieties.

Chinese water chestnuts and horse chestnuts (the ''spreading chestnut tree'' of Longfellow's village smithy) belong to different species.

Chestnuts deserve a far larger use as a vegetable than they currently have. Mashed or braised whole, they combine beautifully with red cabbage, mushrooms, Brussels sprouts, onions and carrots.

How to Buy

Fresh chestnuts, imported mainly from Spain and Italy, are available from October through March, peak season during December and January. *Buy* plump, glossy, fresh-looking nuts, free from blemishes, which are heavy for their size. *Avoid* dried-out, shriveled, cracked or blemished nuts that are light for their size.

Canned chestnuts and chestnut purée, both either unsweetened or sweetened, are available in gourmet stores. They are used like cooked fresh chestnuts. Most come from France, though some imports come from Hungary. The sweet Hungarian chestnuts are not as sweet as the French. Sugar-glazed chestnuts, called *marrons glacés,* need not concern us here.

Shelled dried chestnuts are sold in Italian and Spanish markets and, after reconstituting in water, are used like fresh ones. However, they are not as flavorful.

Chestnut flour is sold in the same markets during the fall and winter months only since it only keeps for a relatively short time. It is used for making a polentalike mush that serves as a starch and in baking.

1 pound in the shell—approximately 35 to 40 raw chestnuts.

1 pound, shelled and peeled—approximately 2½ cups.

How to Keep

Keep fresh chestnuts in a cool, dry place; they dry out easily. Cover open cans or jars of canned chestnuts and refrigerate. Keep shelled dry chestnuts as you would beans or lentils, in a covered container in a cool dry place. The same applies to chestnut flour, which should be used within a month of buying it.

Fresh, unshelled, kitchen shelf—1 week.

Fresh, shelled, cooked and covered, refrigerator shelf—3 to 4 days.

Canned, preserved, open and covered, refrigerator shelf—1 week.

Dried, kitchen shelf, uncooked—2 months.

Dried, cooked and covered, refrigerator shelf—3 to 4 days.

Flour, kitchen shelf—1 month.

Nutritive Values

Chestnuts are high in carbohydrates and a moderate source of protein and minerals.

3½ ounces, fresh—194 calories.

3½ ounces, dried—377 calories.

3½ ounces chestnut flour—362 calories.

How to Use

Before they can be eaten the chestnuts' hard outer shells and the thin brown bitter inner peel must be removed. This is usually done by cooking or roasting which makes the process easier. The outer shell only can be removed from raw nuts, though with some difficulty.

To cook and shell chestnuts, make a horizontal slash in the flat side of the chestnut using a sharp, pointed knife. Place the chestnuts in a saucepan with ample cold water to cover. Bring to the boiling point and boil for 3 minutes. Remove from heat. With a slotted spoon, scoop 2 or 3 chestnuts at a time from the hot water. With the same sharp pointed knife, remove the outer shell and the inner skin, taking care to keep the chestnuts whole. This is easier said than done; invariably many of the chestnuts break and have to be used with other vegetables, in stuffings or mashed. Keep the unpeeled chestnuts in the hot water until their turn or the inner skin won't come off. If the water gets cold, boil it up once more.

To roast chestnuts, slash the flat side as described above. Place on a baking sheet in a hot (400° F) oven for 15 to 20 minutes, stirring occasionally. Serve piping hot, with a glass of wine. Or to roast chestnuts over an open fire, punch rows of holes into a large flat tin like a metal lid or large pie pan. Prepare the chestnuts as above and place on a grill over white coals. This is the method of the street chestnut vendors.

To purée chestnuts, cook and shell the nuts. Depending on the later use, cook them further until tender in boiling water, milk or bouillon to cover. Do not overcook them or they will fall apart. Cover the pot and use low heat. Drain and mash like potatoes, or press through a sieve or whirl in the blender with a little of the cooking liquid. Season and use as in recipe.

To reconstitute dry chestnuts, soak overnight in water to cover. Then simmer, covered, in about 5 inches of water until the chestnuts puff up and are tender. Use as fresh cooked chestnuts, cup per cup.

PURÉE OF CHESTNUT SOUP

6 servings

1 pound chestnuts, peeled
¼ cup carrot, minced
¼ cup onion, minced
2 bay leaves
6 cups chicken consommé
salt

freshly ground pepper
1 cup heavy or light cream
1 tablespoon butter
1 tart apple, peeled, cored and
   thinly sliced
2 tablespoons minced parsley

Combine the chestnuts, carrot, onion, bay leaves and consommé in a large saucepan. Bring to the boiling point and lower the heat. Simmer covered until the chestnuts are very soft and falling apart. Remove the bay leaves. Press through a sieve or purée in a blender. Check the seasoning; if necessary, add a little salt and pepper. Stir in the heavy cream. Return to lowest possible heat or place on an asbestos plate and keep hot. Heat the butter in a small frying pan. Quickly sauté the apple slices in it until they are golden. Float them on the soup and sprinkle with the parsley just before serving.

BRAISED CHESTNUTS

4-6 servings

1 cup chicken consommé	1 bay leaf
¼ cup dry white wine or dry sherry	salt
	freshly ground pepper
1 pound chestnuts, peeled	1 tablespoon flour
4 tablespoons butter	

Combine the consommé and the wine in a saucepan. Bring to the boiling point and lower the heat. Add the chestnuts, 2 tablespoons of the butter and the bay leaf. Simmer covered over lowest possible heat for 15 to 20 minutes or until the chestnuts are tender. Remove the bay leaf. Taste; if necessary, add a little salt and pepper. Knead together the remaining butter and the flour. Drop in pea-sized pieces into the chestnut liquid, stirring carefully in order not to break the chestnuts. Serve hot.

Variation: 1. Add 1 pound cooked Brussels sprouts to the finished braised chestnuts and heat together.

2. Add ¼ pound lean diced ham or prosciutto to the braised chestnuts (or braised chestnuts with Brussels sprouts) and heat through.

CHICK PEA
Cicer arietinum

Chick peas are the seeds of a branching bush annual which is well adapted to arid and semiarid regions. It is a very nutritious legume, widely cultivated in the Mediterranean (garbanzo in Spain, ceci in Italian), Mexico and Latin America (garbanzo) and the Arab countries (hommos or hummus). India is a very large producer of chick peas, where as *gram* it is made into the typical basic Indian dish of *dhal*. And a kind of coffee substitute is made from chick-pea meal.

The chick pea is a very old crop, being known to the Egyptians, Hebrews, Greeks and Romans who all eat quantities of chick peas to this day. In this country, it figures only in ethnic cooking. There are black, white and red varieties, though the white chick pea is the most commonly used kind. The red varieties are grown in the Orient and the black is now a curiosity. As the peas dry they wrinkle and are fancifully described as resembling a ram's head. Occasionally they are eaten fresh, but most commonly they come to market dried and are cooked like dried beans. They have a rich nutty flavor that lends itself to soups and stews, salads, mashed or marinated dishes as an appetizer. Chick peas deserve far greater use by American cooks.

How to Buy

Dried chick peas are available the year round. They are sold in bulk in ethnic markets and in pound packages in American ones. Chick peas are also canned like beans and ready to use. Chick-pea meal is available in Italian and other Latin stores. *Buy* full, clean chick peas. *Avoid* shrunken, blemished ones.

½ cup dry chick peas—approximately 1¼ cups cooked and drained.

How to Keep

Keep dry chick peas in a covered container in a cool dry place.
Dry, kitchen shelf—1 year.
Cooked or canned, opened and covered, refrigerator shelf—1 week.

Nutritive Values

Chick peas are an excellent source of proteins and carbohydrates, thiamine and iron and a fair source of other minerals.

3½ ounces, dry—360 calories.

How to Use

Wash in several changes of water. Soak overnight in plenty of water to cover. Using the same water, place in saucepan, bring to the boiling point and simmer over low heat for about 2 hours or until tender. Or place washed chick peas in large saucepan with water to cover plus 2 or 3 inches. Bring to the boiling point. Remove from heat and cover. Let stand for 1 to 2 hours. Then bring to the boiling point again, cover and simmer over low heat until tender, adding more hot water if necessary. As with beans, cook chick peas slowly so that they will retain their shape. Unless you are making soup and need the cooking liquid, drain and use peas as specified in recipe. If the cooked chick peas are to be stored, pour a little of their cooking juice over them to keep them moist. If they are to be puréed in a blender, use a little of the cooking liquid.

CHICK PEA APPETIZER *(Hummus bi Taheeni)*

4-6 servings

Sesame oil is available in Middle Eastern grocery stores and gourmet food stores. In storage (do not refrigerate) the paste oil will separate into paste and oil, but remain perfectly good. Just stir before using.

1½ cups cooked chick peas
⅓ cup sesame oil
½ cup fresh lemon juice
1 garlic clove, mashed
salt

freshly ground pepper
lettuce
2 tablespoons minced parsley or
  chopped fresh mint

Press the chick peas through a food mill or a sieve. Stir in, alternately, the sesame oil and the lemon juice. Stir in the garlic and season lightly with salt and pepper. There should be a smooth purée with the consistency of commercial sour cream. If too thick, beat in a little water, 1 tablespoon at a time. Pile on a plate lined with lettuce and sprinkle with the parsley or mint. Chill before serving. Serve as a dip with raw vegetables or flat Arab bread.

Note: This may be made in a blender, though the texture will be rougher because the chick pea skins are blended in. To make, blend together the sesame oil, lemon juice and garlic. Add the chick peas. Cover and blend at high speed. If too thick, add a little water, 1 tablespoon at a time. Then proceed as above.

ROMAN CHICK PEA STEW

6-8 servings

This is a heavy and utterly delicious stew, good for people who have exercised on the beach or the ski slopes. I take it along on picnics and reheat it to lukewarm on the site. To make a meal, have some tomato salad, bread, cheese and fruit.

¾ cup olive oil
3 large garlic cloves, minced
8 anchovy fillets, minced
1 cup chopped parsley
about 5 cups cooked chick peas
    (2 cups raw) or 2 1-pound
    cans chick peas
4 large tomatoes, peeled,
    seeded and chopped

1 tablespoon dried rosemary,
    crumbled
1 quart water
1 pound elbow macaroni,
    cooked *al dente*
salt
freshly ground pepper
freshly grated Parmesan or
    Romano cheese

In a large kettle, combine the olive oil, garlic, anchovies and parsley. Cook over low heat, stirring constantly, for about 5 minutes. Add the chick peas (if using canned chick peas, do not drain), tomatoes, rosemary and water. Simmer covered over low heat for about 30 minutes, stirring occasionally. Cook the macaroni while the soup is simmering. Add to soup. Check the seasoning; if necessary, add a little salt and pepper. Simmer covered for 5 to 10 more minutes, stirring occasionally. Serve with plenty of freshly grated cheese.

SAUTEED CHICK PEAS

4-6 servings

Serve with roast meats.

2 tablespoons olive oil
4 cups cooked chick peas,
    drained
1 large tomato, peeled, seeded
    and chopped
2 tablespoons minced fresh
    basil or 1 tablespoon dried
    basil

1 teaspoon dried thyme
salt
freshly ground pepper

Heat the olive oil in a deep frying pan. Add the chick peas. Cook, stirring constantly, for 3 minutes. Add all the other ingredients. Cook covered over medium heat for 5 to 10 minutes. Serve hot.

CHICORY
Cichorium intybus

There are three common forms of chicory. One is used for greens, one is grown for its large roots which are dried and made into a coffee supplement and one whose roots are forced to produce a compact cluster of blanched leaves is used as a salad green and a cooked vegetable. This latter form is the popular Belgian endive, or witloof, see page 77.

The chicory used for greens has dark green, lobed, toothed leaves which somewhat resemble dandelion leaves. They have a pleasantly bitter flavor and are used as salad greens and potherbs. The long fleshy taproots, which taste somewhat like parsnip, can be boiled or braised like any other root vegetable.

Chicory was introduced into the United States in the late 1890's and appeared as a farm crop for the sake of its root in the early years of the century. But cultivating the root took considerable manual and mechanical labor, so its cultivation was dropped. It did not take as a coffee supplement either, since the foreign-born population who used it for coffee claimed that the American varieties were not as good as the European ones, which, to boot, came in under a low tariff. And to this day, except in Louisiana, Americans do not care for the bitter flavor of coffee with chicory. European use of chicory as a coffee stretcher has greatly declined also, since real coffee is now more widely available and though not cheap, is not the luxury product that it once was.

Chicory is now cultivated as a green or gathered wild.

How to buy

Though fresh chicory for salads and as a potherb is available the year round, it is not as commonly found in vegetable markets as other products. It is sold by weight or in bunches.

Buy crisp, bright, young and tender unblemished greens. *Avoid* wilted, old greens and greens with blight spots or insect damage. When buying roots, choose firm, relatively unwrinkled ones.

Roasted chicory is available in packages in supermarkets and occasionally in bulk in ethnic groceries.

Allow 1 pound for 3 to 4 servings as salad, 2 servings as a vegetable.

How to Keep

Treat like any fresh greens; use as soon as possible.
Place unwashed greens in a plastic bag and refrigerate.
Uncooked, refrigerator shelf—2 days.
Cooked and covered, refrigerator shelf—1 to 2 days.

Nutritive Values

Fresh chicory is an excellent source of vitamin A.
3½ ounces, raw—20 calories.

How to Use

For salad use, trim and wash the chicory as for any other fresh salad greens. Large leaves may be torn into smaller pieces. Dry well and chill before using. To cook as a vegetable, trim and wash the chicory. Drop into boiling salted water, cook for 1 minute and drain. This step removes the bitterness and may be repeated. Serve with melted butter, lemon juice or herbs like any other leafy green vegetable. Roots may be boiled and peeled, or peeled and braised and served with any suitable sauce.

ROMAN BRAISED CHICORY

4 servings

¼ cup olive oil
1 large garlic clove
6 anchovy fillets, minced, or 2
 tablespoons anchovy paste
3 medium tomatoes, peeled
 and chopped

2 heads chicory, washed and
 coarsely chopped
salt
freshly ground pepper
hot water or beef bouillon

Heat the olive oil in a deep frying pan. Cook the garlic in it until it is brown, then discard the garlic. Add the anchovy and cook, stirring constantly, for about 2 minutes. Add the tomatoes and cook for 2 more minutes. Add the chicory and mix well. Check the seasoning; if necessary, add a little salt and pepper. Simmer covered over low heat for about 10 minutes or until the vegetable is cooked but still crisp. Stir frequently and check for moisture; if necessary, to prevent scorching, add a little hot water, 2 tablespoons at a time.

CHILE
Chili, Chilli, Chilie
genus *Capsicum*

Chiles are members of the pepper family, of which the succulent green (sometimes red or yellow) bell peppers are most familiar. Fresh or dried, sweet, pungent or hot, they are a characteristic ingredient in Mexican cooking and have been so for long before the coming of the Spaniards. Chiles are natives of Mexico and tropical America. They are also widely used in Africa, India, Southeast Asia, China, Japan and the Pacific Islands and to a certain extent, in Italy and Spain.

About fifteen or so varieties of mild and hot chiles are used fresh or dried in Mexican cooking. Their specific use is excellently explained in *The Complete Book of Mexican Cooking* by Elisabeth Lambert Ortiz (M. Evans & Co., New York, $8.95). I am indebted to Mrs. Ortiz for her information on chiles and other exotic products.

Chiles, both dried and fresh, have long been staples in California and in Southwestern states. In recent years, however, chiles have begun to come into more general use. Vegetable and supermarkets carry a number of varieties, especially in Latin neighborhoods, since dried red chiles are also used in Latin cooking. Chiles are also sold canned in water or lightly pickled; they are peeled and ready to use. Southwestern markets also frequently carry ground chiles, such as ancho, mulato and pasilla. Commercial chile powder is a different proposition since other herbs and spices are added to it. So are the canned tamale and other sauces which contain chiles as well as other ingredients.

Chiles are sold under a confusing variety of names. When in doubt if a green or red chile is sweet or hot, ask the person who sells it. Although he may be very vague and inaccurate about the name, he will know if it is hot or not. Except for connoisseurs of Mexican food, there is not a great difference in flavor between chiles of any one kind. I feel that fresh sweet ones, fresh hot ones, or dried chiles of various kinds can be substituted for similar kinds. Adjustments may have to be made, though, in the case of hot chiles, some of which rank only hotter and hottest. And all chiles, in whatever shades of green, yellow or red, turn red if left sufficiently long on the vine. The same variety may at times produce sweet as well as hot specimens. The Mexican chiles most commonly used are:

FRESH GREEN SWEET CHILES

California pepper or guero, very pale yellowish green, tapering, medium size.

Valenciano, similar to the above, but deeper green and larger.

FRESH GREEN HOT CHILES

Serrano, about 1½ inches long, tapering.

Jalapeño, dark green, about 2½ inches long, very popular.

Poblano, almost black-green, shaped like a triangular bell pepper.

DRIED RED CHILES

Ancho, most frequently used, wrinkled, a deep reddish brown, about 3 to 4 inches long, broad; flavor from rather mild to pungent.

Mulato, somewhat resembles the ancho, but longer, brownish-black, very pungent.

Pasilla, long (about 5 to 6 inches), slender, brownish-black, very pungent.

Chipotle, smaller than mulato, almost brick red, with a distinctive flavor; very hot.

Guajillo, about 4 inches long and pointed with a smooth, brownish-red skin, extremely hot.

Cascabel, small, round, brownish skin, hot.

Pequin, tiny, red and extremely hot.

Ha-paka, very hot dried Japanese chile found in Japanese markets.

How to Buy

Many fresh chiles are available throughout the year. *Buy fresh* chiles that are plump, with clear, bright skins. *Avoid* blemished, shriveled chiles. *Buy* clean *dried* chiles, available all year, free of dirt and insects, with no signs of crumbling or deteriorating.

It is impossible to give accurate measurements for the use of chiles since they vary in flavor and piquancy. Experimentation is the only answer; go easy at the beginning. Take a dish with which you are familiar, such as tomato sauce or some soup, and try out the various chiles.

How to Keep

Only store fresh, plump chiles. Do not wash or wrap, but store loosely in the vegetable drawer and keep very dry since heat and moisture ripen them. Store dried chiles in a well-tied plastic bag in the refrigerator or in a cool dry place. If in touch with the air they become dry and brittle and lose flavor. Check all stored chiles and throw out any deteriorating ones. Refrigerate canned chiles in an open can in their own juice.

Fresh chiles, refrigerator—2 weeks.

Dried chiles, wrapped—2 months.

Cooked or canned, covered—1 to 2 weeks.

Nutritive Values

Chiles, especially dried red ones, are an excellent source of vitamin A and a fair source of minerals.

3½ ounces green, without seeds, raw—37 calories.

3½ ounces red, dried pods—321 calories.

How to Use

CAUTION I The juice of chiles, as well as the seeds, membranes or veins and stems, are the hottest parts and for this reason they are usually removed from the flesh. After handling any chiles, wash your hands immediately and thoroughly with soap and several changes of hot water. Never touch your face, especially your eyes, with hands that have touched chiles, or you will suffer devastating pain.

CAUTION II When adding chiles to a dish, add a very little at a time, since chiles can be unexpectedly hot. If you are adding fresh chiles, mince them as well as possible. *Remember, a little goes a long way*.

FRESH CHILES

It is better to peel the bigger chiles before using in a cooked dish. To peel a few chiles, spear each on a long-handled kitchen fork. Over the surface heat of the kitchen range, rotate the chile until its skin is black and charred. Put into a small paper bag for 2 to 3 minutes to let the chile steam. Then peel off charred skin under running cold water, using your fingers and the point of a knife. Remove the stem, membranes and all seeds, and dry on paper towels. Or boil chiles in water to cover for 10 minutes, then remove the skin. The first method is more satisfactory. If more than a few chiles are to be peeled at a time, spread them on the broiler pan. Under high heat, roast them until they are charred, turning frequently with a long-handled fork. Place in paper bag for 10 to 15 minutes to let the chiles steam. Then peel them under running cold water. Remove stems, membranes and seeds, wash again, drain and dry. *Do not freeze* uncooked chiles; cook them first for 10 minutes in boiling water to cover, then drain and dry.

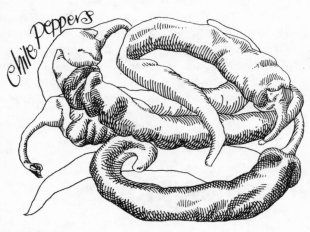

DRIED CHILES

Crumble small dried chiles between the fingers before removing seeds.

Wash dried chiles in several changes of cold water. Remove the stems, membranes and seeds. If large, tear into pieces. Place in a bowl and cover with hot water, about 1 cup for 6 chiles. Soak for 1 hour. Then either purée in a blender with the soaking liquid to be added to other ingredients, or purée with the liquid together with the other ingredients. Blend in small quantities and for a minimum of time, to preserve the flavor. Or push through the coarse disk of a food mill together with the soaking liquid.

To use ground chiles, moisten with a little water or bouillon.

FRESH CHILI-PEPPER CORN BREAD

one 9-inch-square bread

1 cup flour
1 cup cornmeal
½ teaspoon baking soda
2 teaspoons baking powder
¾ teaspoon salt
2 eggs, beaten
1 cup corn cut off the cob

1 cup sour milk
½ cup water
¼ cup diced hot green peppers, seeded
¼ cup melted butter or bacon fat or drippings
butter

Sift together the flour, cornmeal, baking soda, baking powder and salt. Stir in eggs, corn, sour milk, water and the hot peppers. Mix only until all the ingredients are moistened; do not overmix. Stir in the butter. Generously grease a 9 × 9 × 2 baking pan. Place briefly on direct heat to heat the pan. Turn the batter into the hot baking pan and bake in a preheated hot oven (425° F) for about 30 minutes or until the bread shrinks away from the sides of the pan. Serve hot with butter.

CHINESE CABBAGE

East Asia, notably China, has produced several so-called cabbages, which differ from the European varieties, but nevertheless belong to Brassicaceae, the cabbage family. In China, they have been cultivated since before the Christian era, but until fairly recently they have remained unknown or oddities in other countries. In the United States, with its large Chinese population, two varieties have been cultivated extensively for sale in Oriental markets. Now, these Chinese cabbages are increasingly found in other markets, and their use is no longer limited to Oriental cooking. They both are confusingly called "Chinese cabbage."

Bok choy, Chinese chard, Chinese mustard, *Brassica chinensis*. The vegetable consists of a long (10 to 20 inches) cluster of thick, broad-based white or greenish-white stalks with loose, broad dark green leaves resembling chard rather than an ordinary cabbage. Some varieties have tuberous roots, which are cooked and eaten like turnips. Bok choy is widely cultivated and available the year round. *Choose* fresh looking, crisp firm heads and *avoid* limp, yellow-leafed vegetables. Refrigerate unwashed in a plastic bag for 1 to 3 days. Bok choy is also dried and added to soups and stews.

Bok choy has a light, delicate flavor and a delightful crisp texture. It must be cooked quickly or both are lost. The vegetable may be cooked like chard (see page 333). If mature, cook stalks and leaves separately since the stalks will take a longer time. Or cut into bite-sized pieces and stir-fry to add to any mixed meat and vegetable or vegetable combinations or wherever some crisp texture is desirable in a dish. Or use the hearts only, raw in salads, or blanched as a prized Chinese vegetable.

Bok choy is a good source of vitamin A, calcium and other minerals.

3½ ounces—approximately 14 calories.

Pe-tsai, Chinese cabbage, celery cabbage, *Brassica pekinensis*.

This vegetable looks somewhat like a pale head of romaine lettuce, with broad-ribbed pale green, strong-veined, wavy and somewhat crinkled leaves. The heart is pure white and used as a delicacy. Pe-tsai is available the year round. In California it is called nappa nappa. *Buy* heads with crisp outer leaves. *Avoid* very large or very firm heads, which have a strong flavor. Refrigerate unwashed in plastic bag for 1 to 3 days.

Pe-tsai has a more delicate flavor than other cabbages and practically no odor while cooking. Cook as you would any cabbage.

3½ ounces raw—14 calories.

JUDY HYUN'S INSTANT KIMCHI

4 servings

Kimchi is a national Korean relish. It can be extremely hot and elaborate, ripening for weeks, or it can be quick. I prefer this less powerful version. Use it as you would coleslaw.

1 Chinese cabbage, trimmed
2 garlic cloves, mashed
1 teaspoon hot pepper sauce or
 flakes

1 or 2 tablespoons soy sauce
1 teaspoon vinegar
1 tablespoon salt
1 tablespoon sugar

Chop the cabbage into 1½-inch pieces. There should be about 3 cups. Wash and drain. Combine the cabbage and all the other ingredients and mix well. Taste and if necessary adjust the flavor with more pepper, soy sauce and vinegar. Cover and let stand at room temperature for about 1 hour.

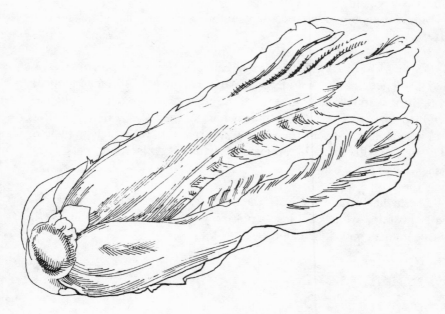

SAUTÉED CHINESE CABBAGE

4 servings

This is my favorite way with any cabbage. Speed is of the essence, though non-Chinese cabbages may have to cook a few moments longer. If desired, add 1 tablespoon crushed fennel or aniseed to the cooked cabbage.

2 tablespoons butter or salad oil   salt
1 small Chinese cabbage,   freshly ground pepper
   trimmed and shredded

Heat the butter in a deep frying pan. Add the cabbage. Cover and cook over medium heat for 3 minutes, stirring 3 times. Remove from heat and season with salt and pepper.

CHINESE PARSLEY
(See page 146)

CHINESE SPINACH
(See page 317)

CHINQUAPIN
Castanea pumila

A tree related to the chestnut which grows in the southern United States and yields small, single-fruited burrs which are eaten like chestnuts. Chinquapins are old Indian food and the name comes from the language of the Algonquins of Virginia.

CHIVES
Allium schoenoprasum

A relative of the onion, with small elongated white bulbs and fresh green tubular leaves which grow in clumps. The fresh leaves are snipped into small bits to flavor and season all kinds of food which are enhanced by the chive's delicate onion flavor. They are always used raw.

Potted chives in the markets tell us spring is here. They grow well by a sunny window. To keep the plants looking respectable, do not snip off the tops since they will brown where cut. Instead, snip a few leaves at a time. Keep several plants and don't cut one plant more than four times a season. If you plan to keep your plants, you must divide them every two or three years. Use the tiny bulbs for pickling; they are delicious.

Fresh chives are excellent flavorings for soups, egg dishes, cottage and cream cheeses, sauces and salads. Cut and add them to the food just before serving since they are apt to lose their fresh, delicate flavor.

Chopped frozen and chopped freeze-dried chives are also available. When added to foods they regain some of their fresh appearance, texture and flavor. Use about ½ teaspoon for each serving in all dishes where you would use fresh chives.

Chives are an excellent source of vitamin A.

3½ ounces raw—28 calories.

CHUFA
Nut Grass
Cyperus esculentus

Chufa is a weed found in Europe, Africa, Asia and America, where it is grown in back yards rather than commercially, or gathered wild by wild-food lovers. It is a member of the sedge family that includes bulrushes and the variety used by the ancient Egyptians for making papyrus, or paper. The edible parts are the tuberous roots, which are eaten much like peanuts, raw, or boiled and roasted, or made into a flour as a coffee substitute. The flavor is slightly nutlike and sweet, and the texture is crisp. Chufas contain a white milky juice which in Latin countries is made into a refreshing beverage called *horchata de chufas,* a kind of almond milk. It is made by soaking a pound of the tubers for 48 hours in water to cover. Drain if there is any excessive liquid left, mash the tubers, add 2 quarts of water and 1 pound of sugar. Let stand for 1 hour. Squeeze through a sieve or cheesecloth. Use as a cold drink, as you would use coconut milk. (I have not tried this recipe.)

COLLARDS
Collard Greens
Brassica oleracea, acephala

Though collards are a humble but very healthful member of the cabbage family, they do not have a head but are cultivated as a vegetable for their dark green, smooth, thick, tender, broad or curly leaves which grow in a kind of loose rosette on top of a tall stem. Collards are a close relative of kale, with which it is sometimes confused. Together they are the most primitive members of the cabbage group, originating in the eastern Mediterranean or Asia Minor, and not much changed from the wild forms of cabbage eaten by prehistoric man.

Collards are a hardy vegetable, withstanding heat and drought to a far greater extent than cabbages; like kale, cold weather and even a light freeze improves their quality. They are largely cultivated as a winter vegetable in the South, where they have achieved an honored place in that region's cooking under the name of "greens," generally cooked with bacon or salt pork.

How to Buy

Available the year round, peak season January through April. Usually sold by the pound. They are also sold frozen. *Buy* fresh, crisp, green, tender young leaves that are free from insect injuries. *Avoid* wilting, yellowing, blemished leaves.

1 pound uncooked—2 to 3 servings.

How to Keep

Remove wilted leaves and wash and shake dry thoroughly before refrigerating in a plastic bag.

Refrigerator shelf, uncooked—3 to 5 days.
Refrigerator shelf, cooked and covered—3 to 4 days.

Nutritive Values

Collards are a superior source of vitamins A and B and contain large amounts of calcium, phosphorus and other minerals.

3½ ounces raw—40 calories.
3½ ounces cooked and drained—33 calories.

How to Use

Cook like spinach, chard, cabbage or kale. Wash thoroughly in several changes of cold water to remove sand and earth. Trim off the tough stems and the midribs of the leaves. Cut large leaves into pieces for cooking, or shred like cabbage. Cook covered in 1 inch of boiling salted water for 5 to 10 minutes, or the shortest possible time for tenderness. Drain, season and add butter. When collards are cooked in the Southern manner with some form of pork, the resulting juice is called "pot likker." This is an extremely nutritious broth and it should be eaten or sopped up with corn bread.

SOUTHERN COLLARD GREENS

4-6 servings

The long cooking is essential for the typical flavor. Serve with corn bread.

1½ quarts water
1 ham hock or ½ pound salt
  pork
4 pounds collard greens,
  washed and prepared for
  cooking

½ teaspoon hot pepper flakes or
  to taste (optional)
¼ cup salad oil or butter
salt
freshly ground pepper

Put the water and the ham hock in a large pot with a tight-fitting lid. Bring to the boiling point. Lower the heat to very low and simmer covered for 30 minutes. Add the collards and the hot pepper flakes. Simmer covered for about 2 hours, stirring occasionally. Add the salad oil and simmer covered for 30 more minutes. Check the seasoning; if necessary, add a little more salt and some pepper.

COLLARDS ALL' ITALIANA

4 servings

Serve with pork chops.

3 tablespoons olive oil
1 medium onion, thinly sliced
1 cup chopped peeled tomatoes
salt
freshly ground pepper
½ teaspoon dried marjoram

2 pounds collard greens,
  trimmed and prepared for
  cooking
¼ cup freshly grated Parmesan
  cheese

Heat the oil in a saucepan large enough to hold the collards. Add the onion and cook, stirring constantly, until soft. Add the tomatoes and cook for 5 minutes longer. Season with salt and pepper and marjoram. Add the collards. Simmer covered over low heat for about 15 or 20 minutes or until tender. Stir frequently and check the moisture; if necessary, add a little water, 2 tablespoons at a time. Sprinkle with Parmesan cheese and serve hot.

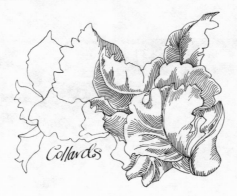

CORIANDER
Cilantro, Culantro, Chinese Parsley
Coriandrum sativum

A member of the parsley family cultivated for its feathery dark green leaves as well as its seeds. The leaves are constantly used like parsley in Mexican and other Latin cookery, and a wide use is made of them in Chinese (where it is known as yuen-sai) and Japanese (koyendoro) cookery. The flavor of the leaves is very unlike that of the parsley it resembles; it has a distinctive flavor described by some as fetid, though to millions of others, including myself, it is divine.

The tiny seeds have a fragrant taste reminiscent of aniseed, cumin and orange. They are used whole or ground in a variety of foods, from cheeses and salads to cakes, cookies and candies. Most blended spices like curry powder and condiments contain coriander. An old-fashioned candy consisted of sugar-coated coriander seeds, and a coriander seed was the reward when as a child you worked youself through a jawbreaker. Coriander seeds have long been chewed for a sweeter breath, and a crushed seed in the bottom of a demitasse cup makes a welcome change from the habitual lemon peel.

Coriander is probably a native of the Mediterranean and the Near East. Seeds have been found in Egyptian tombs and it certainly existed in Persia centuries before the Christian era. In the Bible, Exodus 16:31, coriander is mentioned thus: "And the house of Israel called the name thereof Manna; and it was like coriander seed, white; and the taste of it was like wafers made with honey."

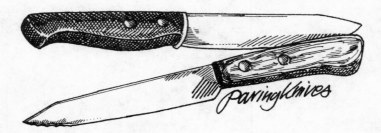

Paring Knives

CORN
Maize, Indian Corn
Zea mays

Corn is the only cereal of American origin and one of the most widely cultivated food plants in the world, exceeded in acreage only by wheat. Its products, such as starch and oil, have produced large industries. Corn is without a doubt the most popular American vegetable, yet it has never become a mainstay of our diet, as it is in Mexico; more than three-quarters of the United States corn crop is fed to livestock.

Corn's proper name is maize, a word of Indian origin which is understood throughout the world. Calling the vegetable corn is an exclusively American practice, dating back to colonial times. "Corn" is an Anglo-Saxon word meaning small particles (such as peppercorns); and in England and Germany, the word "corn" stands for wheat. When the early American settlers came to this country, they were introduced to maize by the Indians. The settlers saw maize flourish while their former staple crop, wheat, failed. As maize became the more familiar crop, the settlers began referring to it as "corn."

Corn is a grass that had been domesticated and cultivated long before the white man arrived in the New World; it has never been found in a wild state. The grass probably originated in the lowlands east of the Andes and was carried to Peru, where various varieties have been found in Inca tombs. From there it went north to become part of the Maya and Aztec civilizations, and to our own Southwestern Plains, and Northern Indians.

The mythology of corn and its religious significance to these great Indian civilizations has filled many volumes. Corn was their basic food; corn was the deity that made them live, to be propitiated with gifts and dances. Even in Christian times in Mexico, some religious images were life-size statues mainly made of cornstalks. In the Central and South American corn belts, the Indians' use of corn went further than food. It was used as currency and the husks wrapped around tobacco made simple cigars and served as an introduction to smoking for many a contemporary boy and girl.

Corn was also popular with the settlers of our country. Ground into a meal, it went into the many dishes that sustained North and South alike. Johnny cake, hush puppies, corn muffins and corn pone are pure Americana; the latter served as the subject of a 15½ hour long Senate filibuster by Huey Long in 1935. The exclusive Hasty Pudding Club of Harvard owes its name to the pudding originally known as Indian pudding, made with corn. Finally, let us not forget popcorn, the joy of an American childhood that lasts into adulthood, for what would the movies be without a bag of popcorn?

How to Buy

Fresh sweet corn is available practically all the year round, peak season from May to September. Large amounts of corn are frozen on the cob or as kernel corn or canned as kernel or cream corn. *Buy* ears with fresh, snug, green husks with dark brown silk at the husk end. The kernels should be firm, plump and juicy-looking, and large enough to leave no space between the rows. Ears should be filled to the tip, with no rows of missing kernels. The stem ends should not be too discolored or dried out. Medium-sized kernels are preferable. *Avoid* soft, tired-looking ears with spots, signs of decay or worm damage. Avoid tiny soft kernels which mean that the corn is immature or very large, tough kernels which indicate overmaturity.

Allow 1 to 2 ears per serving.

Two ears equal approximately 1 cup fresh corn kernels.

How to Keep

Use as quickly as possible; the best fresh corn is that cooked as soon as picked. The sooner used the sweeter and more tender: flavor and texture are lost within the first 24 hours after picking and the sugar content turns quickly into starch at higher temperatures. To store, wrap the whole unhusked ear in damp paper towels and store in the coldest part of the refrigerator.

Fresh, refrigerator shelf—as soon as possible.

Fresh and cooked or canned, covered, refrigerator shelf—2 to 3 days.

Nutritive Values

Fresh corn contains mostly agreeable carbohydrates, as well as a fair amount of vitamin A and some vitamin C, protein and minerals.

1 small ear—approximately 85 calories.
3½ ounces kernels, cooked on cob—91 calories.
3½ ounces cornmeal, cooked—50 calories.

How to Use

To husk fresh corn, remove the outer husk and the silk; a small vegetable brush is helpful for removing silk. Rinse in cold water. For fresh whole kernels, cut lengthwise from the cob with a sharp knife, scraping well to get all the milky juice. For fresh cream-style corn, slit through the center of each row of kernels with the point of a sharp knife. Press out the pulp and the juice with the blunt edge of the knife.

To boil fresh corn, husk and place into a large kettle of rapidly boiling water. Do not salt the water as salt toughens, but add 1 tablespoon of sugar for sweetness. After the water reaches the boiling point again, cover and cook for 3 to 5 minutes. Do not overcook. Drain and serve immediately with butter, salt and pepper. To roast fresh corn pull back the outer husk, remove the silk, smooth the husk back into place and tie with string. Soak prepared corn in salted cold water for 5 minutes, drain and place into a shallow baking dish. Roast in a preheated moderate oven (350° F) for 30 minutes, or roast without first soaking. Or grill over an open fire for 10 to 15 minutes. Roast unhusked ears buried in hot coals for 10 to 15 minutes or wrap them in heavy aluminum foil and roast in a preheated moderate oven (350° F) for 40 minutes or so (or over hot coals for 10 minutes). Or husk corn and spread kernels with melted butter seasoned with soy sauce, curry or other spices, wrap in heavy aluminum foil, and roast in hot coals for 10 to 15 minutes. Cook fresh kernels in a covered saucepan in a small amount of water, milk or light cream for 3 to 5 minutes or until just tender and season with salt, pepper and butter.

HOMINY

Hulled corn that is broken into various sizes and soaked in weak lye. This pioneer food is now marketed as grits, also known as samp, and popular in the South. See page 189 for main entry.

MASA HARINA

A corn product widely used in Mexico and other Latin countries made from hulled corn kernels soaked and boiled in lime water, drained and ground many times into a very fine meal; used for tortillas and other foods. It is now packaged and available in most American and all Latin markets.

PARCHED CORN, SHAKER-DRIED CORN

Drying was one of the principal ways of preserving food well into the 19th century. The Shakers were known for their dried corn. The Pennsylvania Dutch also use it to this day, mostly in soups. Dried corn is reconstituted like dried beans. It is surprisingly tasty.

COLACHE

4 servings

A little more or little less of this or that vegetable does not hurt the dish.

2 tablespoons bacon fat or salad oil
1 pound zucchini, trimmed and sliced (about 3 cups)
½ green pepper, minced
3 ears corn cut off the cob
2 medium tomatoes, peeled and diced
½ teaspoon sugar
salt
freshly ground pepper
½ teaspoon ground cumin seed or to taste
½ cup grated Monterey or Cheddar cheese

Heat the bacon fat in a heavy casserole. Cook, stirring constantly, the zucchini and the pepper in it for about 2 minutes. Add all the other ingredients except the cheese and mix well. Simmer covered for 10 to 12 minutes or until the vegetables are tender. Sprinkle with the cheese before serving.

FRESH CORN SALAD

6 servings

This is a good buffet dish. Add julienne sticks of Swiss cheese, strips of cooked cold meats or chicken or cooked shrimp to make a main-dish salad.

8 ears corn, husked
½ cup olive oil
¼ cup cider vinegar
1 tablespoon fresh lemon juice
2 teaspoons Dijon mustard
salt
freshly ground pepper
¼ cup minced parsley
2 tablespoons minced fresh
    basil leaves or 2 teaspoons
    dried basil or 1 or 2
    tablespoons minced fresh
    tarragon leaves

2 large tomatoes, peeled,
    seeded and chopped
1 small green pepper, peeled
    and cut into strips
½ cup minced green onions
lettuce

Fill a large kettle with water and bring to the boiling point. Add the corn and cover the kettle. Bring back to the boiling point. Remove from the heat and let stand for 5 to 10 minutes. Drain and cool. Cut the kernels off the cobs. Combine the olive oil, vinegar, lemon juice and mustard. Mix well. Taste; add salt and pepper. Add the parsley, basil or tarragon and mix well. Add the corn and toss. Add the tomatoes, pepper and green onions and toss again. Line a salad bowl with lettuce and pile the corn salad on the lettuce.

CORN FRITTATA

4 servings

4 slices bacon
2 tablespoons minced onion
4 ears corn cut off the cob
4 eggs
3 tablespoons water

¼ cup grated Parmesan cheese
salt
freshly ground pepper
¼ teaspoon dried thyme

In a large frying pan, cook the bacon until it is crisp. Drain the bacon on paper towels, crumble and reserve. Pour off all but 2 tablespoons of the bacon fat. Cook the onion and the corn in the bacon fat for 3 to 5 minutes or until tender. Beat together all the remaining ingredients and stir in the crumbled bacon. Pour the mixture over the corn. Cook over low heat, without stirring but shaking the frying pan to prevent sticking, for about 5 minutes or until set. Cut into 4 wedges. Turn each wedge over with a large spatula. Cook until set. Or place the frying pan under the broiler and cook until the top is set. Serve hot or lukewarm.

CORN SALAD
Field Salad, Lamb's Lettuce
Valerianella olitoria

A spring and summer salad green that springs up wild in fields of corn and other grains. The plant is four to six inches tall with leaves that, depending on the varieties, are spoon-shaped or round, smooth edged or slightly toothed, growing in compact rosettes. Their texture is quite firm and their flavor bland and vaguely lettucelike.

Corn salad is cultivated to a small extent in this country, especially in home gardens. In Europe, it is extremely popular and grown accordingly and widely sold in bunches. Corn salad is the French salad called *mâche,* also called *doucette* and *salade du chanoine.* In England, it is known as lamb's lettuce, and the thought of baby lambs grazing on it in the spring is a pretty one. There is a longer-leafed, somewhat hairy Italian variety, whose Roman name is *insalatina,* little salad.

Corn salad appears mainly in Italian markets. It is very perishable and should be treated as other perishable salad greens. It may also be briefly cooked like spinach.

CRESS
(See page 354)

CUCUMBER
Cucumis sativus

Cucumbers, which belong to the squash-gourd family Cucurbitaceae, are one of the most widely cultivated vegetables and one of the oldest, going back some 3,000 years. The Emperor Tiberius, known for his dubious personal life, was so fond of cucumbers that he had to eat them every day, wherever he was, so that they were grown in special movable frames. Charlemagne grew cucumbers in his gardens in the 9th century, and the English did in the 14th century. But then, with their periods of constant war, they forgot how and only took to cucumber growing 250 years later when the vegetable was reintroduced from the continent. Since then the popularity of the cucumber, fresh or pickled, has become immense, especially in Germanic and Slavic countries where it may be considered, beside cabbage, the national vegetable.

The New World owes cucumbers to Columbus, who had them planted in Haiti in 1494. The Spaniards reintroduced them to the Indians on the Atlantic coast, and the English grew them in their settlements in Virginia in 1609 and Massachusetts in 1629.

The cucumber, which strictly speaking is a fruit, is used as a vegetable, grows on a trailing vine, a graceful plant that has been known to yield 25 to 125 cucumbers. There are many varieties which can be divided into three main groups. The large, smooth green-house-green English cucumber grows to as much as two feet in length with flesh more delicate and tender than the field-grown or garden-grown cucumber. This cucumber is the one that commonly serves us for table use along with the small pickling varieties. There are also Japanese cucumbers, found in Oriental markets, which may be smooth and rounded or pointed, with soft spines. The pale apple or lemon cucumber is yet another; it produces rounded fruits the size of an orange. The latest in cucumbers are seedless ones which will grow at the same rate to the same size so that they can be harvested mechanically.

Besides being very low in calories, inexpensive and widely available, cucumbers have healing and cosmetic virtues. Rubbed on the skin, cucumbers will keep it white and soft and soothe sunburn and other irritations. Cucumber juice is said to get rid of or at least soften freckles. Especially in France, soap and other cosmetic products made from cucumbers are very highly thought of as beautifiers.

How to Buy

Almost all commercially sold cucumbers have waxed skins which slow up their spoiling. Since it is impossible to remove all the wax, even under hot water, they have to be peeled. As anyone who has eaten a fresh, nonwaxed cucumber knows, a good deal of the flavor resides in the peel. It is sad to think that the coming generations, unless they have their own gardens, will never know the joys of unwaxed cucumbers.

Available all year, peak from May through August.

Buy cucumbers that are fresh, firm, well shaped and not too large. They should be bright green in color with whitish tips. *Avoid* soft, rubbery, dull cucumbers or very large ones.

Allow 1 medium cucumber for 2 to 3 servings.

How to Keep

Do not peel or slice until ready to use. Cucumbers, especially cut cucumbers, whether raw or cooked, in any form, give off a strong odor that other refrigerated foods will rapidly absorb. Wrap whole unpeeled cucumbers in plastic wrap and refrigerate. Cover any cut or cooked cucumbers very tightly with plastic wrap or aluminum foil before refrigerating. Do not freeze.

   Unpeeled, refrigerator shelf—1 week.

   Salad, covered—3 to 4 days.

   Cooked and covered—3 to 4 days.

Nutritive Values

Cucumbers are 95 per cent water. They have small amounts of vitamins and minerals and are by volume very low in calories.

   6- to 7-inch cucumber—approximately 25 calories.

   3½ ounces raw, peeled—15 calories.

How to Use

Wash, trim ends and either slice, cut into strips or dice. Peel if the skin is tough or heavily waxed. If lightly waxed, try to remove the wax under hot water; some of it may come off. Do not peel young cucumbers with a tender skin. To flute for decorative slices: score the skin lengthwise with a fork before slicing. For shells, peel or not, cut into halves lengthwise and scoop out the seeds with a sharp spoon or the tip of a knife. To crisp, cut into thin or thick slices or sticks. Refrigerate in salted ice water for 1 to 2 hours. Drain thoroughly. To wilt, thinly slice cucumbers; place in a bowl and sprinkle with salt (about 1 to 2 tablespoons per cucumber). Cover and weigh down with a weight such as a filled can. Let stand at room temperature for 30 to 60 minutes. Drain and rinse out salt under running cold water. Drain again and squeeze dry with hands. Dress with sour cream, yoghurt, or vinegar and sugar.

   Cucumbers are excellent cooked, sautéed, deep-fried or stuffed. To cook, peel and cut into thick slices or large sticks or quarters. Cook covered in an inch of boiling water for 3 to 5 minutes; do not overcook. Drain and serve with butter, lemon juice or herbs. To sauté, cut into ¼-inch slices or sticks. Dip in flour and sauté in hot butter for 2 to 3 minutes. Or deep fry by dipping ½-inch slices or sticks in beaten egg and bread crumbs or flour and dropping into hot oil (375° F on frying thermometer) and fry until golden-brown. Serve immediately with lemon wedges.

Note: When cooking cucumber, do not add salt until it is cooked. It is a watery enough vegetable, and salt during cooking draws even more water.

ICY CUCUMBER SOUP

6 servings

This soup should not be buttery, because cold buttery soup is not attractive. The cream will add the needed richness. Remember that thorough chilling always takes more time than one thinks.

2 tablespoons butter
2 leeks, chopped, white parts
  only, or 1 medium onion,
  chopped
1 bunch green onions, chopped,
  white and tender green parts
  (remove coarse outer leaves)
6 cucumbers
1 cup watercress leaves or 1
  cup parsley leaves
2 medium potatoes, peeled and
  chopped
6 cups chicken consommé
salt
freshly ground pepper
½ teaspoon dry mustard or
  ground cardamom
1 cup heavy cream
1 cup radishes, finely chopped
  (optional)

Heat the butter in a deep kettle. Over low heat, stirring frequently, cook the leeks and the onion in the butter until the vegetables are tender. Do not let them brown. Peel the cucumbers, cut them lengthwise into quarters, scrape off the seeds and chop. Add the cucumbers, watercress, potatoes, chicken consommé, salt and pepper to taste and the mustard or cardamom to the onion mixture. Simmer covered over low heat for about 20 minutes, or until the potatoes are tender. Strain through a fine sieve or blend in a blender. Check the seasonings. Pour into a bowl; tightly cover the bowl with aluminum foil or plastic wrap. Chill the soup thoroughly. Stir in the cream before serving and sprinkle with the chopped radishes.

SOUR CREAM CUCUMBER SALAD

4 servings

If the cucumbers are not waxed, do not peel them but wash them and score them lengthwise with the tines of a fork. Good with curries.

3 or 4 medium cucumbers
1 tablespoon salt
¾ cup sour cream
1 to 1½ tablespoons white
    vinegar
2 tablespoons salad oil (do not
    use olive oil)

¼ teaspoon sugar
salt
freshly ground pepper
3 tablespoons minced dill or
    minced parsley

Trim the cucumbers. Slice them as thinly as possible. Sprinkle with salt, mix and let stand at room temperature for 1 hour. Drain and rinse under running cold water to remove the salt. Squeeze dry. Combine the sour cream, vinegar, salad oil, sugar and salt and pepper. Pour over the cucumbers. Cover and chill for 1 hour or more. Sprinkle with the minced dill before serving.

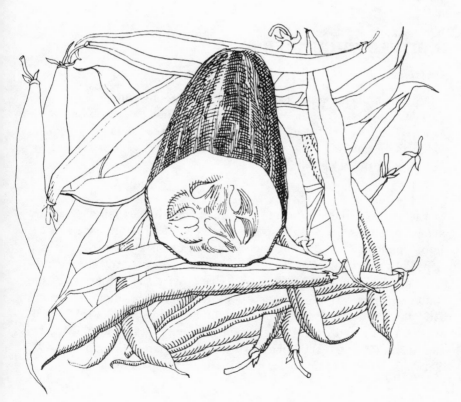

SCANDINAVIAN PICKLED CUCUMBERS

4 servings

In Scandinavia, cucumbers are not peeled. Since ours are generally coated with wax, it will be necessary to peel them.

½ cup white vinegar	2 to 3 tablespoons sugar
2 tablespoons water	¼ cup minced dill
salt	2 large cucumbers or 4 small
freshly ground pepper	Kirby cucumbers

Combine all the ingredients except the cucumbers and mix well. Slice the cucumbers as thinly as possible—they should be almost transparent. Place in a serving dish. Pour the dressing over the cucumbers. Cover and refrigerate 3 or more hours. Check the seasoning and drain before serving.

SAUTEED CUCUMBERS

4 servings

3 large cucumbers, about 1 pound each	3 tablespoons butter
⅓ cup flour	1 tablespoon grated onion
½ teaspoon salt	¼ cup minced parsley
⅛ teaspoon freshly ground pepper	

Wash and peel the cucumbers. Cut them into halves lengthwise and scrape out the seeds with a spoon. Split each half lengthwise and cut into 1-inch pieces. Dry the pieces with a clean kitchen towel. In a paper bag, mix together the flour, salt and pepper. Add the cucumbers. Shake to coat the pieces and shake off excess flour. Heat the butter in a deep frying pan and cook the onion for about 1 minute. Add the cucumbers. Cook over medium-to-high heat, stirring constantly with a fork, for 4 or 5 minutes or until crisp and golden. Do not overcook or the cucumbers will be soggy. Drain on paper towels. Serve in a hot serving dish sprinkled with the parsley.

DAIKON
Oriental Radish

Raphanus sativus longipinnatus

The daikon is an Oriental radish that produces large-growing white roots. There are also two smaller, turniplike versions which the Chinese prefer. All of these radishes are somewhat spongy in texture and mildly pungent.

Daikon is eaten raw or pickled. Raw, shredded or grated, the radish goes into Oriental salads or is served as a side dish in Japanese meals. Or it may be dipped into soy sauce. It can be pickled by itself or in combination with other ingredients to be used as a side dish to Oriental and Indonesian meals. Daikon also serves ornamental purposes; the flowers that garnish Japanese dishes so prettily are usually carved from daikon. The leaves of young plants with undeveloped longish roots are used as a somewhat pungent green vegetable. They are sold in bunches in Oriental stores (roots removed) and should be cooked in the water in which they were washed for the shortest of times.

3½ ounces raw—19 calories

PICKLED DAIKON

about 3 cups

1½ pounds daikon
1 cup sugar
½ cup white or rice vinegar

1 cup water
¼ cup salt

Peel and wash the daikon and slice very thinly. Place in a glass or china bowl. Combine the remaining ingredients in a saucepan. Bring to the boiling point, remove from heat and cool. Pour over the daikon slices. Cover the bowl. Refrigerate for 3 days and drain before serving.

DANDELION

Taraxacum officinale

The dandelion is a weed that exasperates those who care for beautiful lawns but pleases others who like a fresh tasting, pungent green on their tables. The name seems to come from the French *dent du lion*, lion's tooth, describing the toothed jagged edges of the leaves. The name of the vegetable in France is not as romantic; as *pissenlit* it refers to the dandelion's diuretic effects.

A native of Eurasia, dandelions have been a popular green since the days of the Romans in all of Europe and a good part of the Orient. The young leaves of the plant can be eaten raw in salads and all the green leaves may be cooked like spinach or used as a potherb. The flowers of this adaptable green have long been used for home-made wines and the roots, dried, roasted and ground, serve as a coffee substitute. Dandelion teas, from the leaves or the roots, have been famed for centuries for their therapeutic uses. All the medieval herbals list them for their health-giving properties. Our colonial ancestors depended on them as the first spring green after a winter of monotonous root vegetables.

Apart from the wild varieties, several kinds of large-leafed dandelions are now grown commercially in the United States as well as in France and other European countries. Interestingly, a Russian variety yields a latex (wild rubber) juice.

How to Buy

Wild and cultivated dandelions, gathered in bunches, are marketed in the early spring and summer. The cultivated dandelions are lighter green in color and less bitter than the wild ones.

Buy fresh, tender, crisp, clean and comparatively large green leaves. If the roots are still attached, the leaves are juicier. *Avoid* wilted, flabby and yellowed leaves and leaves that are very dirty and have insect damage.

Allow 1 pound raw leaves for 2 to 3 servings.

How to Keep

Trim away damaged or yellowed leaves and roots. Wash thoroughly and shake dry. Wrap in plastic wrap and refrigerate.

Raw, refrigerator shelf—3 to 5 days.

Cooked and covered, refrigerator shelf—3 to 4 days.

Nutritive Values

Dandelions are an excellent source of vitamin A and a good source of iron and other minerals.

3½ ounces, raw—45 calories.

3½ ounces cooked—33 calories.

How to Use

To cook: wash leaves and shake dry. Cut or tear into 2- to 3-inch pieces. If young, use no water, but cook covered, like spinach, in the water that clings to them for 5 minutes or until just tender. If older, cook covered in ½ inch boiling salted water. Drain and season to taste.

Use the small tender leaves for salads, whole or chopped.

WILTED DANDELION GREENS

4 servings

6 slices bacon, cut into strips
1½ pounds dandelion greens,
   prepared for cooking

⅓ cup vinegar
½ teaspoon sugar
salt

Cook the bacon in a deep frying pan until crisp. Drain off all but 3 tablespoons of the fat. Add the dandelion greens, vinegar, sugar and a little salt. Mix well. Cover and simmer until the greens are wilted. Stir frequently and taste; if necessary, add a little more vinegar to flavor the greens. Serve hot.

DASHEEN
Colocasia esculenta

Dasheens are oblong starchy tubers, a variety of the numerous taro family (page 336) which are grown in warm climates as a potato substitute. When cooked, and dasheens must be cooked, the flesh becomes cream colored and nutty in flavor. The leafy tops of the vegetable are, like other taros, called callaloo and are used for the soup of the same name (page 100).

Dasheens and all the other taros are one of the staple foods of millions of people in the Caribbean, Central and South America, Southeastern and Eastern Asia, the Pacific and especially in Hawaii, where poi, a thin paste made of cooked taro is an important food. The name dasheen is said to mean "de la chine" since the vegetable was thought to have come from there.

How to Buy

Available all year in Latin markets where they are also known as yautia. *Buy* firm, fresh looking dasheens which are full and heavy for their size. *Avoid* wizened vegetables.

Allow 1 pound for 2 to 3 servings.

How to Keep

Keep in a dark, cool, well ventilated place, like potatoes, though dasheens don't keep as long.

Raw—1 week.

Cooked and covered, refrigerator shelf—2 to 4 days.

Nutritive Values

Dasheens are higher in carbohydrates than potatoes and they contain a good deal of water.

3½ ounces tubers, raw—98 calories.

3½ ounces, leaves and stems, raw—40 calories.

How to Use

Any potato recipe can be used for dasheens. Preferably do not peel the raw vegetable because its juice is somewhat irritating to the skin. Scrub with a vegetable brush and boil in salted water for 15 minutes or until tender. Peel and mash, or cube or slice and serve with salt and pepper and butter or add to other dishes according to recipe.

MASHED DASHEEN

4 servings

2 pounds dasheen, scrubbed	salt
boiling water	freshly ground pepper
4 tablespoons butter	1 cup hot milk or light cream

Cook the dasheen in boiling water for about 15 minutes or until tender. Peel and mash. Beat in the butter and season with salt and pepper. Beat in the milk and beat until fluffy. Serve immediately or keep hot in the top of a double boiler over hot water.

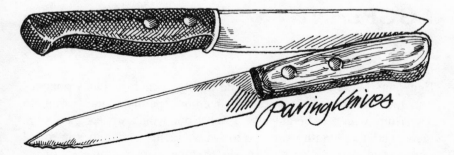

Paring Knives

EDIBLE FLOWERS

Cooking with flowers is an art practiced since ancient times. Chinese, Arabs, Greeks and Romans used peonies, lotus, roses, violets and other blossoms to flavor and beautify their cookery. The healthful properties of flowers as food run through many culinary writings of the Middle Ages and later times; flower cookery was at its height in the 18th and 19th centuries when the French and British used flowers in tarts, puddings, cakes, wines and liqueurs.

Flower cookery is not much practiced today, with a few exceptions. In Japan, the petals of chrysanthemums similar but not identical to ours are pickled. In Italy and France, squash flowers dipped in a batter and quickly deep-fried, are an appreciated side dish.

For those interested in the possibilities of flower cookery, I recommend an amusing and learned book, *Flower Cookery, The Art of Cooking with Flowers,* by Mary MacNicol, Fleet Press Corporation, New York, 1967. I also recommend *The Art of Cooking With Roses* by Jean Gordon, Noonday Press, Farrar, Straus & Giroux, paper $2.65.

EGGPLANT
Aubergine
Solanum melongena

Eggplants belong to the nightshade family, which includes potatoes, tomatoes and pepper, tobacco, belladonna, petunias and jessamine. The fruit, which is botanically a berry but which we eat as a vegetable, varies in length from two to twelve inches and comes in round, oblong and pearlike shapes. Its slick, shiny skin, reminiscent of patent leather, is most commonly dark purple, but it may also be whitish, reddish, yellowish and even striped. There is no question that the eggplant is indeed a beautiful vegetable. Americans admire it, but do not consider it a major vegetable, unless they are of French, Italian, Oriental or Near Eastern origin.

The origins of eggplant are like that of so many other vegetables, unclear. It is said to have originated near India, where many food plants have originated. There are many names for it in those parts, in Sanskrit, Bengali and Hindustani, which prove that it has been cultivated since antiquity. Another, quite different variety seems to have developed in China. There, eggplant is mentioned in 5th-century books, and, as in India, it is still a popular food. In any case, the vegetable traveled West and settled in the Mediterranean and Near Eastern lands where it is perhaps best appreciated. In the United States, eggplants were grown for ornamental uses only until fifty or sixty years ago.

Eggplants grow on an annual bushy plant, which need a relatively warm climate and long growing conditions. The varieties grown commercially in the United States are the large fruited ones, but in Italian, Oriental and Near Eastern markets, it is possible to find the small long fruit, and occasionally even the round pale eggplant or the tiny, finger-length ones, which are preferred by Chinese and Japanese.

How to Buy

Eggplant is available the year round, peak August and September. Whether you are buying the common, large commercial eggplant or the small ones or any of the varieties, *buy* fruit that are firm, smooth, of a uniformly glossy color and heavy for their weight. Choose small rather than large fruit. *Avoid* oversize fruit or fruit with large, rough, spongy places and with dark brown spots which are a sign of decay.

Allow 1 medium eggplant (about 1½ pounds) for 4 to 6 servings.

How to Keep

Eggplant is perishable. Use as soon as possible. Until then, keep in a dark, cool and humid place, such as a basement. Or refrigerate briefly.

Raw, refrigerator shelf—3 to 4 days.
Cooked and covered, refrigerator shelf—3 to 4 days.

Nutritive Values

There is little nutrition in eggplant, but it adds interesting flavor and texture variety to menus.

3½ ounces cooked and drained—19 calories.

How to Use

Eggplant can be prepared in many ways, depending on its size and the nationality of the cuisine. Whether it should be peeled or not depends on the size and variety and the toughness of the skin. The commonly sold large eggplants have a tough skin, but the skin of the small, long skinny ones or the tiny ones is tender and edible. Eggplant is a watery fruit, and there are two schools of thought as to whether the water which is a little bitter should be drained before cooking. Again, it depends on the size and variety and use.

If the water is to be drained, wash, trim off the stem, peel or not. Cut the eggplant into halves lengthwise and cut several ¼-inch gashes lengthwise into the flesh. Or cut into ¼- to ½-inch slices. Sprinkle about 1 tablespoon salt on the flesh for each eggplant half or corresponding slices. Lay the halves (cut side down) or slices on a kitchen towel or several thicknesses of paper towels. Let stand at room temperature from 15 to 30 minutes. Press the eggplant halves or slices gently with the back of a spoon to extract as much moisture as possible without damaging the fruit. Dry the halves or slices with another kitchen towel or more paper towels before using.

Or else, peel or not. Cut into slices, julienne strips or cubes. Do this just before using because eggplant darkens quickly when the cut surfaces are exposed to the air.

To boil

Eggplant is seldom boiled by itself; more likely, it is added to stews or dishes with liquid in which it will cook. In this case, it is best to quickly sauté the sliced or cubed eggplant first in a little hot butter or oil; this step helps it keep its shape and adds to its flavor.

To pan fry

Slice, cube or cut the eggplant into julienne strips. Sauté in a little hot butter or oil, turning over once, for 5 to 7 minutes or until golden brown. Or dip in flour and sauté as above. Season with salt and pepper.

To deep fry

Cut into strips. Roll in seasoned flour, dip into egg beaten with milk or water (1 egg and 2 tablespoons of milk or water) and roll in fine dry bread crumbs. Fry in deep hot fat (375° F to 385° F on frying thermometer) for a few minutes (time depends on the size of the strips) and drain on paper towels. Serve immediately with lemon wedges.

To broil or grill

Cut washed and trimmed eggplant into 4 or 8 wedges, depending on size. Or cut into ¾-inch slices. With a pastry brush, brush all the cut surfaces with melted butter, salad or olive oil. Sprinkle with salt and pepper and any desired herbs. Place on broiler pan or barbecue grill and broil or grill about 3 to 4 inches away from heat for about 10 minutes. Turn over once or twice to insure even cooking and brush repeatedly with melted butter or oil.

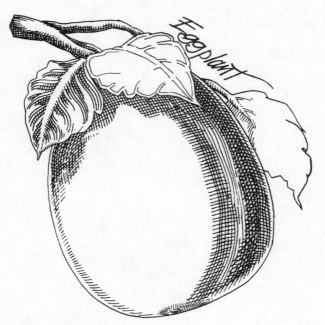

POOR MAN'S CAVIAR WITH BEANS

4-6 servings

1 large eggplant, about 3
   pounds
6 tablespoons olive oil
½ cup minced onion
1 garlic clove, minced
2 large ripe tomatoes, peeled,
   seeded and chopped
¼ cup minced parsley
2 tablespoons minced fresh
   basil or 2 teaspoons dried
   basil

1 to 2 cups cooked navy beans
   (if canned, rinse under
   running cold water and drain
   thoroughly)
2 to 3 tablespoons fresh lemon
   juice
salt
freshly ground pepper
2 tablespoons drained capers
   (optional)

Put the eggplant in a baking dish and prick 3 times with the tines of a fork. Bake in a preheated moderate oven (350° F) for 30 to 45 minutes or until soft. Cool. Slit open the skin. Remove most of the seeds with a teaspoon. Mash the pulp with a fork. Heat 4 tablespoons of the oil in a frying pan. Cook the onion and garlic in it until soft and golden. Stir into the eggplant and mix well. Add the tomatoes, parsley, basil, and the beans. Mix gently, taking care not to break the beans. Combine the remaining 2 tablespoons oil and the lemon juice. Stir into the eggplant mixture. Season with salt and pepper and if necessary add a little more lemon juice. Sprinkle with the capers.

EGGPLANT PARMIGIANA

6 servings

1 large eggplant, about 3
   pounds
salt
flour
2 eggs beaten with 2 teaspoons
   olive oil
fine dry bread crumbs
olive oil

2 tablespoons minced fresh
   basil or 2 teaspoons dried
   basil
1½ cups tomato sauce, heated
8 ounces mozzarella, thinly
   sliced
⅔ cup grated Parmesan cheese

Trim but do not peel the eggplant. Cut into ¼-inch slices. Put the
slices on a large platter and sprinkle each slice with about ⅛ teaspoon
salt. Let stand at room temperature for about 30 minutes to draw out
excess moisture. Drain and dry the eggplant slices between paper
towels. Dip each slice into the flour and shake off excess. Dip into
the beaten eggs, shake off excess egg and dip into bread crumbs.
Heat about ⅛ inch olive oil in a large frying pan. Fry the eggplant
slices, a few at a time, until golden on both sides, turning over once.
Drain on paper towels. Stir the basil into the tomato sauce. Spoon a
little tomato sauce into a buttered 2-quart baking dish. Arrange one-
third of the fried eggplant slices, overlapping, on the sauce. Top with
a layer of a third of the mozzarella, a third of the tomato sauce and
a third of the grated Parmesan. Repeat until all the ingredients are
used. Bake in a preheated moderate oven (350° F) for 20 to 30
minutes or until bubbly.

Vegetable Steamer

CAPONATA SICILIANA (Pickled Eggplant)

8 servings

Whatever is not eaten at one sitting can be stored in a closed container in the refrigerator for 2 or 3 weeks.

4 medium eggplants, about 1 pound each

1½ cups olive oil (it must be olive oil)

4 large onions, thinly sliced

1 cup Italian-style canned tomatoes, forced through a sieve

4 celery stalks, white part only, thinly sliced

½ cup drained capers

½ cup minced parsley

12 black olives, pitted and halved

2 tablespoons pine nuts

½ cup wine vinegar

¼ cup sugar

salt

freshly ground pepper

Peel the eggplants and cut them into 1-inch cubes. Heat 1 cup of the olive oil in a large, deep frying pan. Cook the eggplant in it until it is soft and brown, stirring constantly. Remove the eggplant with a slotted spoon to a dish and reserve. Add the remaining oil to the frying pan. Cook the onions, stirring constantly, until they are soft and golden. Add the tomatoes and celery. Cook over medium heat, stirring frequently, until the celery is tender. To prevent scorching, add a tablespoon or two of water, if necessary. Add the capers, parsley, olives, pine nuts and the fried eggplant. Mix well. Cook for about 1 minute and remove from heat. Heat the vinegar in a small saucepan and dissolve the sugar in it. Stir the vinegar into the eggplant mixture. Season with salt and pepper. Simmer covered over lowest possible heat for about 15 minutes. Stir frequently and add a tablespoon of water if there is danger of scorching. Go easy on the water because the finished dish must not be soupy. Cool before serving.

BAKED EGGPLANT, MOZZARELLA, EGGS AND TOMATOES

3-4 servings

4 small eggplants, each about 6
   inches long
salt
4 anchovies, drained and
   minced
2 large ripe firm tomatoes,
   peeled and cut into ¼-inch
   slices
3 hard-cooked eggs, sliced
1 mozzarella cheese weighing
   approximately 8 to 12
   ounces, cut into ¼-inch
   slices

freshly ground pepper
1 cup Italian parsley sprigs
¼ cup fresh basil leaves or 2
   tablespoons dried basil
2 garlic cloves
¼ cup olive oil

Trim and peel the eggplants. Cut into ¼-inch slices. Put the slices on a large platter and sprinkle each slice with about ⅛ teaspoon salt. Let stand at room temperature to draw off excessive moisture. Drain and dry the eggplant slices between paper towels. Spread a little minced anchovy on each tomato slice. In a buttered shallow oven-proof dish or pie plate which can go to the table make well-overlapping rows of eggplant, egg, tomato and mozzarella slices in that order. Sprinkle with very little salt (the eggplant slices and the anchovies are salty) and pepper. Mince together the parsley, basil and the garlic cloves. Sprinkle the mixture over the vegetables and cheese; sprinkle with the olive oil. Cover the dish with aluminum foil. Bake in a preheated moderate oven (350° F) for 30 minutes. Remove the aluminum foil and bake for about 10 more minutes to let the excessive moisture in the dish evaporate. Serve either hot, lukewarm or cold, but not chilled.

TORTINO DI MELANZANE (Eggplant and Egg Puff)

4-6 servings

A good main dish served with tomato salad.

4 small eggplants, each about
  6 inches long
salt
flour
olive oil
10 eggs
¼ cup milk

⅓ cup minced parsley
1 tablespoon fresh marjoram,
  minced, or ½ teaspoon dried
  marjoram
salt
freshly ground pepper

Trim and peel the eggplants. Cut into ¼-inch slices. Put the slices on a large platter and sprinkle each slice with about ⅛ teaspoon salt; let stand for 30 minutes to draw out excess moisture. Drain and dry. Coat the slices with flour, shaking off excess flour. Pour about ¼ inch olive oil into a large frying pan. Heat the oil to the smoking point. Fry a few eggplant slices at a time for about two minutes on each side in the hot oil, turning as each side gets golden brown. Add more oil to keep a ¼-inch level. Remove eggplant with a slotted spoon and drain on paper towels. Arrange the fried eggplant slices in overlapping rows in a 1½-quart deep baking dish. Beat together the eggs, milk, parsley, and marjoram. Season with very little salt and pepper, taking into account that the eggplant slices have been salted. Pour the mixture over the eggplant. Cook in a preheated hot oven (400° F) for about 20 minutes or until puffed and golden brown.

ENDIVE
Curly-leaf Endive
Cichorium endivia crispa

Endive is a leafy green vegetable generally used for salads which grows in a loose head, with crisp, narrow white or rose-tinted ribs in ragged-edged leaves which curl at the ends. The center leaves form a yellowish heart. Another type is Escarole, with straight, broad leaves (page 175) with which endive is often confused. Both are members of the chicory family, as is their cousin the Belgian endive, or witloof (page 77). Confusingly, endive is often not only sold as escarole, but as chicory as well.

Endives, like escarole, are almost exclusively used for salads in the United States. In European and Near Eastern cookery both are used as cooked vegetables, in soups or in composite dishes, a splendid use that deserves recognition in the United States. Their very slightly bitter, or perhaps pungent, flavor adds sparkle to both salads and cooked dishes.

Endive is sold wherever lettuce is sold, among the salad greens. Two other kinds, very popular salad greens among Italians, can be found in Italian markets and are well worth looking for: the cicoria San Pasquale, with light green leaves, and radichetta, with dandelion-like leaves and a delicious, somewhat peppery flavor.

How to Buy

Curly endive is available all year, peak June through October.

Buy fresh, clean, heads with crisp ribs and leaves; look for a tightly packed head. *Avoid* flabby, wilted heads with a yellowish-green color, bruised stems and browning outer leaves, or heads with insect damage.

Allow 1 pound for 3 to 4 servings.

How to Keep

Remove and discard any wilted or bruised outer leaves. Wash the heads under running cold water. Drain and shake off as much water as possible. Pat dry with paper towels. Store in refrigerator vegetable drawer or refrigerate in a plastic bag.

Raw, refrigerator shelf or vegetable compartment—3 days.

Nutritive Values

Endive is a good source of vitamin A and a fair source of iron.
  3½ ounces raw—20 calories.

How to Use

Endives are used like lettuce in salads, but they may also be cooked
as a green. In order to keep endive fresh and crisp, remove from
refrigerator just before using. Cut away any tough part of the stem.
Separate the leaves or cut them into bite-sized pieces. Wash thoroughly, if necessary in several changes of water; drain and dry
between paper towels or with a kitchen towel. To crisp, place dried
endive in a dry kitchen towel or plastic bag and refrigerate 1 to 2
hours. For salads serve with salad dressing or use in a mixed tossed
salad.

Experience has taught me that washing endive, lettuce or any other
greens in a colander does not get all the dirt out. The proper way of
washing them is to fill a very large bowl, or better still the kitchen
sink, with cold water. Drop in the greens and swirl around carefully
so as not to bruise the leaves. If the greens are very sandy or dirty,
repeat the process. Drain in a colander and then pat dry.

If the center of an endive is not as white as wanted, it can be
bleached further by placing a damp cloth over the center overnight.

To cook endive, wash and drain but do not pat dry. Cut into ½- to
1-inch pieces. Place in a saucepan with 2 tablespoons butter for each
medium head. Cook, stirring constantly, for about 2 minutes. Season
with salt and pepper and simmer covered for 5 minutes. Check the
moisture; if necessary, add a tablespoon of water at a time.

Or add cut endives to soups, stews or casserole dishes; the slightly
bitter flavor improves these dishes.

STIR-FRIED ENDIVE

4 servings

4 slices bacon
¼ cup sesame seeds (optional)
½ cup scallions, thinly sliced
½ cup mushrooms, thinly sliced
1 medium head endive,
   trimmed, washed and
   coarsely shredded

salt
freshly ground pepper

Cook the bacon in a large frying pan until crisp. Drain and crumble. Cook the sesame seeds in the bacon fat, stirring constantly, until they are golden. Add the scallions, mushrooms and endive. Season with salt and pepper. Cook over high heat, stirring constantly, for 3 minutes or until the endive is tender but crisp. Sprinkle with the bacon and serve very hot.

ESCAROLE
Cichorium endivia latifolia

Escarole is the broad-leafed variety of endive, and a close relative of the curly endive, with which it is at times confused. The heads look somewhat flattened, with broad, white-ribbed somewhat curly green leaves which in the center form a yellowish heart. Escarole has a faintly bitter flavor and a firm texture. It is used mostly as a salad green and among people of French and Mediterranean descent as a cooked vegetable.

The history of the escarole is the history of curly endive. Since the uses of the two greens are sufficiently similar, please refer to Endive, page 173. However, some typical European recipes for cooked escarole follow.

ESCAROLE AND RICE SOUP

6 servings

½ cup olive oil
1 garlic clove
1 medium tomato, peeled and
　chopped
1 large head escarole, trimmed,
　washed and coarsely
　shredded

8 to 10 cups hot chicken
　consommé or water
2 teaspoons salt
1 cup long-grain rice
freshly grated Parmesan cheese

Heat the olive oil in a soup kettle. Brown the garlic in the oil and discard. Add the tomato and the escarole. Cook, stirring constantly, for about 3 or 4 minutes or until the escarole is soft. Add consommé and salt. Bring to the boiling point and add the rice. Lower the heat. Simmer covered, stirring frequently, for 15 to 20 minutes or until the rice is cooked. Serve with plenty of freshly grated Parmesan cheese.

BRAISED ESCAROLE WITH ANCHOVIES

4 servings

4 tablespoons olive oil
1 large garlic clove
4 to 6 anchovy fillets, minced
1 large head escarole, trimmed,
　washed and coarsely
　shredded

salt
freshly ground pepper

Heat the oil in a frying pan. Brown the garlic and discard. Stir the anchovies into the oil and cook for 1 minute. Add the escarole and mix well. Cook over high heat, stirring constantly, for 3 or 4 minutes or until the vegetable is tender but crisp. Season with salt and pepper and serve very hot.

FENNEL
Finocchio, Fenouil
Foeniculum vulgare

The common fennel, to translate its botanical name, is an aromatic plant native to the Mediterranean. The commercially grown variety, also known as sweet or Roman or Florence fennel and especially by its Italian name of finocchio, is the one used as a salad plant and vegetable. Finocchio is a bulbous vegetable composed of broad leaf stalks which overlap each other at the base of the stem forming a bulb which is firm, white, crisp and three to four inches across. The stalks end in feathery bright green leaves which can grow to a height of two feet. Since there are several leaf stalks to each bulb, finocchio looks somewhat like a hand with feathery fingers. The flavor of the bulb and the leaves is reminiscent of licorice or anise. However, finocchio has nothing else in common with the herb anise (*Pimpinella anisum*), which produces the seed used in baking and candies.

The common fennel, which also tastes somewhat like anise, is a tall perennial grown for its fine feathery leaves, which are used to flavor foods as dillweed is used, and for its very aromatic seeds which are also used as flavoring in the way dill seeds are used. Fennel oil is used medically and for soaps and perfumes. The stalks, fresh and dried, are used as fuel for grills since they flavor grilled foods such as fish deliciously. There is a third variety rarely found outside of Italy, Sicilian fennel, whose tender young stalks are eaten raw.

Fennel is an old food plant. Pliny relates how serpents eat fennel when they shed their skin to renew their youth. Victorious Roman athletes wore fennel wreaths on their brows. Throughout the centuries, it was used to cure eye trouble, draw poison and to increase the milk supply of nursing mothers. It was held in the highest esteem in England. Poor folks used fennel to still the pangs of hunger and to make food palatable, or for a treat, they coated fennel seeds with sugar and ate them like candy. In Shakespearean England, fennel stood for flattery; but in Italy, the word finocchio, applied to a person, means that he is a homosexual.

How to Buy

Dried common fennel is sold in some herb stores. Dried fennel seeds are found on the spice shelf of supermarkets. It is generally sold whole but occasionally is ground.

Finocchio is a winter vegetable, available October through April in all Italian and many American markets. It is beginning to be better known than it used to be.

Buy firm, crisp bulbs with no more than one coarse outer branch at each side of the bulb, with at least 10-inch tops which insure succulence. The color of the bulb should be a very pale greenish-white with fresh looking green tops. *Avoid* soft, coarse bulbs with brownish-edged base and stalks and wilted tops, discolored or cracked bulbs.

Allow 1 medium bulb for 2 servings.

How to Keep

Wrap bulb and stalks in a plastic bag and refrigerate.
Raw, refrigerator shelf—3 to 4 days.
Cooked and covered, refrigerator shelf—2 days.

Nutritive Values

All fennel is rich in vitamin A and a good source of potassium and calcium.
3½ ounces raw—28 calories.

How to Use

Fresh fennel leaves or the leafy tips of finocchio are used for garnishes and chopped to add flavor to salads, stews and other dishes, in the manner of dillweed. *Dried* stalks of the common fennel are used in French Provençal cooking as fuel for grilling fish, giving it a superior flavor. Fennel seeds are used to spice soups, stews, sauces and especially fish dishes, as well as pies, cookies and breads. They are also used in Indian curries and for pickling.

Finocchio is eaten raw as an appetizer or as a salad or cooked as a vegetable. Do not cut off the feathery tops until the finoccio is used. To prepare, cut off feathery tops at bulb level. Remove the tough outer stalks. Wash and drain. Cut off hard base. If the vegetable is to be used for an appetizer or salad cut with the grain into slices. Place on a serving dish, sprinkle with salt and pepper, and dribble with a little olive oil and lemon juice or vinegar. As a cooked vegetable, if the finocchio is small, cut it into halves lengthwise. If it is medium-sized or large, cut it into quarters lengthwise. Place in saucepan and add boiling salted water or bouillon to cover. Cook covered for 5 minutes or until tender but still firm. Dress with butter and serve.

FINOCCHIO À LA GRECQUE

4-6 servings

Serve as an hors d'oeuvre or with cold roast chicken.

3 cups dry white wine
4 tablespoons olive oil
2 tablespoons tomato paste
grated rind of 1 lemon
1 bay leaf
8 coriander seeds

½ teaspoon dried thyme
salt
freshly ground pepper
4 large heads finocchio,
    trimmed and cut into quarters

Combine all the ingredients except the finocchio in a heavy casserole. Bring to the boiling point. Lower heat to very low and add the finocchio. Simmer covered for 15 to 20 minutes or until the finocchio is tender but still firm. Transfer the finocchio to a deep serving dish. Over high heat, cook the pan liquid until it is reduced by a third; this process intensifies the flavor. Pour over the finocchio. Chill before serving.

FINOCCHIO AU GRATIN

4 servings

Serve with broiled meats.

4 large or 6 medium or 8 small heads finocchio, trimmed	salt
boiling salted water or chicken consommé	freshly ground pepper
	⅔ cup butter, melted
	⅔ cup freshly grated Parmesan

Cut the large and the medium finocchio into quarters lengthwise; cut the small finocchio into halves lengthwise. Cook in boiling consommé to cover for about 5 minutes or until barely tender. Drain thoroughly. Place half of the finocchio in a buttered shallow baking dish. Sprinkle with a little salt and pepper (the cheese is salty), half of the butter and half of the grated cheese. Top with the remaining finocchio, butter and cheese. (No more salt is needed.) Cook in a preheated hot oven (400° F) for about 10 minutes or until the top is golden brown.

FINOCCHIO AND MUSHROOMS

4-6 servings

Instead of finocchio, you may use 2 medium-sized thinly sliced artichokes.

2 large heads finocchio, trimmed	1 pound mushrooms, sliced
2 tablespoons butter	¼ cup hot chicken consommé
2 tablespoons olive oil	salt
1 garlic clove	freshly ground pepper
1 large tomato, peeled and chopped	½ teaspoon dried thyme

Cut the finocchio into thin slices lengthwise. Heat the butter and the olive oil in a saucepan. Cook the garlic in it until browned; discard. Add the tomato and the finocchio. Simmer covered, stirring frequently, for 5 minutes or until finocchio is half tender. Add the mushrooms and consommé and season with salt, pepper and thyme. Simmer covered over low heat for about 10 minutes or until the vegetables are tender but still firm. There should be just a little sauce in the pan since mushrooms draw water; you may have to simmer it without a cover to reduce the cooking liquid.

FIDDLEHEAD
Ostrich Fern
Matteuccia struthiopteris

The best known of the ferns that grows on the shores of Northern streams and lakes; named after the shape in which the head of the frond grows. The flavor is delicious, a cross between asparagus and mushrooms.

The soft budding stem of the fiddlehead fern is a delicacy of Northern New England and Canada, one that was known to the Indians. The stems are picked when still young and tender, when they're about eight inches tall, washed thoroughly and steamed like asparagus and broccoli, but for three to five minutes only. They are served like these vegetables with salt and pepper, butter, Hollandaise or any other suitable sauce, or raw as a salad, dressed with vinegar and lemon juice.

Canned or frozen fiddleheads can occasionally be bought in specialty stores.

GARLIC

Allium sativum

This most pungent and famous of all flavorings is a plant that, together with chives, onions, leeks and shallots, belongs to the lily family. Its edible part, like that of the onion, lies underground, consisting of a compound bulb made up of an unpredictable number of white or purplish almond-shaped segments called cloves which are enclosed by a thin common skin. Each clove is also enclosed by its own skin. Of the several varieties, the most common are white or purple.

Various forms of wild garlic grow in the United States, such as crow garlic and field garlic. Since they grow mostly in pastures, a strong garlic flavor is found in the milk of the animals that graze there in the spring. I remember the delicious, thick fresh cream and butter from the pastures of the Eastern Shore of Maryland which came to me weekly when I lived in Annapolis. In the spring, the garlic flavor and odor were so strong that they could be used only for non-sweet dishes.

Garlic has been cultivated in both temperate and hot climates for thousands of years. Its origin is obscure, but it appears to have originated in Southern Asia and the Mediterranean. The slaves who built the pyramids of ancient Egypt are said to have lived on garlic and onions in the 5th century BC. The Israelites in the Wilderness spoke about a lack of garlic to Moses (Numbers XI:5); and in 13th-century China, Marco Polo observed that the higher classes ate their meat preserved in several spices whereas the poor ate theirs steeped in garlic juice.

Throughout the centuries, garlic also served as a medicinal. Ancient and medieval herbals speak of its power to cure toothache, dog bites, poisoned-arrow wounds, the plague, and skin diseases to mention a few. The belief in garlic's power to repel evil has been strong since antiquity. Demons, witches and especially vampires are said to vanish at the sight of it, a belief that is still held in many parts of the world including the United States, where people wear garlic or keep it in the house to ward off such as the evil eye and head colds.

Garlic has long been an essential in Mediterranean and some Far Eastern, such as Chinese, cooking. It would be impossible to think of the cookery of Provence or of some Italian cooking without the presence of the potent bulb. In the United States until the end of World War II, garlic was largely limited to ethnic or to gourmet cooking, and many took a derogatory view of it. But American soldiers brought home a taste for the foods they had known abroad, and as a consequence all sorts of little known ingredients such as garlic found their place in our cooking.

Today, garlic may form part of almost any non-sweet dish including pickles and sausages. Its power varies according to the ways it is used. Peeled raw garlic, mashed in a garlic press or with the blunt part of a knife, is the strongest, stronger than peeled raw chopped, minced or sliced garlic. Pure garlic juice is unbearable, though some Southern Europeans will drink it as a panacea for all ills. When garlic is cooked with food the taste will be different depending on whether the cloves are peeled or not. Unpeeled garlic, unbruised so as not to release its volatile oils, and cooked whole assumes a sweet, nutlike flavor unlike its raw self. These cooked cloves may be peeled and mashed or their contents may be squeezed into one's mouth like a berry. And they will leave no odor on your breath. Thus dishes containing 40 garlic cloves, or others with 2 pounds, sound terrifying, whereas in practice they are subtle gourmet fare.

Large quantities of garlic are processed into flakes, powders and salts to be sold as fresh garlic substitutes and to be put into all manner of packaged foods from ketchup, sausages, cold meats, and prepared mustard to dog food, for it appears that dogs like the flavor. However great their convenience, they are no match for the real garlic, and they will always have a somewhat synthetic flavor.

How to Buy

Garlic is available the year round. Most of it is imported from Italy and Spain. Some garlic is sold as single cloves in little plastic bags but it is usually dried out and flavorless.

Buy firm, plump bulbs which are heavy for their size. Their skins should be clean, dry and unbroken. Buy small amounts at a time. *Avoid* soft bulbs with broken skins, dried out, dirty or shriveled bulbs or bulbs that are sprouting.

How to Keep

Keep garlic away from other foods. Place in a small open basket and keep in a cool, dry, well ventilated place. Do not refrigerate.

Cool, dry place—1 month.

Nutritive Values

Garlic contains only a negligible amount of minerals.

3½ ounces raw, unpeeled, about 3 bulbs—137 calories

How to Use

Peel garlic just before using. Rub a salad bowl with a peeled, cut garlic clove. Drop a peeled clove into French dressing for 24 hours and remove since it will deteriorate. Add peeled garlic cloves to soups, stews and casseroles and if desired remove with a slotted spoon before serving. If a large quantity of garlic is to be peeled, drop unpeeled bulbs into boiling water and cook for 2 minutes. Drain and peel. For sauces, cook a few cloves of blanched garlic in butter over low heat for 10 minutes or until very tender. Mash and add to sauces. Never allow garlic to brown or it will be bitter.

ROCAMBOLE
Giant Garlic, Sand Leek

Allium scorodoprasum: A pretty plant whose elongated edible bulbs which bunch at the top are used like garlic because they taste like it.

GARLIC CHICKEN

6 servings

In spite of the large number of garlic cloves, this dish is fragrant rather than offensive.

¼ cup salad oil
1 large onion, diced
2 large carrots, sliced
4 celery stalks, sliced
2 3-pound chickens, cut into
   pieces (no backs or wings)

salt
freshly ground pepper
juice of 2 lemons
20 to 30 garlic cloves, unpeeled
   and left whole
6 slices buttered or fried toast

Heat the oil in a frying pan. Add the onion, carrots and celery and cook, stirring constantly, until they are soft. With a slotted spoon transfer the vegetables to a casserole with a tight-fitting lid or to a clay pot. Remove any fat from the chicken pieces and, if desired, skin them. Lay the chicken pieces on top of the vegetables. Sprinkle with the salt, pepper and lemon juice. Put the garlic around and on the chicken pieces. Cover tightly; *this is essential,* because the chicken must cook in its own juices. Cook in a preheated moderate oven (350° F) for 1 hour. Do not uncover until ready to serve. Serve each diner some of the garlic and a slice of buttered toast. The diner squeezes the garlic between first finger and thumb out of its skin and onto the toast. Spread the toast with the garlic.

FOUR GARLIC SAUCES

All of these are "more-or-less" cookery.

PESTO

about 1¼ cups

This Genovese basil sauce is commonly used as a pasta sauce. However, a tablespoon ladled into a dish of hot soup, preferably vegetable soup, improves the soup immensely. The basil *must* be fresh.

3 to 5 garlic cloves, minced
2 cups fresh basil leaves
⅓ cup grated Parmesan cheese
4 to 6 tablespoons olive oil

¼ cup pignoli nuts
salt
freshly ground pepper

Pound the garlic and the basil together in a mortar. Pound in the grated cheese, turning always in the same direction, together with a drop or two of oil to make the mixture stick together. Pound in the nuts and a little more oil. Stir in the remaining oil, a few drops at a time, using 4 tablespoons. If a thinner sauce is wanted, stir in the remaining oil. Season with salt and pepper to taste.

The sauce may be made in a blender almost as satisfactorily, but a blenderized sauce has a different consistency from one made in the mortar. For the blender sauce: Combine all the ingredients and 4 tablespoons of oil in a blender. Purée and scrape down the sides with a rubber spatula. If too thick, add the remaining oil and purée again.

PISTOU

This is the French Provençal version of Pesto, not surprising since Genoa and Provence are not far apart. It is basically the same, but no pignoli nuts are used. Pistou is part of soupe au pistou, a vegetable soup. Since not all people like garlic equally well, it is best to serve the pistou separately.

AÏOLI

about 2½ cups

The famous garlic mayonnaise of Provence, is used as a dip for fresh or cooked vegetables and salt cod. This mayonnaise should not be made in a blender, because blender mayonnaise does not have the thick, silken consistency that is its great virtue. Use a marble mortar and a wooden pestle and have the egg yolks and the oil at room temperature; this is important. Or make the mayonnaise in the traditional way, in a bowl, with a wooden spoon.

4 to 6 large garlic cloves, peeled
2 egg yolks, lightly beaten
about 2 cups olive oil or 1 cup olive oil and 1 cup peanut oil (the mixture makes a lighter aïoli)

lukewarm water
squeezed juice of 1 lemon
¼ teaspoon salt

Pound the garlic cloves to a paste. Add the egg yolks. Mix with the pestle, always turning in one direction, until the garlic and eggs have assimilated and are just beginning to get pale. While beating the garlic and the eggs, add about 4 tablespoons of the oil very very slowly, drop by drop, in a steady stream, never stopping turning the pestle in the same direction. The mixture should be thick. Add 1 teaspoon of water and 1 teaspoon of lemon juice and continue turning the pestle, adding the oil in a very thin stream. When the mixture gets too thick again, add 1 more teaspoon each lukewarm water and lemon juice. Repeat until the desired consistency is reached and the oil has been used. Season with salt.

If the mayonnaise separates, not all is lost. Put it into a clean bowl. Wash and dry the mortar and pestle. Add a garlic clove, a pinch of salt, 1 teaspoon of lukewarm water and 1 egg yolk. Crush and mix together. Add the separated mayonnaise by teaspoons to the mortar, turning the pestle constantly in the same direction.

BAGNA CAUDA

about ¾ cup

A sauce or dip from Piedmont, meaning literally "hot bath." Use it as a dip for raw vegetables or as a sauce for plain hot cooked vegetables, boiled fish or meats. The sauce must *never* brown or boil.

½ cup butter
¼ cup olive oil
6 garlic cloves, sliced paper
   thin, or to taste

1 2-ounce can anchovy fillets
   (without capers), minced

Over lowest possible heat (use an asbestos plate), cook together the butter, the olive oil and the garlic for 15 minutes. Do not let the mixture boil. Stir in the anchovies. Cook, stirring constantly, until the anchovies have dissolved. Keep hot over a candle warmer or chafing-dish lamp.

GREEN ONION
(See page 244)

HEARTS OF PALM

These are the edible inner portion of the *Sabal palmetto* palm tree, which is also the official Florida state tree, also known as cabbage tree. To obtain the hearts, the outer husks of palms are shucked and the inner layers chopped off until the edible part is reached. It is immediately placed in water to avoid darkening. Hearts of palm are off-white in color, reasonably firm and vaguely reminiscent of artichoke in their flavor. They reach us canned, imported from Brazil or packed in Florida. They are used as a delicate salad vegetable or sauced or deep fried. Since they are bland, they need to be well seasoned.

HEARTS OF PALM IN LEMON BUTTER

4-6 servings

Palm hearts are packed in cans of different sizes, which are not always available. However, this does not matter in the following recipe; decrease or add the butter and lemon juice depending on the amount of vegetable. Good with fish and seafood.

⅓ cup butter
3 cups canned palm hearts,
   drained, thinly sliced
1 teaspoon grated lemon peel
1 or 2 tablespoons fresh lemon
   juice

salt
freshly ground pepper
1 tablespoon minced chives
1 tablespoon minced parsley

Heat the butter in a large frying pan; do not let it brown. Add the palm heart slices. Cook over very low heat, stirring carefully with a fork so as not to break the slices, until the vegetable is coated with the butter and very hot. Do not brown. Stir in the remaining ingredients and serve very hot.

HOMINY

The word means kernels of hulled corn from which the germ has been removed and which have been broken into parts. Hominy is apparently a word of Algonquian Indian origin, implying small particles. It is a truly American food, not known anywhere else.

Ground hominy is called grits. Hominy and grits are boiled in water or milk and then fried, baked, served with a sauce or dished up any way cereals are served. The larger sizes are used as a vegetable, and the smaller ones for breakfast. Hominy is a standard food of many parts of the United States, such as the South and Southwest.

How to Buy

Sold in bulk or canned as pearl hominy, lye hominy or granulated hominy.

Pearl hominy is parched corn with the hull removed by machinery. Also known as samp. Lye hominy is parched corn with the hull removed by soaking in lye water. Granulated hominy is parched corn with the hull removed and slightly ground.

Grits are ground in three degrees: fine, medium and coarse.

How to Keep

Kitchen shelf—stores indefinitely.

Cooked, covered, refrigerator shelf—4 to 5 days.

Nutritive Values

Hominy is a good source of carbohydrate.

3½ ounces hominy and grits, cooked—51 calories.

How to Use

Pour hominy slowly into salted boiling water (1 part hominy to 4 parts water). Cover and cook over low heat for 1 hour or until hominy is tender. Stir often during cooking. Use as is or beat butter into the hominy before serving. Beating whitens hominy. Milk or cream (½ cup for every 1 cup raw hominy) may be beaten into the hominy before serving.

HOMINY AND TOMATO SKILLET

4-6 servings

⅓ cup olive oil
1 medium onion, minced
1 large tomato, peeled and
   chopped (about 1 cup)
salt

freshly ground pepper
½ teaspoon dried thyme
about 3 cups cooked hominy (1
   30-ounce can, drained)
dash Tabasco

Heat the olive oil in a deep frying pan. Add the onion and cook, stirring constantly, until the onion is soft. Add the tomato, salt and pepper and thyme. Mix well. Cook over high heat, stirring constantly, for about 5 minutes. Add the hominy. Lower the heat and cover. Simmer covered, stirring frequently, for about 10 minutes or until very hot. Stir in a dash of Tabasco and serve very hot.

BAKED HOMINY

4-6 servings

Serve instead of potatoes or rice.

2 cups cooked hominy	salt
4 tablespoons butter, melted	freshly ground pepper
3 eggs	⅛ teaspoon ground nutmeg
⅔ cup milk	
⅓ cup grated Swiss cheese (optional)	

Turn the hominy into a buttered 1½-quart baking dish. Beat the butter into the hominy. Beat together the remaining ingredients. Add them to the hominy and mix well. Set the baking dish into a baking pan with 1 inch of water. Bake in preheated moderate oven (350° F) for about 1 hour or until set and golden.

HOP

Humulus lupulus

Hops are perennials native to Europe and Western Asia. The dried female hop flower clusters are used in brewing. What concerns us here are hop shoots, the young shoots of the plant which are thinned out in spring and serve as a luxury vegetable in France and Belgium under the name *jet de houblon*. These squirmy thin little bits of vegetable are tender, creamy in color with a delicate flavor reminiscent of asparagus. They are considered a delicacy and justly so. Hop shoots are lightly boiled and served with butter or a cream sauce. In Belgium, they are served as a first course with poached eggs.

HUSK TOMATO
**Ground Cherry, Strawberry Tomato, Cape Gooseberry,
Chinese Lantern Tomatoes**
genus *Physalis*

These small fruit come in several varieties, colored vividly from
yellow to orangy-green and bright red. A papery husk, resembling a
Chinese lantern, encloses the berries which are smaller than cherry
tomatoes. Their flavor is that of a somewhat tart, sticky tomato, and
they are eaten raw as is, or in salads, in sauces and in preserves.
Small amounts of these gourmet fruit come into our markets during
the autumn. However one variety, the Mexican tomatillo, or little
tomato, is widely available in our Southwest, where it is used for
chili sauces. All in all, husk tomatoes are a pleasant conceit and a
prettier centerpiece than a food.

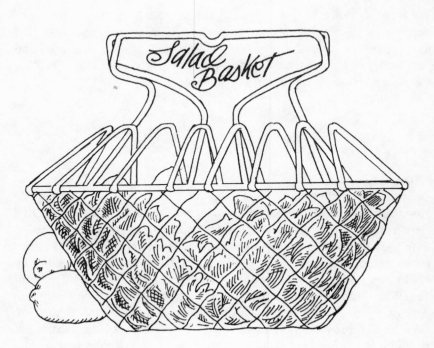

JAPANESE ARTICHOKE
Crosne du Japon
Stachys sieboldi

These tubers are two to three inches long, white when they are fresh and browning quickly thereafter. Generally speaking, they resemble Jerusalem artichokes in flavor, and they are prepared in the same manner. Japanese artichokes are also indigenous to China and they are eaten in both countries. They are virtually unknown in the United States, but quite popular in France, a country that also fancies Jerusalem artichokes.

CROSNES À LA CRÈME

4 servings

Jerusalem artichokes may be cooked in the same manner.

3 cups water
juice of 1 lemon
1 tablespoon flour
1 pound *crosnes* or Japanese
   artichokes
3 tablespoons butter

1 tablespoon olive oil
½ cup heavy cream
salt
freshly ground pepper
⅛ teaspoon ground nutmeg

Combine water, lemon juice and flour in a saucepan. Bring to the boiling point and lower the heat to medium. Scrub, wash and drain the *crosnes*. Drop into the water and cook for about 10 minutes or until almost tender. Drain. Heat the butter and oil in a deep frying pan. Add the *crosnes* and cook, stirring with a fork, for 3 or 4 minutes or until they are well coated with the butter. Stir in all but about 2 tablespoons of the cream. Season with salt and pepper and nutmeg. Cook, shaking the pan to prevent sticking, until the cream has thickened and reduced to about half. Stir in the remaining cream and heat through briefly. Turn into a heated serving dish and serve immediately.

JERUSALEM ARTICHOKE
Helianthus tuberosus

The edible parts of this native North American plant are the underground tubers, which resemble small knobbly potatoes. Their skin is very thin, with either yellow, brown, red or purple tinges; the flesh is white and crisp with a sweetish flavor.

Jerusalem artichokes are no relation whatsoever to the globe artichoke, although their flavors are vaguely similar. Nor have they anything to do with Jerusalem; their name is an adaptation of the Italian *girasole* or sunflower, which is not surprising since the Jerusalem artichoke plant is a 6- to 12-foot tall sunflower.

Jerusalem artichokes have been cultivated for centuries by the Indians; Champlain reported seeing them in the gardens of the Cape Cod Indians in 1605. The plant was introduced to Europe around 1616, and it always has been cultivated much more extensively there than in this country. The French are especially partial to Jerusalem artichokes.

How to Buy

Available from October to March in a limited number of markets. Jerusalem artichokes in plastic bags are available in some supermarkets under the brand name Sunchokes.

Buy firm tubers with clean skins that are free from mold and heavy for their size. *Avoid,* soft, wrinkled, blemished tubers.

Allow 1½ pounds for 3 to 4 servings.

1 pound, peeled and thinly sliced—approximately 2½ cups.

How to Keep

Store tubers in a cool, dry, well ventilated place. Or refrigerate in a plastic bag.

Raw, cool dry place or refrigerator shelf—1 week.

Cooked and covered, refrigerator shelf—2 days.

Nutritive Values

Jerusalem artichokes contain few nutrients. Their caloric values change from approximately 7 calories for 3½ ounces of freshly harvested tubers to approximately 75 calories for 3½ ounces of long-stored tubers.

How to Use

Jerusalem artichokes can be served raw as appetizers or salad; raw they have a sweet, nutlike taste. Or they can be served cooked as a vegetable like potatoes. To prepare, scrub with a vegetable brush or peel with a vegetable peeler. Do not worry about any skin that remains between the knobs; when cooked it will be like the skin of new potatoes. Jerusalem artichokes discolor easily when cut. Drop cut pieces into cold water as you work. Cook whole, or slice, dice or cut into julienne strips or bake in their jackets.

Cook cut up Jerusalem artichokes covered in about an inch of boiling salted water for 5 to 8 minutes. Do not overcook or the vegetable will be mushy. Season with salt and pepper and dress with butter and lemon juice.

JERUSALEM ARTICHOKES IN CREAM

4 servings

2 pounds Jerusalem artichokes,
   cooked and peeled
1 cup heavy cream, heated
salt

freshly ground pepper
dash Tabasco (optional)
2 tablespoons minced parsley or
   chives

Cut the Jerusalem artichokes into ½-inch slices. Place in a casserole that can go to the table. Add the cream and season with salt and pepper and Tabasco. Over lowest possible heat, preferably over an asbestos plate, cook only until thoroughly heated; do not boil. Sprinkle with the parsley and serve immediately.

CREAM OF JERUSALEM ARTICHOKE SOUP

4-5 servings

2 pounds Jerusalem artichokes,
   peeled and sliced
2 medium onions, sliced
4 tablespoons butter
3 cups hot water or chicken
   consommé
salt

freshly ground pepper
2 cups milk, heated
1 cup light cream, heated
⅛ teaspoon ground cardamom
   (optional)
⅓ cup slivered toasted almonds

Combine the Jerusalem artichokes, the onions and 3 tablespoons of the butter in a saucepan. Cover tightly and cook over low heat, stirring frequently, for 8 or 10 minutes. Add the hot water and salt and pepper to taste. Cook 10 minutes longer. Purée in a blender or press through a sieve. Return to the saucepan. Stir in the milk, the cream, the remaining tablespoon of butter and the cardamom. Heat through, but do not boil. Sprinkle with toasted almonds before serving.

WHITE BEANS AND JERUSALEM ARTICHOKES

6 servings

2 pounds Jerusalem artichokes,
   prepared for cooking
salted water
2 tablespoons olive oil
1 garlic clove, minced
¼ cup minced parsley
2 teaspoons dried basil

1 cup chopped fresh tomatoes
   or canned tomatoes, drained
salt
freshly ground pepper
2 cups cooked white beans
   (navy beans)

Place the artichokes into a saucepan with salted water to cover. Bring to the boiling point and lower the heat. Simmer covered for about 5 minutes or until they are easily pierced with a knife. Drain and cool. Cut into ½-inch slices. Heat the oil in a large, deep frying pan. Cook the garlic, parsley and basil in it for 2 minutes. Add the tomatoes and season with salt and pepper. Cook over medium heat, stirring fre-

quently, for 5 to 10 minutes. Add the beans and the Jerusalem artichokes. Mix together gently with a fork and simmer until thoroughly
heated through.

JICAMA
Exogonium bracteatum

This plant, which belongs to the morning glory family, has long been
cultivated in Mexico for the food value of its tubers as well as for its
showy white blossoms. They are also known on our Pacific coast, but
in the East they are only found in Latin markets, and not always
there. The tubers are brown, large, weighing one to six pounds,
somewhat turnip shaped with a four-leaf clover outline. The flesh is
white, bland, juicy and crisp and very much like that of water chestnuts.

Jicama can be used like any sweet potatoes. It is delicious sliced
raw as an appetizer or in salads. Cooked it adds the same kind of
crispness as water chestnuts to any braised or sautéed dishes. To buy,
choose well-formed jicama free of spots and blemishes. Refrigerate
unwashed for 1 to 2 weeks. Cover cut pieces tightly with plastic wrap
and refrigerate. Allow 1 pound for 4 servings.

KALE
Brassica oleracea acephala

Kale, like collards, is the member of the cabbage family which most
closely resembles cabbage in its wild form. Unlike cabbage, kale
does not form a head but consists of a bunch of coarse loose leaves
with curly or crisped edges. Two main varieties are grown in the
United States: Scotch Kale with very curled, divided, bright-green to
greenish-yellow leaves and Blue, with plumelike frilled-edged leaves
that are deep green with a bluish tinge. Kale is a humble, prolific and

extremely healthful vegetable which even improves after a fall frost has hit it; it has a robust flavor that does not appeal to all.

How to Buy

Kale is most plentiful and inexpensive during the winter months, peak season December through April. Kale is sold frozen, but it tends to be mushy. *Buy* crisp leaves with a good dark green color. *Avoid* wilted, bruised or crushed leaves.

Allow 1 pound for 2 to 3 servings.

How to Keep

Use as soon as possible. Refrigerate unwashed in a plastic bag or vegetable drawer.

Raw, refrigerator shelf—3 to 5 days.

Cooked and covered, refrigerator shelf—2 to 3 days.

Nutritive Values

Kale is valuable for bulk as well as for an extremely high content of vitamin A, and a good supply of calcium and other minerals.

3½ ounces raw, leaves and stems—38 calories.

3½ ounces cooked, leaves and stems—28 calories.

How to Use

Remove tough outer leaves and thick midribs. Cut large leaves into pieces. Wash thoroughly and shake dry. Cook covered in an inch of boiling salted water for 5 minutes; do not overcook or kale will be mushy. Season with salt and pepper and melted butter. The robust flavor of kale takes to foods like sausages and bacon.

CREAMED KALE

4 servings

A Danish recipe to serve with pork.

2 pounds kale
1 teaspoon salt
water
4 tablespoons butter
4 tablespoons flour
1 cup milk

1 cup light cream
salt
freshly ground pepper
⅛ teaspoon ground nutmeg or
    more to taste

Cut off the tough stalks and cut the kale leaves into bite-sized pieces. Wash and drain. Put the kale into a saucepan and sprinkle with the teaspoon of salt. Add just enough water to cover. Bring to the boiling point and cook, covered, for 15 to 20 minutes or until tender. Drain well and chop the kale. Heat the butter and stir in the flour. Cook, stirring constantly, for about 2 minutes. Stir in the milk and the cream. Cook over low heat, stirring all the while, for about 5 minutes. Cook 5 minutes longer, stirring frequently; the cooking removes the raw taste of the flour. The sauce should be smooth and thick. Season with the salt and pepper and stir in the nutmeg. Add the kale. Heat through thoroughly.

COLCANNON

4-6 servings

A tasty Irish dish traditionally eaten on Halloween. The kale and the potatoes must be cooked separately, preferably just before serving.

1 pound potatoes, peeled and
   cut into quarters
boiling salted water
1½ pounds kale, trimmed,
   washed and drained and
   shredded
½ to 1 cup milk or light cream

2 small leeks or 6 green onions,
   trimmed, washed and drained
   and sliced
salt
freshly ground pepper
⅛ teaspoon ground mace
½ cup butter, melted

Cook the potatoes in boiling salted water to cover for 10 minutes or until very soft. Drain, mash and keep warm. While the potatoes are cooking, cook the kale in boiling salted water for 10 minutes or until very soft. Drain and chop fine. Keep warm. Heat together the milk and the leeks; the milk should just cover the leeks. Cook covered over very low heat until the leeks are very soft and mushy. Beat the milk and the leeks into the potatoes. Stir in the kale. Beat until the mixture is light green and fluffy and the consistency of mashed potatoes. Season with salt and pepper and mace. Turn the colcannon into a heated deep serving dish. Make a well in the center and pour in the melted butter. Serve the vegetable with a spoonful or two of the melted butter poured over it.

KOHLRABI
Brassica oleracea

Kohlrabi is a member of the cabbage family and a native of Northern Europe. Its name is taken over from the German meaning "cabbage turnip" which describes the vegetable quite accurately. The turnip-like globe of the kohlrabi is not a root but the oblong swollen base of the stem, sprouting leaves like any normal stem. Kohlrabi may get as big as a grapefruit, but it is eaten before fully grown, when measuring two to three inches in length and two inches across. The texture is somewhat crisp and the flavor reminds one of a delicate turnip. There are two kinds of kohlrabi, green and purple.

Kohlrabi is much more popular in Europe than in the United States. It may not be a vegetable that appeals to small children, but steamed and buttered, it deserves its place as an excellent accompaniment to broiled and roast meats. Young, tender kohlrabi is a good ingredient for mixed salads.

How to Buy

Available May through November, peak months June and July. It is becoming more readily available in American markets. *Buy* small kohlrabi with fresh tops and a thin rind that can easily be pierced with a fingernail. *Avoid* large heads which are tough and woody and heads with cracks or other blemishes.

Allow 1 medium kohlrabi for 1 serving.

How to Keep

Do not trim before using. Store in a cool dry, well ventilated place or refrigerate in a plastic bag.

Raw, cool dry area or refrigerator shelf—1 week.

Cooked and covered, refrigerator shelf—2 to 3 days.

Nutritive Values

Kohlrabi is a fair source of vitamin C and minerals.

3½ ounces uncooked—29 calories.

3½ ounces cooked and drained—24 calories.

How to Use

Both the bulb and the leaves that shoot from it are good to eat. Cut off the *leaves and stems,* and chop the stems. Wash and drain. Cook separately or with prepared bulb.

If the kohlrabi bulb is very young and tender, it need not be peeled. Peel more mature bulbs to remove tough outer skin. Slice, dice, or cut into julienne strips. Serve in salads or steamed with butter.

KOHLRABI IMPROVED

4-6 servings

1½ pounds kohlrabi	1 cup chicken consommé
2 tablespoons butter	4 teaspoons flour
½ teaspoon sugar	1 cup heavy cream
salt	¼ cup minced parsley
freshly ground pepper	

Peel the kohlrabi and cut into ½- to ¾-inch cubes. Wash and drain, but do not shake dry. Heat the butter in a large saucepan. Stir the sugar into it and cook, stirring constantly, until the sugar has melted. Add the kohlrabi and season lightly with salt and pepper (the consommé will be salty). Cook over medium heat, stirring constantly, for about 2 minutes. Add the consommé. Simmer covered over low heat, stirring frequently, for about 10 minutes or until tender. Stir the flour into the cream. Stir the mixture into the kohlrabi and mix well. Stir in the parsley. Simmer over very low heat, stirring constantly, until the cream has thickened and is of sauce consistency. The dish should be heated through thoroughly.

Note: As with all dishes of this kind, it is not possible to give totally accurate ingredient amounts. The way the vegetable absorbs the liquid depends on its age; the way the sauce thickens depends on the size of the pan and the heat.

KUDZU
Pueraria thunbergiana

Kudzu is a vine indigenous to China and Japan which is cultivated in the tropics for its often enormous edible tuberous roots. The roots have a yellow-brown fibrous covering and the flesh is white, firm and somewhat fibrous. Only the small roots are eaten by Orientals and by people of Oriental ancestry in the United States. Kudzu roots are boiled in salted water until tender and then usually mashed and seasoned. Their flavor is on the bitter side and takes getting used to. In the Orient, a fine white food starch is also produced by kudzu roots.

LEEK
Allium porrum

Leeks, which belong to the onion family, are shaped like cylinders with a thickened white base and flat, compactly rolled leaves that shade from white to dark green at the top. Their average length is eight to fourteen inches and they are one and one-half to two inches across. Leeks have a mild onion flavor and they are used as a vegetable or potherb. With the exception of the roots and the tough part of the leaves, the whole leek serves in cooking.

Leeks were known throughout the Middle Ages and today they are an important crop and a favorite vegetable in almost all of Europe. In France, the leek or *poireau* is called "the poor man's asparagus" and considered an essential ingredient in French cookery. Leeks are also the emblem of Wales. On St. David's Day Welshmen wear a leek to commemorate the victory of King Cadwallader over the Saxons in 640 AD. Before this battle the Welsh gathered leeks from a nearby garden and wore them in their hats to distinguish themselves from the enemy and avoid accidental attacks on their own troops.

Leeks are an inexpensive vegetable wherever they are grown except in the United States. Here they almost achieve luxury status, possibly because blanching the base and part of the leaves requires a certain amount of manual labor. Their high price is indeed a pity, for leeks are lovely vegetables whether added to soups and stews or cooked and sauced on their own.

How to Buy

Available the year round, peak season September through April. They are sold singly or in bunches. *Buy* leeks which are well blanched 2 to 3 inches from the base and which have tightly rolled leaves with fresh green tops. Small or medium leeks are more tender. *Avoid* leeks that are soft or have soft spots, bruised, wilted, yellowish tops, flabby, fibrous bases and unduly loose leaves.

Allow 1 to 2 medium leeks for 1 serving.

How to Keep

Cut off rootlets and the unusable upper part of the leaves. Do not wash until ready to use. Refrigerate in a plastic bag or in the vegetable drawer of the refrigerator. Do not leave unwrapped leeks in the vicinity of other refrigerated foods because these will absorb some of the leeks' oniony flavor.

Raw, refrigerator shelf or vegetable drawer—3 to 5 days.

Cooked and covered, refrigerator shelf—1 to 2 days.

Nutritive Values

There is little nutrition in leeks except for a small amount of minerals.

3½ ounces, raw—52 calories.

How to Use

From the way leeks grow, dirt is found between the layers of the leaves. Trim off the rootlets and remove the two or three layers of tough outer leaves. Cut off any unusable upper part of the leaves. Split leeks lengthwise and hold under running cold water to remove dirt. Or slice or cut into 2-inch pieces. Place slices and pieces in a bowl with cold water and swish around. Repeat the operation until there is no dirt in the bottom of the bowl. Drain.

Cook cut or whole leeks covered in about an inch of boiling salted water or bouillon for 3 to 10 minutes, depending on size. Do not overcook or leeks will be mushy. Or chill and serve with French dressing. Or braise in a covered saucepan with butter and a little water for about 5 minutes, depending on size, season and serve.

LEEK HORS D'OEUVRE

4-6 servings

12 medium leeks
½ cup olive oil
1 to 2 cups water
2 cups dry white wine
salt
freshly ground pepper
2 cups black olives, pitted and halved

¼ cup seedless raisins or currants, plumped in warm water and drained (optional)
3 large onions, cut into thick slices
4 tablespoons minced parsley

Trim the leeks and remove all but 2 inches of the green tops. Cut into 4-inch pieces. Wash in several changes of water to remove all sand. Drain. Heat half of the olive oil in a large, deep frying pan. Add the leeks and cook, stirring with a fork, for 3 minutes. Add the water and the wine and season with salt and pepper, remembering that the olives may be salty. Cover and simmer over low heat for about 10 minutes or until the leeks are tender but still firm. Add the olives and the raisins and simmer for 5 more minutes. Drain the leeks and reserve the cooking liquid. Transfer leeks, olives and raisins to a serving dish. Heat the remaining oil in the frying pan. Cook the onion rings in it until they are soft and golden. Stir carefully with a fork in order not to break the slices. With a slotted spoon, put the onions on top of the leeks. Drizzle a little of the reserved cooking liquid over the vegetables and sprinkle with the parsley. Cover and chill before serving.

COLD VICHYSSOISE

6 servings

2 tablespoons butter
4 medium potatoes, thinly
   sliced
4 medium white onions, thinly
   sliced
4 leeks, white parts only, thinly
   sliced or 3 bunches green
   onions, white parts only,
   thinly sliced

1 large garlic clove, mashed
4 cups chicken bouillon
1 cup milk
1 cup heavy cream
salt
freshly ground pepper,
   preferably white
2 tablespoons minced chives or
   parsley

Heat the butter in a large heavy saucepan. Add the potatoes, onions, leeks, garlic and 1 cup of the chicken bouillon. Simmer covered over very low heat until the vegetables are very soft. Stir frequently. Add the remaining chicken broth. Simmer covered for 10 more minutes. Add the milk and cream. Bring to the boiling point but do not boil. Cool. Season with salt and pepper to taste. Purée the soup in a blender. If too thick, thin with a little cold milk. Chill very thoroughly. Check the seasoning before serving and sprinkle with chives.

LEEKS AU GRATIN

4-6 servings

Serve as a main dish with rice and a green salad.

12 medium to large leeks
1¼ cups beef or chicken
　consommé
1 cup dry white wine
4 tablespoons butter

4 tablespoons flour
1 cup (4 ounces) grated Swiss
　or Parmesan cheese
salt
freshly ground pepper

Trim the leeks and cut off all but 2 inches of the green leaves. Wash thoroughly in several changes of water. Drain. Combine the consommé and the white wine in a saucepan. Bring to the boiling point. Lower the heat and add the leeks. Simmer covered over low heat for 5 to 7 minutes, or until the leeks are barely tender. Drain and reserve the cooking liquid. There should be about 2 cups; if not, add enough consommé to make 2 cups. Place the leeks in a buttered shallow baking dish. Heat the butter and stir in the flour. Cook, stirring constantly, for about 3 minutes; do not brown. Stir in the leek liquid. Cook, stirring all the time, until thickened and smooth. Stir in ¾ cup of the cheese. Taste and if necessary, season with salt and pepper; the consommé and the cheese may have been salty. Cook until the cheese is melted. Pour the sauce over the leeks. Sprinkle with the remaining cheese. Place under the broiler or in a preheated hot oven (425° F) and cook until the top is golden brown.

LEGUME

A legume is a food plant with pods which open along two seams when the seeds are ripe. Usually the seeds are the edible part of the legume. Peas, beans, chick peas, lentils, lima beans, peanuts and soybeans are the best known legumes, of which there are more than 11,000 species. Many are used as fodder for animals and for medicinal purposes as well as for food.

The generally high protein content of legumes makes them an essential food in countries where little meat is eaten. Since they also contain carbohydrates, fats, some minerals and even some vitamins they supply many of the nutrients people need to survive.

Another enormous advantage of legumes is that they are easily grown under varying climates and conditions. They mature easily and when dried, they store easily thanks to their small size, low water content and hard coating.

LENTIL
Lens culinaris, Lens esculenta

Lentils are the small round seeds of a small shrubby plant believed to have originated in the Eastern Mediterranean and in India. They are among the oldest leguminous crops, known to the ancient Egyptians and the Greeks. To this day they are one of the staple foods of India and the Near East and they are widely used throughout Europe. The Bible often speaks of lentils, the most famous reference being that of Esau who sold his birthright for bread and a "pottage of lentils" (Genesis 25:29-34).

There are two distinctive varieties of lentils. One is the common French kind which is brown or grayish, sold with the seed coat on. The other is the Egyptian or Syrian kind, which is red or orange-red, smaller and rounder without a seed coat and split, which means that it cooks much more quickly. Lentils are never used fresh, but when fully ripe they are dried.

Soup is the most common American use for lentils. In Europe and the Near East, however, lentil salad, braised lentils and lentil and meat stews are staple dishes. And in India, lentils make one of that country's basic pottages or *dhals*. It has been my experience that Americans, who never thought of lentils except as in a soup, are surprised and delighted by the many different ways they appear in the various domestic and exotic cuisines.

How to Buy

Brown lentils are usually sold in 1-pound packages, but in ethnic markets they are sold in bulk. Red lentils are available in Near Eastern and Indian groceries.

1 cup dried lentils—2 to 2½ cups cooked.
1 pound dried—2⅔ cups cooked.

How to Keep

Store in original package or tightly covered container in a dry place.
Raw, kitchen shelf—6 to 8 months.
Cooked and covered, refrigerator shelf—1 week.

Nutritive Values

Lentils are a good source of carbohydrates, phosphorus and iron and have fair amounts of vitamins and minerals.

3½ ounces cooked—106 calories.

How to Use

Pick over lentils. Wash even packaged lentils and drain.

Modern packaged lentils generally need no soaking; follow package directions. If lentils are to be soaked, place in a bowl, cover with water and soak for 8 hours. Or bring to the boiling point in a saucepan, boil for 2 minutes, remove from heat, cover and let stand for 1 hour. Cook lentils in the water in which they were soaked. Or add the liquid called for in the recipe to the measured lentils. Lentils may be cooked in water or in bouillon. Place measured lentils in a heavy saucepan, add the liquid, cover and bring to the boiling point. Reduce heat to simmer and cook for about 1 hour or until tender but still whole. Lentils in soup should be cooked longer, until they mash readily. Drain and season cooked lentils with salt and pepper; like beans, if they are salted during cooking they will be tough. Use as directed in recipe. All lentils dishes should be well seasoned.

LENTIL SALAD

4-6 servings

Any lentil dish should be well seasoned. Serve with hot or cold roast meats or ham.

3 cups lentils	2 bay leaves
water	6 green onions, white and green
1 large onion stuck with 2	parts, thinly sliced
cloves	Lemon French dressing
2 garlic cloves, peeled	salt
1 medium carrot, cut into 2	freshly ground pepper
pieces	tomato wedges
1 celery stalk, cut into 2 pieces	¼ cup minced parsley

Put the lentils into a large saucepan. Add water to cover plus 3 inches. Bring to the boiling point and lower heat to very low. Add the onion, garlic, carrot, celery and bay leaves. Simmer covered for about 30 minutes or until the lentils are tender but not mushy; they must retain their shape. Drain the lentils and remove the vegetables. Turn the lentils into a bowl while they are still hot. Add the green onions and the French dressing. Mix well. Taste and season with salt and pepper. Cool the lentils, then cover the bowl and refrigerate for 2 hours to blend the flavors. At serving time, drain off any excess dressing. Turn into a flat serving dish, garnish with the tomato wedges and sprinkle with the parsley.

LEMON FRENCH DRESSING

Combine ⅓ cup olive oil, 3 tablespoons fresh lemon juice (or to taste), 1 mashed garlic clove, ¼ teaspoon dried thyme and salt and pepper. Stir and mix well before using.

LENTIL SOUP

4-6 servings

2 cups dried lentils
2 quarts cold water
¼ pound bacon in one piece
1 large onion, finely chopped
1 large carrot, finely chopped
1 celery stalk, finely chopped

2 tablespoons bacon fat
½ cup minced onion
2 tablespoons flour
2 tablespoons vinegar
salt
freshly ground pepper

Wash the lentils under running cold water. Pour the 2 quarts of water into a large kettle and bring to the boiling point. Add the lentils, bacon, onion, carrot and celery. Cover partially and simmer over low heat for 30 minutes. Heat the bacon fat in a large heavy frying pan. Add the minced onion and cook, stirring constantly, until the onion is golden brown. Stir in the flour and cook, stirring all the time, until the flour is golden brown. Ladle about ½ cup of the lentil soup into the frying pan and stir thoroughly until the mixture is smooth and thickened. Stir in the vinegar. Turn the whole contents of the frying pan into the lentil soup, scraping the bottom of the skillet with a rubber spatula. Season with salt and pepper. Stir thoroughly. Simmer over low heat covered for 30 more minutes or until the lentils are tender. Before serving, remove the bacon and cut it into ½-inch dice; return to soup, and check the seasoning.

LENTILS, RICE AND SPINACH

6-8 servings

Esau may have sold his birthright for a dish like this. Serve as a meatless main dish with a cucumber salad.

¼ cup olive oil
2 large onions, thinly sliced
1 cup lentils
5 cups water
½ cup long-grain rice
salt

freshly ground pepper
½ pound spinach, trimmed and
    coarsely chopped
⅛ teaspoon allspice
juice of 1 lemon

Heat the olive oil in a frying pan. Cook the onions, stirring constantly, until they are golden brown; do not scorch. Put the lentils into a large saucepan. Add the water and bring to the boiling point. Lower the heat, cover the saucepan and simmer for about 15 minutes, stirring frequently. Add the rice and season with salt and pepper. Simmer covered for 10 minutes. Add the spinach and half of the cooked onions. Mix well. Cook, stirring frequently, until the rice is tender. Stir in the allspice. Turn into a serving dish. Spread with the remaining onions and sprinkle with the lemon juice. Serve hot or cold.

LETTUCE
Lactuca sativa

Cultivated lettuce, the world's most popular salad plant, is descended from wild forms of lettuce found in some form or other all over the globe. The milky juice exuded by lettuce gave it its name, whose Latin root is *lac* or milk, from which come the French *laitue* (milky) and the English lettuce.

According to many ancient Greek and Roman writers, lettuce was known in a number of varieties, including blanched ones, which speaks of its great popularity. Hippocrates, 430 BC, said that it was good for people. We know that lettuce was an English crop from Chaucer, who in 1340 in his Prologue to the *Canterbury Tales,* writes, "well loved he garlic, onions and lettuce."

Lettuce hybridizes easily; there are unbelievable numbers of variants, and the seed catalogs come out every year with new, improved kinds. Lettuce is generally grouped in five classes, all of which come in a number of varieties.

CRISPHEAD LETTUCE

var. *capitata,* is popularly known as iceberg lettuce, which is wrong since iceberg lettuce is a red-tinged variety of no commercial importance. Crisphead lettuces have firm heads about 6 inches in diameter with pale green highly folded inner leaves with a brittle texture. There are two main varieties: Great Lakes, with dark green, crisp, serrated tough leaves and a generally coarse texture; and the more desirable Imperial, with thin, medium smooth-edged green leaves whose quality is good to excellent. Crisphead lettuces are the most commonly grown lettuces because, as a report says, they withstand long distance transportation and the stresses and shocks associated with harvesting and marketing practices. They were developed for just such purposes, triumphs of modern plant breeding. They are resistant to the mildew and other blights which were wrecking the California and Arizona lettuce industry in the 1920's.

BUTTERHEAD LETTUCE

var. *capitata,* is a smaller-headed lettuce with soft, delicately flavored leaves that bruise easily. They look somewhat like full-blown green roses with yellow-green hearts. The principal commercial varieties are Boston lettuce and Bibb lettuce which are grown traditionally in the East, from New York to North Carolina, and in the Midwest. Before the development of the California lettuce industry butterhead lettuces were the main lettuces of the East. Then they went into a decline, but picked up again in the 1950's, when Eastern customers became dissatisfied with crispheads, and new butterhead varieties were developed for local markets. Boston lettuce is medium large with a firm, well defined slightly pointed head and broad, smooth, thick, medium green leaves which at times are tinged reddish brown at the edges. Bibb lettuce, named after its first producer in 1850, is small, very tender, with dark green leaves which have a delicate buttery flavor and is the most desirable of the lettuces.

ROMAINE OR COS LETTUCE

var. *longifolia,* have long loaf-shaped heads, broad, stiff, upright leaves which are crisp, rather coarse and sweet. The leaves of some varieties curve inward at the tips and form a well blanched closed head. Romaine lettuce became popular along with mixed green tossed salads since it gives them flavor and texture. It is not suited to long distance shipping, though winter demands have evolved some Western varieties that will ship better. The best known romaines are Dark Green and White Paris. Romaine lettuce is excellently suited to cooking; French and other European cookery make extensive use of it.

LOOSELEAF OR BUNCHING LETTUCE

var. *crispa.* Different varieties are grown in different areas, but basically, the leaves do not form a head, but are attached to a short central stem. The leaves are tender, curly, smooth or cut-edged or oak-leaf shaped, varying from a fresh green to reddish or rusty-green color. The flavor is fresh and delicate. Looseleaf lettuce is a perishable crop and mostly grown in home gardens, or if commercially, in local greenhouses and on truck farms.

STEM LETTUCE, ASPARAGUS LETTUCE, CELTUCE

var. *angustana.* This variety is native to China, where it has been cultivated for centuries as an ingredient for many dishes. The edible part is not the leaves, but the seedstalk, that is, the enlarged stalk which has a mild flavor reminiscent of water chestnuts. The stalk may be peeled and eaten raw or creamed. Stem lettuce is little used in this country except by people of Chinese origin, in whose markets alone it is to be found. The variety grown in the United States is celtuce.

How to Buy

Available the year round, mostly from California which produces more than two-thirds of the total crop. Arizona is the next largest producer, a long way behind. Peak months for butterhead, romaine and looseleaf are the summer months, generally from May to October. For all lettuce, *buy* fresh, crisp, blemish-free heads. Look for a bright color, whatever the shade of green. *Avoid* soft, wilted, faded heads; check leaves for bruises, tipburn or browning of leaf edges which may indicate soft rot. With the exception of iceberg lettuce, many vegetable markets water their lettuces to keep them fresh in warm weather. This practice is permissible if not overdone; if the lettuces are heavily watered it means they are not fresh. Watch leaves for bruises.

Crisphead or iceberg lettuce heads should be even shaped, firm, but not hard, heavy for their size. Very large, pale heads are overmature and wanting in flavor.

Butterhead lettuce should be fairly compact, clean and free of blemishes.

Romaine should be crisp with unwilted bright green fresh-topped outer leaves.

Looseleaf lettuce should have crisp leaves without nicks or bruises.

1 medium lettuce of any kind—about 3 to 4 servings.

How to Keep

Lettuce should be refrigerated as soon as possible after buying or picking. During storage, it needs some moisture, but it must not be wet. Wash in several changes of cold water, drain well and dry between paper towels. Store in plastic bag in the vegetable compartment of the refrigerator.

Refrigerator shelf or vegetable compartment—3 to 5 days, depending on variety.

Nutritive Values

Aside from some vitamin A, lettuce has few nutrients and few calories.

3½ ounces raw—13 to 18 calories.

How to Use

Use as soon as possible. For salads, lettuce can be cut into wedges, shredded or torn apart, which, unlike cutting with a knife, prevents it from turning dark at the cut edge. For whole lettuce leaves, remove the core and let water run into the hole. Spread the leaves gently apart and gently tear off. All washed lettuce should be well drained and dried between paper or kitchen towels. To keep crisp, wrap in dry paper or towel or place wrapped lettuce in a large plastic bag and refrigerate.

Lettuce, especially the butterhead varieties, wilts easily, especially under the influence of the vinegar and salt in a salad dressing and even more so if it was not properly dried after washing. It is best to dress a lettuce salad just before using, even at the table, as is the habit of some gourmets. However, if this solution is not possible, do this: measure the salad oil and the vinegar for the dressing separately. Place the prepared lettuce in a large salad bowl. For a medium head, measure 1 tablespoon of the oil and pour it over the lettuce. Toss it gently with two forks to coat the leaves evenly with the oil. Add the remaining oil and toss again. Add the vinegar, salt and pepper and any herbs and toss and mix only at serving time. Another method of keeping salad crisp is to pour the dressing into the salad bowl and pile the greens on it lightly; toss only at serving time.

Note: Cut tomatoes have a great deal of juice and will water down any salad. It is better to omit them altogether. If they must go in, peel them first by plunging into boiling water. Retrieve with a fork and slip off the peel. Cool. Cut off the stem end. Cut the tomato into lengthwise slices (they water less this way). Arrange them nicely on top of the salad and toss only at serving time.

Cooked lettuce, especially romaine, lends itself to many delicious dishes, such as soups and purées or as additions to other vegetables. The tougher outer leaves, which are usually thrown away, serve very well for the purpose, not only for economy reasons, but also because they are usually more flavorful than the lighter inner ones.

CREAM OF ROMAINE SOUP

4-6 servings

2 tablespoons butter
1 large head romaine lettuce,
  shredded
12 to 18 green onions, sliced
1½ quarts chicken bouillon
salt

freshly ground pepper
2 tablespoons cornstarch
2 tablespoons water
2 egg yolks
⅓ cup heavy cream
butter-fried croutons

Combine the butter, lettuce and onions in a deep heavy saucepan. Cook over medium heat, stirring occasionally, for about 5 minutes or until the lettuce is wilted. Add the bouillon and season with salt and pepper. Simmer covered over low heat for 15 minutes. Blend the cornstarch and the water to a smooth paste and stir into the soup. Cook for 5 minutes longer. Purée the soup in a blender or strain through a food mill. Beat together the egg yolks and the cream. Spoon a little of the hot soup into the eggs and then stir the mixture back into the remaining soup. Heat through but do not boil. Serve hot with the croutons.

BIBB LETTUCE IN CREAM

4 servings

The lettuce must be very young, very tender and very fresh.

3 small Bibb lettuces, trimmed
  and washed
¼ cup sugar
¼ cup white vinegar

¾ cup light cream
salt
freshly ground white pepper

Wrap the lettuces in a kitchen towel and chill for 1 hour. Tear apart and place in a glass or china bowl. Stir the sugar into the vinegar until it is melted. Stir in the cream. Pour over the lettuce and toss. Refrigerate for 5 to 10 minutes. Just before serving, pour off any excess dressing and season extremely lightly with a little salt and pepper. Serve immediately.

STUFFED ICEBERG LETTUCE

4-6 servings

1 firm medium head iceberg
  lettuce
2 packages (3 ounces each)
  cream cheese, at room
  temperature
⅓ cup crumbled blue cheese, at
  room temperature
¼ cup mayonnaise
2 tablespoons minced green
  pepper

2 tablespoons minced onion
2 tablespoons chopped chives
2 tablespoons finely chopped
  walnuts
1 teaspoon Worcestershire
  sauce
dash Tabasco
sliced tomatoes

Core the lettuce and carefully hollow out the center leaving a shell about 1 inch thick. Wash and drain the lettuce thoroughly and dry on paper towels. Beat together the cream cheese, blue cheese and mayonnaise until smooth. Beat in the green pepper, onion, chives, walnuts, Worcestershire sauce and the Tabasco. Mix thoroughly. Fill the lettuce shell with the mixture. Wrap the lettuce first in wet paper towels and then in foil; tie it with string to keep it in shape. Chill for 2 hours or more. To serve, cut into wedges and surround with sliced tomatoes.

LETTUCE AND BACON

4-6 servings

Serve with hot roast meats, poultry or game.

6 small heads romaine lettuce
boiling water
½ pound lean bacon, diced
1 large onion, minced
1 large tomato, peeled and
    seeded (optional)
salt
freshly ground pepper
sprinkling of a favorite herb
    such as fresh or dried basil,
    thyme or marjoram
hot chicken bouillon or water
    (if necessary to prevent
    scorching)

Trim the romaine heads but leave them whole. Wash through several changes of cold water until no sand remains in the bottom of the basin. Shake dry. Plunge the lettuce into a large saucepan filled with boiling water and cook for about 2 minutes. Do not overcook; the lettuce must remain firm. Drain and lay in a strainer to allow the lettuce to drip off excess moisture. Dry between paper towels. In a deep frying pan, cook the bacon until crisp. Pour off about two-thirds of the fat in the pan. Add the onion and tomato, and cook, stirring constantly, until the onion is tender. Add the lettuce. Season with salt and pepper and sprinkle with the herb. Cook covered over low heat for about 10 minutes. Check for dryness; if necessary, add a little hot bouillon or water, 1 or 2 tablespoons at a time, to prevent scorching. The cooked lettuce should be dry. Serve very hot.

LOTUS
genus *Nelumbo*

Lotus is a decorative water plant belonging to the water lily family whose spectacular flowers and bell-shaped leaves float well above the water surface on long stalks. Surprisingly to most Westerners, it is a food plant in the Orient and in the United States as well, though not remotely to the same extent. All the parts of the lotus are edible: leaves, seeds, and rhizomes, which are the fleshy underwater stems.

The American lotus, *Nelumbo lutea,* a wild plant native to the Eastern seaboard, was long prized by the Indians for its seeds and roots. When roasted the seeds become deliciously nutty and the cooked roots provide starch. Dried roasted lotus seeds are occasionally found in health stores and as for the roots, I suppose one gathers them oneself. Not so in the Orient, where lotus is important as a food plant. *Nelumbo nucifera,* the sacred lotus of India and China, grows from the Caspian Sea to Japan and serves both decorative and culinary purposes. The leaves are boiled as a vegetable and the ripe seeds are dried or roasted, then pickled in various ways or sweetened with soy and then ground to make lotus jam to fill Eastern pastries. The lotus roots are best used when young since they can achieve lengths of four feet and diameters of thirty inches. They are divided into sausagelike segments whose red-brown surface hides flesh that ranges from white to orange. They can be boiled whole, scraped and mashed, dried to make a flour, or scraped and sliced and added to soups. Sliced lotus root is used in many Chinese dishes much as water chestnuts are used. The flavor of the roots is not as pronounced as that of seeds, which for non-Orientals takes some getting used to.

Lotus root is grown as a commercial crop in the Far East and in Hawaii, from where it is shipped fresh to Chinese markets in the United States during the late summer and fall. It is also available sliced and preserved, at times pickled or else in a sweet soy sauce. The canned seeds are also found in Chinese markets.

LOTUS ROOT SALAD

4-6 servings

1 quart plus ¼ cup water
2 tablespoons white vinegar
3 medium segments lotus root,
    about 1½ pounds
¼ cup sake

3 tablespoons sugar
½ teaspoon salt
1 green or red pepper, cut into
    rings

Combine 1 quart of the water and the vinegar in a saucepan. Scrub and peel the lotus root. Cut into ½-inch slices. Drop the slices immediately into the vinegar water to prevent discoloring. Bring the water with the lotus slices to the boiling point. Cook for about 2 or 3 minutes until the slices are tender but still crisp. Drain and turn into a serving dish. Combine the remaining ¼ cup of water, sake, sugar and salt in a small saucepan. Bring to the boiling point. Cook, stirring constantly, until the sugar has dissolved. Pour the hot mixture over the lotus root slices and toss gently with a fork. Let stand at room temperature for 20 minutes. Drain and chill. Serve garnished with the pepper rings.

MALANGA
Tannia, Dasheen, Yautia, New Cocoyam
Xanthosoma sagittifolium

A tropical vegetable cultivated throughout wet tropical America and in Africa, mainly for its starchy roots, but also for its foliage which serves as a potherb and is known as callaloo. Malanga—both roots and foliage—are constantly confused with taro roots and foliages which are also known as callaloo. Though they belong to different botanical families, all these tropical greens and roots taste pretty much the same, the roots being pure starch.

The leaves of the malanga, which has many other names depending on the locality, are several feet tall, large and arrow-shaped. The corm or root or tuber is pointed and can grow up to a foot in length and three inches across, and it produces a number of little three-inch tubers. The skin is thick and rough, yellowish-brown to dark brown and the flesh, depending on the variety, off-white or yellowish. It tastes like something between a moist white and a moist sweet potato, and it contains more starch than either. The root should be boiled or baked first because it is acrid, but after that it can be treated like any potato. The little tubers can be used like new potatoes. Needless to say, malanga is essential in Caribbean and tropical American cooking. It is found in all markets catering to people who come from those parts.

MELON

genus *Cucurbita*

In the United States, melons of different kinds are treated as fruit. But these cousins of the cucumber and squash appear in different varieties in other parts of the world, notably in China, where some are used as a bland vegetable. Two varieties are found in Oriental markets in the United States, to make popular Chinese dishes.

BITTER MELON

Momordica Charantia

is a tapering green-yellow to dark green fruit six to ten inches long and about three inches across with thick smooth warty skin. Inside, like all melons, it is pulpy with showy seeds. Bitter melons are picked for cooking when they are still green and hard; they are yellow when ripe. The flesh has a cool, somewhat bitter flavor. They may be boiled whole, peeled, cut, seasoned, and served with butter or more frequently, peeled raw, sliced or diced, steamed, or added to soup or to stir-fry dishes, or even stuffed and baked or steamed. Bitter melon is also sold dried and canned.

WINTER MELON
Benincasa hispida

This oblong melon is about a foot long, can be eight inches across and weigh 20 or more pounds. The skin is green, covered with a white waxlike bloom, and very thick which gives the winter melon long keeping qualities. The flesh is firm and white and tastes cool with just a tinge of bitterness. To prepare winter melon for cooking, scrape and wash off the waxy bloom. Small tender melons may be steamed whole and served with soy sauce, as in Japan. Or the outer layers of the rind may be peeled off, the pith thrown away and the flesh either sliced or diced and added to stir-fry dishes. The most famous winter melon dish is the famous Winter Melon Soup: the melon itself serves as a soup tureen.

WINTER MELON SOUP

4-6 servings

6 cups chicken consommé
¼ pound ground lean pork
1 pound winter melon, seeded, peeled, and cut into 1-inch pieces
6 Chinese mushrooms, soaked, drained, stemmed and cut into halves

¼ cup bamboo shoots, thinly sliced
¼ cup water chestnuts, chopped
1 tablespoon soy sauce
freshly ground pepper
1 teaspoon cornstarch
1 tablespoon water
1 scallion, minced

In a deep saucepan combine the consommé, pork, winter melon, mushrooms, bamboo shoots and water chestnuts. Mix well and bring to the boiling point. Lower the heat. Simmer without a cover for about 10 to 15 minutes or until the melon pieces are translucent. Stir in the soy sauce and cook for 5 more minutes. Season with pepper to taste. Stir the cornstarch into the water to make a smooth paste. Stir into the soup. Cook, stirring constantly, for about 3 minutes or until thickened. Stir in the scallion and serve very hot.

MUGWORT
Artemisia vulgaris

Mugwort is a pretty plant native to temperate Europe and America which is grown for ornamental gardens in this country. In Japan and China, however, the young leaves and twigs of the plant are used as a seasoning whose taste appeals more to Orientals than to Westerners. Mugwort is also one of those herbs used in Europe from the Middle Ages as a spring tonic and to flavor beer. Herbalists still use it for medical purposes. It has always been associated with witchcraft and inspired many half-witted folk rhymes such as:

> If they'd drink Nettles in March and Mugwort in May
> So many fine maidens would not go to clay.

MUSHROOM
Agaricus bisporus

A mushroom is the fruiting body of certain fungi and botanically one of the simplest plants; it has no roots, stems or leaves. It produces no flowers or seeds and relies on spores, reproductive cells, to reproduce itself. The mushroom lacks chlorophyll and thus cannot carry out photosynthesis to manufacture its own food from sunlight. It has to depend upon nonliving organic matter for its food, a fact that makes mushroom growing totally different from growing other food plants.

There are thousands of mushroom species growing wild in the world; in the United States alone there are over 3,000; some edible, some poisonous. There is only one species cultivated here and in Europe, *Agaricus bisporus,* the French champignon de Paris. It appears in our markets in three strains: white, cream and tan. The first is preferred on the East Coast, the last in California and the West.

To judge from the profusion with which wild mushrooms grow under the most varied conditions, one would think that growing mushrooms commercially would be easy. Far from it. Since it is not a matter of planting a seed, the spawn must be sterile, a pure culture spawn produced in as sterile a lab as a hospital operating room, to be deposited in a scientific compost from which it will draw its nourishment. Mushrooms are grown in special windowless houses in which temperature and ventilation, two all-important factors, can be controlled.

Apart from fresh mushrooms, there is a large variety of canned mushrooms and mushroom sauces available. Among the canned mushrooms, I recommend the varieties imported from France and Germany and the pickled mushrooms in jars from France and Italy; they make very good hors d'oeuvres.

Allow 1 pound fresh mushrooms for 4 servings, or 6 servings as a garnish.

1 pound fresh mushrooms equals approximately—1 quart whole, 20 to 25 medium, 5 cups sliced, or 4 cups chopped or minced.

Dried Mushrooms

Mushrooms are extensively dried in Europe and in the Orient where they are an important part of local cookery. They are imported into this country loose and are generally packed here in plastic containers or plastic bags. The most common dried European variety to reach us is the *Boletus,* but others are chanterelles, morels and the black mushrooms of China. These mushrooms keep their aroma and flavor remarkably well. They are expensive, but a little goes a long way. *Buy* dried mushrooms in good-sized slices, mushrooms which are thoroughly dried out and hard and clean (they may give off a slight dust of their own). All of these imported mushrooms are perfectly safe, but avoid home-dried mushrooms at roadside stands or obscure markets.

To reconstitute dried mushrooms, wash them first in lukewarm water to remove dust and grit. Then soak in lukewarm water to cover for 30 minutes to 1 hour. Use the soaking water in the dish you are cooking as additional liquid.

1 pound fresh mushrooms—approximately 3 ounces dried mushrooms.

How to Buy

Fresh mushrooms are available the year round, peak season October to June. They are sold by the pound. Size has nothing to do with flavor. Lately, so-called washed mushrooms wrapped in plastic packages have appeared on the market. They are apt to be soft and have less flavor then regular mushrooms. It is essential that mushrooms be as fresh as possible. They are highly perishable so that growers pick, pack and ship them to market under refrigeration within 24 hours. Their shelf life is short and they do not keep well in storage. Fresh mushrooms are recognized by caps closed so tightly that the gills beneath are not visible. Since they are mostly water which evaporates during shipping and storage, the caps gradually open to show the brown gills. Opened mushrooms are all right for cooking, but not as flavorful as truly fresh ones. *Buy* firm, closed blemish-free mushrooms. *Avoid* wilted, shriveled, wide-open, slimy mushrooms, or bruised, blemished or browned mushrooms. *Avoid* the prepackaged, "washed" mushrooms which have little flavor.

How to Keep

Refrigerate fresh mushrooms as soon as possible. Do not wash before use. Mushrooms are fragile, so they must not be crowded against other foods. They also need air to circulate around them. To keep them perfect lay the mushrooms on a shallow tray and cover them with paper towels dipped in water and wrung half dry. Or place in an open plastic bag which allows ventilation. If you buy a whole standard three-pound basket, take out what is needed, and cover again carefully with the paper that lines the basket and the lid. Keep refrigerated.

Raw, covered, refrigerator shelf—3 days.

Cooked and covered, refrigerator shelf—3 to 4 days.

Keep dried mushrooms in their own container or in a tightly covered jar in a dark, cool place. They will keep up to a year.

Nutritive Values

Mushrooms are mostly water but they are a moderate source of minerals. They fill without fattening, but they can absorb a surprising amount of the fats and creams with which they are cooked.

3⅓ ounces, raw—28 calories.

3⅓ ounces, canned, solids and liquids—17 calories

How to Use

There are different schools of thought on how to clean fresh mushrooms. Everybody agrees that mushrooms must never be soaked; they become waterlogged. Wipe with a damp cloth without damaging the mushrooms or rinse quickly under running cold water, drain and dry between paper towels.

Method three: prepare a bowl of cold acidulated water (2 tablespoons lemon juice to 1 quart water) and drop the mushrooms into it. Swish around quickly with hands, drain and dry. Or dip trimmed mushrooms quickly into lemon juice diluted with a little water. Dry between paper towels.

I tend to the latter two methods and wash after trimming, because I think mushrooms are much dirtier than one thinks, considering the way they are grown. As with salad greens, it is easier for the dirt to seep out when the whole vegetable is surrounded by water than when it is bunched in a strainer. Speed quick and thorough drying are of the essence. The lemon juice keeps the mushrooms bright and firm and its flavor is light enough to disappear; if it is thought objectionable, wash the mushrooms in a bowl of plain cold water.

Never peel mushrooms; much of the flavor lies in the skin. The unfortunate habit of peeling commercial mushrooms is a holdover from the peeling of certain wild ones which have a tough skin that has to be removed before cooking.

To prepare, trim and wash and dry only the number of mushrooms you are going to use; washed mushrooms, however well dried, do not keep. Trim off stem end and halve or quarter or slice the mushrooms lengthwise. Use immediately after preparing. If you are using only the caps, cut off the stems flush with the cap but leave the bit in the middle; it will prevent the cap from shrinking during cooking. The stems can be sliced and added to other dishes or minced for stuffings.

Many books have been written on mushroom cookery (with a wealth of international recipes) that often neglect basic information, such as the fact that mushrooms release a good deal of water during cooking which has to be accounted for in dishes that might turn watery. This trouble can be avoided by first blanching or sautéing the mushrooms. Also, mushrooms should be sautéed quickly, before they draw water; never cook them for a long time or they'll lose texture and flavor. Blanched or sautéed, they are added to the dish just long enough to add to its flavor during the last cooking period.

To blanch mushrooms

Place trimmed and washed mushrooms in a wire basket or strainer and plunge into a saucepan of rapidly boiling water. Keep them in the water for no more than 1 minute for small mushrooms and 2 minutes for large mushrooms from the moment the water begins to boil again after immersion. Be sure to keep track of the time. Have a bowl of cold water ready and dip the mushrooms rapidly in it 2 or 3 times when they are blanched to reduce the heat and keep them firm.

To sauté mushrooms

Trim, wash and slice or chop or mince 1 pound mushrooms. Heat 2 tablespoons butter and 1 tablespoon salad oil in a heavy frying pan over moderate heat. Add the mushrooms. Shake the pan to coat the mushrooms with the fat. Cook, shaking the pan or stirring carefully with a fork, for about 2 to 4 minutes, depending on the size of the pieces. *Do not cover the pan or the mushrooms will draw water.* Serve as a garnish, as a vegetable on buttered toast, or add to other dishes.

MUSHROOMS PICKLED IN WINE

6 servings

2 cups dry white wine	4 bay leaves
1 cup olive oil	12 whole peppercorns
1 medium onion, minced	1 teaspoon salt
yellow rind of 2 lemons, grated	2 pounds mushrooms, thickly
6 whole cloves	sliced or quartered
1 tablespoon dried thyme or	2 tablespoons lemon juice
savory	½ cup minced parsley

Combine the wine, olive oil, onion, lemon rind, cloves, thyme, bay leaves, peppercorns and salt in a saucepan. Bring to a boil. Lower the heat to very low and simmer covered for 10 minutes. Strain into another large saucepan and bring back to simmering. Add the mushrooms. Simmer for 5 to 10 minutes (depending on their size) until they are tender but still firm. Turn into a serving dish and chill. Before serving, pour off what is left of the marinade and stir the lemon juice into the mushrooms. Sprinkle with parsley.

DRIED MUSHROOM SOUP

6 servings

This most flavorful soup is made with the imported dried mushrooms found in all gourmet stores and most supermarkets.

¼ pound (4 ounces) dried imported mushrooms	6 tablespoons butter
8 cups strong beef consommé	2 tablespoons flour
1 medium onion, chopped	salt
	sour cream

Wash the mushrooms quickly under running cold water to remove any dirt and dust. In a large saucepan soak the mushrooms in the beef consommé overnight. Add the onion and 4 tablespoons of the butter to the mushrooms and consommé and bring to the boiling point. Reduce the heat and simmer covered for 1 hour. Purée in the blender and return to the saucepan. Place over low heat. Blend together the remaining 2 tablespoons butter and the flour. Drop pieces the size of a hazelnut into the hot soup, stirring well after each addition. Cook for 5 minutes longer without boiling. Season with salt. When served, top each serving with a tablespoon of sour cream.

Note: For a thinner soup, use 1 tablespoon butter and 1 of flour, or no thickening at all.

MUSHROOM AND SAFFRON CONSOMMÉ

4-6 servings

6 cups well-seasoned beef consommé	salt
½ teaspoon saffron	freshly ground pepper
½ pound mushrooms, trimmed, washed and finely chopped	1 cup dry sherry

Pour 1 cup of the consommé into a saucepan. Stir in the saffron. Add the remaining consommé and bring to boiling. Lower the heat. Add the mushrooms. Simmer covered for 5 minutes or until just tender and thoroughly heated through. If necessary, season with salt and pepper. Have the soup very hot without boiling it. Stir in the sherry and keep on the heat for 1 more minute, or until the sherry is warmed through.

BROILED MUSHROOMS WITH BACON

Wipe large, fresh mushrooms with a damp cloth and remove the stems. Grate 1 medium onion. Put ⅛ teaspoon grated onion into each cap and wrap in a ½-slice of bacon, fastening with toothpick. Put the bacon-wrapped mushrooms on a rack and broil until the mushrooms are tender and the bacon is crisp. Turn twice during broiling. Serve on buttered toast or spear on toothpicks as an hors d'oeuvre.

EASY STUFFED MUSHROOM CAPS

6 servings

1 pound medium mushrooms
1½ cups water combined with
   the juice of 1 large lemon
1 herbed Boursin cheese,
   mashed, or 1 cup mashed,
   heavily seasoned, herbed
   cottage cheese softened to
   spreading consistency with a
   little sweet or sour cream

small parsley heads

Remove the mushroom stems, washing each mushroom cap in the lemon water and drying it immediately with paper towels. Save the stems for soup or sauces. Spread the cavities with the softened cheese, smoothing off the tops. Decorate each mushroom cap with a small parsley head.

MUSHROOM SOUFFLÉ

3-4 servings

Serve as a first course with a sauce of fresh tomatoes.

4 tablespoons butter
½ pound mushrooms, trimmed,
 washed and thinly sliced
1 tablespoon grated onion
1 teaspoon grated lemon rind

3 tablespoons flour
1 cup light cream
4 eggs, separated
salt
freshly ground pepper

Heat 1 tablespoon of the butter in a frying pan. Add the mushrooms. Cook, stirring constantly, for 3 or 4 minutes. The mushrooms should be firm but not watery. Stir in the onion and the lemon rind. Remove from heat and reserve. Heat the remaining 3 tablespoons of butter and stir in the flour. Cook, stirring constantly, until the butter is golden. Stir in the cream and cook, stirring all the time, until the sauce is thick and smooth. Remove from the heat and stir in the egg yolks, one at a time, stirring well after each addition. Season with salt and pepper. Add the mushrooms to the sauce and mix well. Beat the egg whites until stiff and fold them gently into the mushroom mixture. Spoon into a buttered 2-quart baking dish. Bake in a preheated moderate oven (350° F) for about 30 to 35 minutes. Serve immediately.

MUSHROOM SAUCE FOR PASTA

Use this sauce on 1 to 1½ pounds cooked spaghetti or linguine.

6 tablespoons butter
4 medium onions, very thinly
 sliced
2 pounds mushrooms, thinly
 sliced
salt

freshly ground pepper
¼ teaspoon ground nutmeg
1 cup heavy cream
1 to 1½ pounds spaghetti
freshly grated Parmesan cheese

Heat 3 tablespoons of the butter in a heavy saucepan. Add the onions. Cook over medium heat, stirring constantly, for about 4 minutes or until the onions are just beginning to turn golden. Cover the saucepan. Simmer over lowest possible heat for about 30 minutes or until the onions are very soft but still light. Stir frequently. While the onions are cooking, heat the remaining butter in a large, deep frying pan. Add the mushrooms. Over medium heat, and stirring constantly, cook the mushrooms for about 4 minutes or until tender but still firm. Do not brown them. Lower the heat. Add the onions to the mushrooms and mix well. Season with salt and pepper and nutmeg. Keep warm over an asbestos plate. While the vegetables are cooking, cook the spaghetti in plenty of boiling salted water until barely tender. Five minutes before serving time, stir the cream into the onion-mushroom mixture and heat through. Do not boil or the sauce will curdle. Drain the spaghetti and turn into a heated deep serving dish. Add the sauce and toss. Serve with plenty of grated Parmesan cheese.

MUSHROOMS IN CREAM

3-4 servings

I think this simple way of cooking mushrooms one of the best.

2 tablespoons butter
1 pound mushrooms, trimmed
   and sliced
⅔ cup hot heavy cream
salt

freshly ground pepper
⅛ teaspoon ground nutmeg
2 tablespoons minced parsley or
   dillweed
buttered rice

Heat the butter in a deep frying pan. Add the mushrooms. Cook over medium heat, stirring constantly, for about 2 minutes. Add the cream and season with salt and pepper and nutmeg. Cook, stirring all the time, for 2 or 3 more minutes or until the cream has thickened. Sprinkle with parsley and serve on hot buttered rice.

MUSHROOMS À LA PROVENÇALE

3-4 servings

¼ cup olive oil
1 pound mushrooms, thickly
  sliced or quartered
2 whole garlic cloves
salt

freshly ground pepper
½ teaspoon dried thyme or 3
  sprigs fresh thyme
½ cup minced parsley
juice of ½ lemon

Heat the olive oil in a heavy saucepan with a closely fitting lid. Add the mushrooms, garlic cloves, salt and pepper and thyme. Cook covered over medium to high heat for about 5 or 7 minutes, shaking the pan very frequently to prevent sticking. At serving time, sprinkle with the parsley and the lemon juice. Serve very hot.

FRESH MUSHROOM SALAD

4 servings

⅔ cup olive oil
⅓ cup fresh lemon juice
1 teaspoon dried thyme
1 to 2 teaspoons Dijon mustard
salt

freshly ground pepper
1 pound mushrooms, thinly
  sliced
¼ cup minced parsley
lettuce

Combine all the ingredients except the mushrooms, parsley and lettuce and mix well. Add the mushrooms and toss with 2 forks. Cover and let stand at room temperature. At serving time, drain and sprinkle with the parsley. Pile in a serving dish lined with lettuce.

MUSHROOMS ANNETTA

4 servings

WHITE SAUCE

1 tablespoon butter
2 teaspoons flour
½ cup milk
dash of ground nutmeg

2 tablespoons butter
2 tablespoons olive oil
½ cup minced onion
¾ cup minced parsley
1 small garlic clove, minced

1 teaspoon grated lemon rind
1½ pounds fresh, firm
   mushrooms, trimmed and cut
   in quarters
½ cup Madeira
salt
freshly ground pepper
juice of 1 lemon

To make the white sauce, heat the butter in a small saucepan. Stir in the flour. Then stir in the milk. Cook, stirring constantly, until thick and smooth. Stir in the nutmeg. Remove from the heat and reserve.

In a large saucepan, heat together the butter and oil. Add the onion, ½ cup of the parsley, the garlic and the lemon rind. Cook, stirring constantly, until the onion is soft. Add the mushrooms. Cook over medium heat, stirring frequently, for about 3 or 4 minutes. The mushrooms must remain firm and quite white. Add the Madeira. Cook over high heat, stirring constantly, for another 3 or 4 minutes. Most of the liquid in the saucepan should have evaporated leaving about ½ cup of sauce or so. Stir in the white sauce and mix well. Cook for 2 minutes longer or until the white sauce has amalgamated with the mushrooms and their cooking liquid and the dish is thoroughly heated through. Season with salt and pepper. Stir in the lemon juice and remaining parsley and remove from heat. Serve immediately.

MUSTARD
genus *Brassica*

To the cook, mustard is one of two things: an herb of the cabbage family which is used as a pungently flavored green vegetable, or the condiment made from the seeds of this herb. Both kinds of mustard are widely used in the West and in the East; there is no substitute for the condiment mustard, whatever kind. The name is derived from Old French *moustarde,* which in its turn comes from the Latin *mustum,* meaning must, the freshly pressed juice of grapes with which the ground seeds were mixed for a condiment.

Both mustard the herb and mustard the seed have long been used for medicinal purposes and to this day, faith in mustard plasters to draw out a chest cold is by no means dead.

Chinese mustard (Indian Mustard), *Brassica juncea,* has large coarse dark green toothed leaves of different shapes. Oriental cookery uses the seedlings and leaves of immature plants in soups and stir-fry dishes and makes a cooking oil from the seeds. Two varieties, black mustard, *Brassica nigra* and white mustard, *Brassica alba,* are grown mainly for their seeds.

Potherb mustard, Brassica japonica, is the green vegetable simply known as mustard greens. Three main commercial varieties are grown, one with large, smooth, broad oval leaves, a distinct white midrib and toothed leaves; another one with wide, bright green and yellow tinged leaves that are very curly at the edges; and a third with smooth leaves. They all taste the same, pleasantly pungent, bitter, and on the coarse side. These mustards have bright yellow flowers, which make a mustard field in bloom a ravishing sight.

Tuberous-rooted Chinese mustard, Brassica napiformia, has thin, bluish, irregularly toothed leaves. The tuberous roots are eaten in China as a winter vegetable. The three- to four-inch roots look and taste like turnips, they have the same texture and are cooked like them. It was introduced into the United States from China in the late 1800's, but it is only—and not always—found in Oriental markets.

In England, another kind of mustard, *Sinapis alba,* is grown for salads and sandwiches with the traditional cress. The plants are harvested when only a few inches high. It is deliciously peppery like its close contender for looks and flavor, *Brassica rape,* grown for the same purpose. Unfortunately these mustards, so common in the British Isles, are unknown in the United States.

How to Buy

Available the year round, peak season December through April. *Buy* fresh, young, clean mustard greens, with tender leaves and a good green color. Some varieties are lighter green, others show a slight bronze tinge. *Avoid* wilted, yellowish greens with leaves that are soft or insect damaged or are unduly dirty.

Available canned or frozen.

Allow 1 pound for 2 to 3 servings.

How to Keep

Trim and wash the leaves and shake dry. Refrigerate in plastic wrap or in the vegetable drawer.

Raw, refrigerator shelf—2 to 4 days.

Cooked and covered, refrigerator shelf—2 days.

Nutritive Values

An excellent source of vitamins A and C and iron, and a good source of other minerals.

3⅓ ounces, raw—31 calories.

3⅓ ounces, cooked and drained—23 calories.

How to Use

Remove blemished or wilted leaves, and cut off the roots and tough stems. Wash thoroughly by dipping at least three times in and out of a bowl filled with water; change the water after each dipping until there is no trace of dirt left. Drain and shake dry. Cut large leaves into pieces. Cook covered in a half inch of boiling salted water for 10 to 15 minutes or until tender. Drain well, season with salt, pepper and butter or bacon fat. Or cook the Southern way with a piece of salt pork, ham hock or a piece of bacon. Or purée and season like puréed spinach.

NASTURTIUM
Tropaeolum majus

These pretty flowering vines, one tall, one growing low, are natives of Chile and Peru and are grown for their lovely flowers. However, the young tender stems and leaves of our low-growing nasturtium are picked to be added to salads and to sandwiches because of their delicately peppery flavor. The unripe and still green seeds, somewhat more peppery than the leaves, can be pickled to be used in lieu of capers or added to vinegars as a flavoring.

NETTLE
Common Nettle
Urtica urens

Various varieties of nettles are found throughout temperate Europe, Asia, South America and even Australia. In Europe, the heart-shaped, finely toothed tapering green leaves of the common nettle have been used as a potherb and for medicinal purposes since the days of the Romans. It is said that Roman soldiers who could not stand the cold English climate rubbed their bodies with stinging nettles to warm them, and this is just one example of the strange and abundant lore connected with them. Nettles were introduced into the United States by immigrants and they quickly became an obnoxious weed since Americans felt not as drawn to them as a food as the English, Scotch or French. However, they are an edible green, and a surprisingly agreeable one since the stinging hairs are rendered innocuous by cooking. However, caution does not end with picking them with gloved hands; it is best to wear rubber gloves when washing and trimming them like any other greens. Only young, tender nettles should be picked and quickly steamed to be served with butter.

NEW ZEALAND SPINACH
(See page 318)

OKRA
Gumbo
Hibiscus esculentus

The finger-shaped, pointed, somewhat hairy green fruit pod of a tropical plant with a unique gooey, mucilaginous quality which is used as a vegetable and to thicken dishes like stews and soups. The name gumbo by which okra is also known applies more to a certain kind of soup-stew made with it in Louisiana. Both words are of African origin.

The plant is a native of tropical Africa, and it is said to have come from the region that includes Ethiopia and the eastern, higher part of the Sudan. Okra is of considerable antiquity, but relatively little is known about it. Very likely, it came to Egypt and to the Arab countries through traders and slave raiders working out of Ethiopia and the Sudan. The Arabs grew very fond of it, calling it *bamiya;* it is still much used in all Arab cookery. How okra came to Louisiana and other Southern states we do not know for sure; it may have been introduced by the Spanish or French colonists or by the Negro slaves who used it in their home country or, most likely, by both.

Although okra has always been used extensively in Southern cookery, it is only beginning to come into its own in other parts of the country. And, in spite of the large popularity okra enjoys in West Indian, tropical American, Arab, even Indian cooking, it is unknown in Europe and the Mediterranean. Its role in French cookery is limited to that of New World Creole cookery. For people not raised on okra, the flavor may be said to be an acquired one, as is its texture.

Ripe okra seeds serve as the basis of an edible oil used in the East; they may also be roasted and ground and used as a coffee substitute. Recent research at the University of Rhode Island claims that the ripe pods are as high in protein as meat or milk and that they might be ground into flour and serve as a food.

How to Buy

Available the year round, especially in Southern states, peak season July through October. There are several varieties which include a giant Chinese variety with tender pods up to twelve inches long. Okra pods are always tapered and pointed, but they may be long and thin or chunky, smooth or ridged, light green or darker green. Mature okra pods are fibrous; it is therefore necessary to pick them when young, the younger the better. Aside from dwarf varieties, the ideal length is about two to three and one-half inches. Okra is also available canned or frozen; it takes well to freezing.

Buy young, crisp, tender small pods, free from blemishes. *Avoid* flabby, dull, dry, shriveled and discolored pods and stiff and woody pods.

Allow 1 pound for 3 to 4 servings.

1 quart—1 pound

1 pound medium 3- to 5-inch pods—approximately 22 to 28 pods.

How to Keep

Refrigerate in refrigerator drawer or in an open plastic bag to permit ventilation.

Raw, refrigerator shelf—4 days.

Cooked and covered, refrigerator shelf—2 days.

Nutritive Values

A mediocre source of vitamins and minerals.

3½ ounces cooked and drained—29 calories.

How to Use

Okra is always eaten cooked. The most common use is as a thickener in gumbos and Creole stews. As a vegetable, okra is stewed by itself or combined with other vegetables; it has great affinity with corn and tomatoes. Okra is also deep fried or used in salads. In Indian cookery, it is also stuffed, though the effort hardly seems worthwhile to us. Wash and trim off the stem ends. Leave small pods whole. Cut large pods into ½- to 1-inch slices. Cook covered in an inch of boiling salted water for 5 minutes or only until barely tender. Drain immediately, season and serve with butter and lemon juice or tomato sauce. It is important not to overcook okra since overcooking makes it slippery and dulls its color.

OKRA, ONION AND TOMATO STEW

4-6 servings

You may add 1 cup corn kernels to the stew.

6 slices lean bacon
2 medium onions, minced
1 large green pepper, cut into
    strips
1 pound young medium okra,
    trimmed and cut into ½-inch
    slices
4 medium tomatoes, peeled
    and chopped

salt
freshly ground pepper
2 teaspoons dried basil
½ teaspoon hot pepper flakes
    or to taste
¼ cup minced parsley

In a large frying pan, cook the bacon until crisp. Drain, crumble and reserve. Pour off all but 3 tablespoons of the bacon fat. Add the onion and the green pepper and cook, stirring constantly, until the pepper is almost soft. Add the okra. Cook, stirring all the time, until the okra is golden. Add the tomatoes, salt, pepper, basil and pepper flakes. Simmer covered for 10 to 15 minutes or until the okra is tender; do not overcook. Before serving, sprinkle with the crumbled bacon and parsley. Serve hot.

FRIED OKRA

4-6 servings

Serve with fried fish or with an omelet.

1 pound young medium okra
2 eggs, beaten in a bowl with
½ teaspoon salt

1 cup cornmeal, in a bowl
peanut or salad oil for frying

Wash the okra and trim off the stems. Cut into ½-inch slices. Turn into the bowl with the beaten eggs and toss with 2 forks until well coated. With a slotted spoon, transfer the okra to the bowl with the cornmeal. Toss again until well coated with the cornmeal. Heat ½ inch of oil in a large frying pan. Add the okra and stir. Cover the frying pan and cook over medium heat, stirring frequently, until the okra is golden brown and crisp. Drain on kitchen paper and serve very hot.

CHICKEN GUMBO

6-8 servings

The oysters are optional. Gumbo filé, the powdered young leaves of sassafras, is available in gourmet shops.

1 3½- to 4-pound chicken, cut
into serving pieces
¼ cup flour
salt
freshly ground pepper
4 tablespoons salad oil
1 cup chopped onion
½ cup chopped green pepper
⅓ cup chopped celery
1½ cups chopped smoked ham
2 cups chopped peeled tomatoes
1 teaspoon thyme

2 bay leaves
¼ teaspoon cayenne pepper
2 teaspoons curry powder
2½ quarts warm, not boiling,
water
2 tablespoons butter
1 pound young medium okra,
trimmed and cut into 1-inch
slices
2 cups oysters and their liquor
1 or 2 tablespoons gumbo filé
hot boiled rice

Remove all fat from the chicken. I also remove the skin because it fattens up the gumbo. Combine the flour, salt and pepper and toss the chicken pieces in it. Shake off excess flour. Heat the salad oil in a soup kettle. Add the chicken pieces, onion and green pepper. Cook over medium heat, stirring frequently, for 10 to 15 minutes or until lightly browned. Add the celery, ham, tomatoes, thyme, bay leaves, cayenne and curry powder. Add 2 quarts of the water, reserving the remainder to thin the gumbo if it becomes too thick. Simmer covered over low heat for about 1 to 1½ hours. Remove the chicken from the gumbo and take all the meat off the bones. Cut the meat into bite-sized pieces or shred it coarsely. Return it to the gumbo. Heat the butter in a large frying pan. Add the okra. Cook, stirring constantly, for 3 or 4 minutes or until the okra is golden. Add the okra to the gumbo and mix well. Season with salt and pepper. Simmer covered for 20 more minutes. If the gumbo is too thick, and this is a matter of taste, add some of the remaining warm water. Just before serving, add the oysters and heat through thoroughly. Remove from the heat and stir in the gumbo filé. Spoon some boiled rice into each soup plate and ladle the gumbo over the rice.

ONION
Allium cepa

The familiar, dry common onion is a single underground bulb which belongs to the lily family. There are many varieties, varying in shape, size, weight, color and pungency. The cause of the onion's strong smell and flavor is a volatile oil which is rich in sulfur compounds. Onions are used in the cooking of practically every country in the world; without them, most cookery would be flavorless. Possibly it is the one indispensable vegetable flavoring.

The onion is a native of Western Asia. It was cultivated for centuries in the Mediterranean and Near East. In the fourth millenium BC, the slaves who built the Great Pyramids are said to have lived on onions, radishes and garlic. The Children of Israel, fleeing from Egypt, cried out bitterly when they were deprived of the onions they had enjoyed in Egypt, which they preferred to Manna. In Greek and Roman times, as in the subsequent Middle Ages, onions were not only food but medicine as well. Hippocrates, the Greek physician of the third and fourth centuries who is known as the Father of Medicine, declared onions bad for the body but good for the sight.

Through the centuries, onions and their juice were used to cure all sorts of ills including earache, colds, fever, laryngitis and poor complexions as well as warts. In New England there was a belief brought by early settlers that a string of onions hung over the front door would catch disease germs on their way into the house and save those who lived within. These onions were of course never eaten. A diet of nothing but boiled onions was said to cure arthritis, but there is no proven record that it does.

There seems to be nearly universal agreement that the smell of onion on the breath is unattractive. A character in Shakespeare's *Midsummer Night's Dream* sums up general opinion well when he advises: "Eat no onions nor garlic, for we are to utter sweet breath." Not so with earlier men of Iceland, however; they are advised: "Onion is good in the mouth against evil smell."

The onion was introduced by the Spanish into the West Indies soon after their discovery. From there it spread all over America and was grown by the earliest settlers and Indians alike.

President Washington's favorite vegetable was the onion. He was fond of onions any way they were prepared and even ate them cored and stuffed with mincemeat. New England abounds with inns where George Washington is reputed to have slept, but the Munroe Tavern in Lexington, Mass. (now a museum) has a more distinctive claim to Washingtonian fame. "George Washington ate glazed onions here," it could proudly proclaim, for he did just that in 1790. General Grant so firmly believed that onions would cure dysentery and other hot weather ills that in the summer of 1864 he sent a wire to the War department: "I will not move my army without onions," which netted him three wagon loads to the front.

Onion varieties commercially grown in the United States include flat to top-shaped mild onions, mild globe onions with yellow, white or red skins, small and tiny pickling onions, very large mild brown or yellow imported Spanish onions, large, flat, mild, white or yellow Bermudas and sweet red, imported Italian onions which are mild enough to use raw in salads and sandwiches.

How to Buy

Available the year round. Spanish onions are available from September to April. Bermuda onions are available from March to June as are red Italian onions. Size does not affect quality or flavor.

Buy hard, firm, dry onions with small necks. The skins should be papery, dry and crackly and free from blemishes. *Avoid* spongy, soft onions, or onions with wet or very soft necks, hollow woody centers or with fresh sprouts. *Buy* large onions for slicing, medium onions for roasting or boiling, small onions for boiling and tiny onions for pickling.

Small white onions are available frozen. Dried onions, onion salt and similar products invariably have an artificial, dead flavor and should be avoided.

Allow 1 pound dry onions for 4 servings.

Allow 1 medium sweet onion for 1 serving.

Allow 4 to 6 small white onions for 1 serving.

How to Keep

Keep dry onions in a cool, dry, well ventilated place, preferably in a single layer, or wrap in an airtight bag and refrigerate.

Raw, dry room temperature—3 to 4 weeks.

Cooked and covered, refrigerator—4 days.

Nutritive Values

A moderate source of vitamin C and minerals.

3½ ounces raw—38 calories.

3½ ounces cooked and drained—29 calories.

How to Use

If dry onions have begun sprouting and have green tops, simply cut them off. Peel onions under running water to avoid tears. Or wear glasses, preferably wrap-arounds or clear ski goggles. A folk method to prevent tears is to put a piece of bread between the teeth so that it sticks out. Peel and cut onion just before using to preserve flavor; the flavoring substance in onions is a volatile oil which evaporates when exposed to the air. To cut onions: leave large onions unpeeled, cut into halves lengthwise and peel. Put the cut side down on a board. Preferably with a French knife, slice the onion half lengthwise into ⅛-inch slices almost to the base. Then slice crosswise. Chop the ends. Cut onion rings crosswise from a whole, unpeeled onion, remove dry skin from each ring and separate carefully. Chill in ice water to crisp; drain and dry. To peel small boiling onions, score the root end of each onion with a small cross using a sharp pointed knife. Then pour boiling water to cover over the onions and let stand for 3 to 5 minutes. Drain and peel. For onion juice, cut a medium onion into halves. With the edge of a spoon, a grapefruit spoon or the edge of a knife, scrape the onion and catch the juice in a spoon. To grate onion, cut into halves and peel. Grate on the coarse side of a grater; grating on the fine side is too tedious an enterprise to even consider. Grated onion adds a more powerful flavor to a dish than its equivalent chopped.

The closed chopping device, imported from Europe, is excellent for chopping onions effortlessly, all the more since they may be chopped together with garlic, parsley and herbs. A spring, which you push up and down, moves an arrangement of blades on the food to be chopped. Both blades and food are enclosed in plastic so that there is no spattering. I do all my chopping this way with one large and one medium chopper.

GREEN ONION
Spring Onion
Allium cepa

Green onions are onions that are pulled when the tops are still green. They have a definite bulb formation with the same concentric arrangement as dry onions. The varieties pulled before the bulb has formed are scallions. Green onions look like cylinders with tightly furled leaves from eight to twenty-four inches in length and about one quarter- to one half-inch across, white at the root base and green at the top. Their history is the same as that of dry onions, and they are equally popular throughout the world; in China more use is made of spring onions than of dry ones.

Green onions are mostly eaten raw, by themselves as appetizers, in salads, in sandwiches or snipped as a fresh green into cooked dishes. Cooked, they are a delicious, delicate vegetable. Green onions are sold in bunches. *Buy* young tender, clean green onions with well-trimmed bulbs, firm, with fresh, bright green tops. *Avoid* soft, withered, wilted green onions with broken or bruised leaves, diseased or damaged leaves. Refrigerate in vegetable drawer for 2 days and use as soon as possible. Trim, wash and use sliced or chopped in salads or cook whole or cut into two pieces in an inch of boiling salted water for three to four minutes. Drain, season and serve with butter and lemon juice.

3½ ounces raw, bulb and entire top—36 calories.

ONIONS À LA GRECQUE

6 servings

36 small white onions (the
smaller, the better), peeled
⅔ cup olive oil
2 cups dry white wine
1 cup water
½ cup wine vinegar
2 tablespoons tomato paste
2 garlic cloves, mashed

2 cloves
1 teaspoon each dried crumbled
tarragon, salt, coarsely
ground pepper, dry mustard
and mustard seed
½ cup golden raisins
½ cup minced parsley

Combine all the ingredients except the raisins and the parsley in a large deep frying pan. Bring to the boiling point. Lower the heat to very low and simmer covered for 10 minutes. Add the raisins and simmer for 5 more minutes or until the onions are tender but still holding their shape; the cooking time depends on their size. Cool and let stand at room temperature for 2 hours, then chill. Sprinkle with the parsley before serving.

ONION FRITTATA

3 servings

¼ cup olive oil
2 large onions, sliced very
  thinly
1 tablespoon flour
2 tablespoons milk

6 eggs, beaten
salt
freshly ground pepper
⅛ teaspoon ground nutmeg

Heat the olive oil in a heavy frying pan. Add the onions. Cook, stirring frequently, over lowest possible heat until the onions are soft and golden. Stir the flour into the milk. Combine with the eggs and beat to mix thoroughly. Season with the salt, pepper and nutmeg. Pour the egg mixture over the onions. Cook until the frittata is well set at the bottom and golden brown. Put a plate the size of the frying pan over the frittata. Turn the frying pan over so that the frittata is on the plate, cooked side up. Slide back into the frying pan and cook until set. Cut into wedges and serve hot or lukewarm.

CURRIED ONIONS

4 servings

¼ cup golden raisins
¼ cup dry sherry
1 pound small white onions,
  peeled
1 cup water
4 tablespoons butter
salt

freshly ground pepper
1 tablespoon curry powder or to
  taste
approximately 1 cup light
  cream or milk
1 tablespoon cornstarch
juice of ½ lemon

Soak the raisins in the sherry. Put the onions into a saucepan. Add the water, 2 tablespoons of the butter and the salt and pepper. Bring to the boiling point and lower the heat. Simmer covered for 10 minutes or until the onions are tender but still firm; cooking time depends on their size. Reserve the onions. Put the remaining butter into the top of a double boiler and stir in the curry powder. Cook, stirring frequently, over hot water for 10 minutes. When the onions are cooked, drain them into a bowl. Measure the cooking liquid and add enough cream to make 1¼ cups. Stir the cornstarch into the cream and stir this mixture into the curry butter. Cook, stirring frequently, until thickened and smooth. Add the onions, raisins and the sherry in which they were soaked. Cook over hot water, stirring frequently, until the onions are thoroughly heated through. Stir in the lemon juice before serving.

DANISH BROWNED ONIONS

4-6 servings

24 small white onions (the smaller, the better)
½ cup butter

¼ cup light brown sugar
1 teaspoon salt

To avoid tears in peeling, cook the onions in gently boiling water to cover for 5 to 8 minutes or until tender; cooking time depends on their size. Drain, cool and peel. Heat the butter in a frying pan. Stir in the sugar and the salt. Cook over low heat, stirring constantly, for a minute or two or until the sugar is melted. Do not scorch. Add the onions. Cook over lowest possible heat until browned on all sides. Stir with a fork or shake the pan frequently to avoid sticking.

ONIONS AND APPLES

4 servings

Serve with any pork dish.

2 tablespoons bacon fat
2 cups thinly sliced onions
3 cups peeled tart apple slices

salt
1 tablespoon brown sugar
⅛ teaspoon ground mace

Heat the bacon fat in a deep frying pan. Add the onions and apples and season lightly with the salt. Simmer covered over low heat, stirring frequently, for 10 to 15 minutes or until the vegetables are tender and golden brown. Stir in brown sugar and mace and cook for 2 minutes longer.

BAKED ONIONS

Eat these baked onions hot with butter, salt and pepper as you eat baked potatoes. Cold, season with salt and pepper and drizzle with a little olive oil and lemon juice.

Put *unpeeled* medium or large onions into a baking dish. Bake in a moderate oven (350° F) for 30 minutes or until soft. Slip off the skins before serving; they will come off easily.

ONION, ORANGE AND OLIVE SALAD

6 servings

For all roasted or grilled meats. Crisp the onion slices by chilling them in ice water. Drain when needed.

1 bunch watercress
18 paper-thin, crisp slices sweet
   Bermuda onions (the red
   kind)

18 thin orange slices, peeled
12 slices jumbo black olives
⅔ cup French dressing made
   with lemon juice

Pick over the watercress, remove the thickest stems, wash and shake dry. Make a bed with it in a salad bowl. Arrange the onion and orange slices on the watercress in an overlapping pattern. Top with the sliced olives. Pour the French dressing over everything. Bring to the table as is and toss there.

OLD FASHIONED ONION GRAVY

about 3 cups

4 tablespoons meat fat and
   drippings or bacon fat
2 cups thinly sliced onions
2 tablespoons flour
2 cups beef consommé
salt

freshly ground pepper
¼ teaspoon dried thyme
1 tablespoon Worcestershire
   sauce
2 tablespoons drained capers
   (optional)

Heat the fat and cook the onions, stirring constantly, until soft and golden. Stir in the flour and cook for 2 more minutes. Stir in the consommé. Taste (the consommé may be salty) and stir in salt and pepper, thyme, Worcestershire sauce and capers. Simmer covered over low heat for 10 minutes.

PARSLEY
Petroselinum crispum

Parsley is the most popular and widely used of all culinary herbs, a bright green biennial related to carrots, parsnips, anise, caraway and celery. They are all members of the Umbelliferae family, which have umbrellalike flowerheads and volatile oils in their stems and leaves and seeds which give them their characteristic flavor and odor.

There are three basic kinds of parsley grown in this country. The first two are distinguished for their foliage and intensity of flavor. *Curly-leaf, Petroselinum crispum,* has dark or lighter green finely cut deeply curled leaves; *plain-leaf, Petroselinum sativum,* more commonly known as Italian parsley, has deeply cut, flat, heavy, glossy dark green leaves; and *turnip-rooted* (or Hamburg parsley or parsley root), *Petroselinum tuberosum,* is grown for its edible roots which look like a slender parsnip with a taste resembling that of celeriac. Of these three, the curly-leaf parsley is the most common and best known, used as a flavoring and as a garnish. Italian parsley is far more flavorful and is widely used in Continental cooking. Parsley root is used in France as *persil à grosse racine* and in Italy in small quantities as a flavoring mainly for soup.

Parsley originated around the Mediterranean, where it has been used since antiquity. Its name is derived from the ancient Greek, a corruption of *petroselinon,* meaning growing among the rock, which wild parsley frequently does. The Greeks thought highly of parsley, crowning victors at the Isthmus games with it, and as Homer says, feeding it to their horses for added stamina. But they would not eat it because parsley was associated with oblivion and death, all of which proves that many of the ancient legends connected with vegetables are moot propositions. The Romans wore parsley leaves at their banquets in the pious hope it would delay the effects of too much wine, but they also ate it and, according to Galen, the early physician whose authority held until the 16th century, parsley was "sweet and grateful to the stomach."

Parsley is still indispensable in our kitchens, and besides, it is one of the prettiest herbs, well suited to be set up like a bouquet of flowers as a centerpiece for the dining table.

How to Buy

Available the year round. Many American markets carry Italian parsley along with curly-leaf parsley, and occasionally parsley root. However, the latter is best found in Italian markets. *Buy* crisp, firm parsley, with a healthy, all over color; parsley should spring back from the slight pressure of your fingers. *Avoid* wilted, yellowing parsley, bruised leaves or leaves with black, watery areas.

How to Keep

Wash parsley and shake it dry. Put at once into a jar with a tight lid and refrigerate.

Packed in tight jar, refrigerator shelf—2 to 3 weeks.

Nutritive Values

Exceptionally high in vitamins A and C and a good source of minerals.

3½ ounces—44 calories.
1 tablespoon chopped—1 calorie.
10 small sprigs—5 calories.

How to Use

Parsley deserves to be made use of as a vegetable in soups, stews and salads rather than being treated as a garnish only. Wash and chop or mince just before use to keep the fresh color. Though a bunch of parsley looks clean, it is surprisingly dirty. Fill a bowl with water, loosen the bunch into sprigs and wash in the water, changing it two to three times or until clean. Fold into a double or triple layer of paper towels or in a kitchen towel and wring thoroughly to dry. Then chop or mince. Obviously, parsley may be chopped or minced before being washed. In this case, also wash the chopped parsley in several changes of water and wring dry in paper towels. To chop parsley: hold several sprigs together and press the parsley leaves together tightly. Place on chopping board and cut across with a sharp knife. Or hold the parsley heads tightly in your hand and snip at them with a pair of scissors. Do not throw away the stems; they (especially Italian parsley) are as flavorful as the leaves. To dry parsley: cut the heads from the stems. Wash them thoroughly and drain them. Place the heads into a strainer and plunge into a saucepan full of boiling water for no more than 30 seconds. Drain. Measure a piece of heavy-duty foil to fit a baking sheet. Punch holes with a fork all over the foil. Place on baking sheet. Spread parsley heads in one layer over the foil. Or place washed and blanched parsley heads on a wire screen. Place baking sheet or screen in a preheated slow oven (300° F) until they are crisp and dry. Leave the oven door partially open. Store in an airtight container.

FRIED PARSLEY

A delicious garnish for fish and meats as found in fine restaurants. The fried parsley should be crisp and dark green.

Trim off all but 1 inch of the parsley stems. Wash and drain. Dry between paper towels until the parsley is absolutely dry; you will need several changes of paper. Not a drop of moisture must remain on the parsley or the fat will spatter. You will need 4 to 5 inches of fat for each cup of parsley. Heat the fat in a deep saucepan to 400° F on the frying thermometer. Put 1 cup trimmed dry parsley into a frying basket. Lower the basket into the fat for 1 minute or until no hissing noise is heard. Remove immediately and drain on more paper towels. Serve at once.

PARSNIP
Pastinaca sativa

The edible underground root of a plant that is a member of the ubiquitous Umbelliferae that includes parsley, fennel, carrots, celery and chervil. Parsnips are humble vegetables whose name, from the Latin *pastus* meaning food and *sativa* meaning cultivated, spells out exactly what a parsnip is—"just food," poor thing. Since the vegetable likes a cool climate and even improves after a frost which changes the starch in the root into sugar, parsnips were for centuries the vegetable of the poor in Northern Europe as the potato, a New World plant, is today. Parsnip varieties cultivated in the United States have tapered roots up to twelve inches in length and about three inches across at the shoulder with a fairly smooth light skin and fine-grained, sweet white flesh. The parsnips appear early in America, being mentioned on Margarita Island in 1564. The Virginia settlers cultivated it in the early 1600's, and by 1630 it was a common vegetable in Massachusetts. Even the Indians, such as the Iroquois, grew parsnips; General Sullivan destroyed Indian parsnip stores in his forays against them.

In all fairness to parsnips, American cookery does not make the best of them, as the French do (even in England parsnips are very much liked). Served as a vegetable in their own right rather than as a flavoring for soups and stews they can be puréed, braised, made into fritters or deep fried.

How to Buy

Available all year, peak September through May.

Buy small to medium parsnips, no less than an inch and a half across, that are fairly clean and firm and well trimmed. Avoid large parsnips which are woody, soft, bruised and discolored and shriveled roots suffering from insect and other blemishes.

Allow 1 pound for 2 to 3 servings.

Allow 2 pounds for 3 to 4 servings of puréed parsnips.

How to Keep

Refrigerate unwashed in a plastic bag.
Raw, refrigerator shelf or vegetable drawer—1 to 3 weeks.
Cooked and covered, refrigerator shelf—1 to 2 days.

Nutritional Values

Chiefly carbohydrate, a poor source of other nutrients.
3½ ounces raw—76 calories.
3½ ounces cooked and drained—66 calories.

How to Use

When ready to use, trim and wash parsnips. Peel or scrape. Or best, brush, boil first and then skin and prepare for recipe. Leave whole or cut lengthwise into slices, strips or dice. Have pieces the same size for even cooking. If the parsnips look woody, halve or quarter like an apple and remove woody core. Cook whole in boiling salted water for about 20 minutes, depending on size. Drain immediately. Or cook pieces in an inch of boiling salted water for 5 to 10 minutes. Drain, season and serve with butter. Or bake in a moderate oven in a covered baking pan for 20 to 30 minutes depending on size. It is important not to overcook parsnips which easily become mushy when cooked too long.

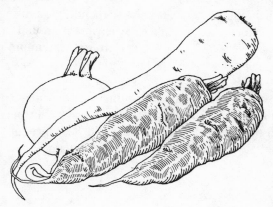

BRAISED PARSNIPS

4-6 servings

2 or 3 tablespoons butter
2 pounds parsnips, peeled and
    cut into thin julienne strips
1 tablespoon grated onion
¾ teaspoon salt

¼ teaspoon freshly ground
    pepper
¼ teaspoon sugar
6 large outer lettuce leaves
3 tablespoons minced parsley

Heat the butter in a saucepan. Add the parsnips, onion, salt, pepper and sugar. Mix gently with a fork. Wash the lettuce leaves and leave them wet. Cover the parsnips with the lettuce. Cover the saucepan and simmer over low heat for 10 to 15 minutes or until the parsnips are tender. Shake the saucepan frequently to prevent sticking. Check for moisture; if necessary, add a little water, 1 tablespoon at a time. Sprinkle with the parsley before serving and serve with the lettuce leaves which will have cooked down.

PARSNIPS IN SOUR CREAM

4-6 servings

2 pounds parsnips, peeled and
    cut into 1-inch cubes
boiling salted water
salt
freshly ground pepper

½ to 1 cup sour cream,
    depending on taste
¼ teaspoon ground mace or
    ground cardamom or ground
    ginger

Cook the parsnips in just enough boiling salted water to cover until tender but still firm. Drain and season with salt and pepper. Stir in the cream and the mace. Return to heat and heat through, but do not boil. Or mash the parsnips as you would potatoes and proceed as above.

PEA

Pisum sativum

The edible seed, grown in a pod, of a variety of herbaceous annuals, peas are probably the most popular of all vegetables. The chief varieties are the familiar green-shelled garden pea, which is eaten fresh or dried; the field pea, which has small colored seeds and is used for making split peas and meal; and the sugar pea, also known as snow pea, which has soft, edible pods eaten whole.

Peas are a very ancient vegetable, since seeds of primitive varieties have been found in the remains of the Bronze Age Lake Dwellers of Switzerland around 5000 BC. Peas have also been found in the ruins of Troy. However, these early peas were smaller than those we know today, and they were largely grown for dry seeds. Green peas, eaten fresh, are a later development.

In 17th-century France peas were considered a rare gift of the gods. The French also refined the pea into the most desirable kind we have today: the tiny, tender sweet *petit pois,* meaning small peas, which are as delicious raw as cooked. Peas have been known in America since the days of the earliest settlers who brought the dry seeds with them to make the pease pudding of the nursery rhyme and which had been a staple in the English diet (and that of Central Europe as well) for centuries. Jefferson was also fond of peas, which he grew at Monticello, where he competed with the neighboring farmers for the first crop. He won the competition—the prize was a dinner—so often that one year he wrote his daughter not to tell his neighbor that he had come out on top again.

Today, in the United States, 95 per cent of the pea crop, amounting to about ½ million tons, is canned or frozen. Admitted that peas are among the least objectionable canned or frozen vegetables, they do not remotely compare to freshly picked young green peas, one of nature's major miracles. Unfortunately, these peas are harder and harder to find, but personally, I prefer an even more mature fresh pea to the preserved varieties.

How to Buy

Available March through November. Unfortunately, tiny fresh peas are not commercially available. *Buy* fairly large, angular, bright green garden pea pods which are well filled and snap easily. *Avoid* light-colored, swollen pods which are overmature and contain tough seeds and also spotted, mildewed pods.

Allow ¾ to 1 pound fresh peas in shells for 1 serving.

1 pound fresh peas in shells—approximately 1 cup shelled peas.

How to Keep

Refrigerate unshelled peas. Use as soon as possible.

Raw, refrigerator shelf—2 to 4 days.

Cooked and covered, refrigerator shelf—2 to 3 days.

Nutritive Values

A fair source of vitamin A and minerals.

3½ ounces fresh, raw—84 calories.

3½ ounces cooked and drained—71 calories.

How to Use

Shell peas just before using. Discard any that are beginning to sprout; though not harmful they are not worth eating. If small and tender, use raw in salads. Cook covered in an inch of boiling water for about five minutes or until just tender; drain. Some people add a teaspoon of sugar to the cooking water for added sweetness. Season. If peas are for later use, drop them into a bowl of cold water, drain immediately and refrigerate, and serve with butter and any desired herb such as mint, tarragon, chives or basil.

BLACK-EYE PEA
Cowpea
Vigna sinensis

In spite of their appearance and name, black-eye peas are botanically closer to beans than to peas according to some botanists. They are the edible pods of an annual leguminous vine, which are marked with a black eye. Black-eye peas are thought to be natives of India, where they are an important staple. As in China, Africa and the Caribbean, black-eye peas are widely grown in our deep South, where they are simply known as peas. Cousins of the black-eye pea are the crowders (brown crowder, cream crowder), so called because the seeds are so crowded in the pods that their ends are flattened. Both black-eye peas and crowders are harvested when the pods begin to fade. They are then shelled and usually cooked with a piece of pork. Dried black-eye peas are treated and cooked like dried beans.

3½ ounces fresh raw—127 calories.
3½ ounces cooked and drained—108 calories.
3½ ounces dried, cooked—76 calories.

PIGEON PEA
Cajanus cajan

The edible seeds of a tropical legume probably originating in Africa, which reached Asia in prehistoric times. Pigeon peas are usually dark gray or yellow, the size of small garden peas, growing tightly crowded in hairy pealike pods. They are extensively grown in all tropical countries. In India, where they are known as "red gram," they are the most important food after chick peas, used to make a basic dish of *dhal*, or porridge. Pigeon peas are also a popular West Indian staple providing useful proteins in the diet of poor people. Frequently split into halves, dried pigeon peas are treated and cooked like dried beans. Recently fresh and also flash-frozen green pigeon peas have reached our Latin vegetable markets, though the latter unfortunately, are already thawed and soft. Their Spanish name is *gandula*.

3½ ounces fresh raw immature seeds—117 calories.
3½ ounces dried mature seeds—342 calories.

SNOW PEA

Edible Pod, Chinese Pea, Sugar Pea
Pisum sativum macrocarpon

A snow pea is a firm crisp flattened pod which tapers at both ends and which measures to about three inches long and about a half inch across. The color is very bright, almost translucent green, through which the tiny seeds are visible. The whole pod is eaten, which accounts for its French name of *mange-tout*, that is, eat-it-all.

Snow peas are an essential vegetable both in Chinese and French cooking. Justly so, for properly prepared, they are delicious. Though they are reaching American markets in increasing quantities, snow peas in season are always sold in Chinese and Oriental greengroceries and markets both fresh and frozen. Fresh snow peas should have both tips snipped off just before cooking time; if there is a string, remove it, too. Wash and drain, and preferably dry to insure crispness. If they are to be stored, seal the unwashed snow peas tightly in a plastic bag to keep in their natural moisture. They must be used as soon as possible. The best way of cooking snow peas is to stir-fry them for 2 minutes so that they will be tender but still very crisp. If they are to be added to other dishes, do so for just the final two to three minutes of cooking, again to keep them crisp. The smallest amount of overcooking robs snow peas of their delicious crisp texture. Frozen snow peas are not nearly as crisp as the fresh vegetable. When growing snow peas in one's own garden, pick the pods when they are about an inch and a half long; commercially grown ones unfortunately are larger.

Allow 1 pound for 3 servings.

3½ ounces raw—53 calories.

3½ ounces cooked and drained—43 calories.

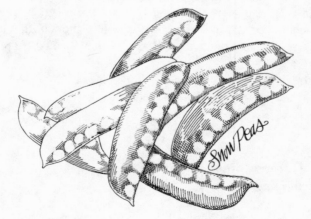

PEA SOUP

4 servings

This soup may be made with tough mature peas.

1 tablespoon butter
¼ cup minced bacon
1 small onion, minced
2 large tomatoes, peeled and
    chopped
3 pounds unshelled peas,
    shelled (about 3 cups)

salt
freshly ground pepper
5½ cups hot chicken
    consommé
toasted slices of French or
    Italian bread
grated Parmesan cheese

Combine the butter and the bacon in a deep saucepan. Cook, stirring constantly, for about 2 or 3 minutes or until the bacon is limp. Add the onion and cook 2 minutes longer. Add the tomatoes and the peas and season with salt and pepper. Cook, stirring occasionally, for about 3 minutes. Add the consommé. Simmer covered, stirring occasionally, until the peas are tender. Put a slice of toasted bread into each soup plate and sprinkle with the Parmesan. Ladle the soup over the bread.

FRENCH SNOW PEAS WITH HAM

4 servings

1½ pounds snow peas, ready
    for cooking
boiling salted water
1 tablespoon butter
½ cup minced smoked ham or
    Canadian bacon

salt
freshly ground pepper
2 tablespoons minced parsley

Cook the snow peas in boiling salted water to cover for 2 minutes. Drain and rinse quickly under running cold water. Drain. Heat the butter in a frying pan and add the ham. Cook, stirring constantly, for about 3 minutes. Add the snow peas and salt and pepper. Over high heat, and stirring constantly, cook for 2 more minutes. Sprinkle with the parsley and serve immediately.

PEA AND PROSCIUTTO SAUCE FOR PASTA

This sauce is excellent for green noodles and will dress 1 to 1½ pounds. The ham must be full-flavored; odds and ends of Virginia and country hams may also be used. Here I curb my antipathy to frozen vegetables.

2 tablespoons butter
2 tablespoons olive oil
⅓ cup minced onion
⅔ cup minced parsley
1 cup finely diced prosciutto
   ham, fat and lean parts
2 10-ounce packages frozen
   peas

¼ cup hot water or beef
   bouillon or tomato sauce
½ to ¾ cup heavy cream
salt
freshly ground pepper
grated Parmesan cheese

Heat the butter and the olive oil in a heavy saucepan. Add the onion and ⅓ cup of the parsley. Cook over low heat, stirring frequently, until the onion is soft. Add the ham and cook 5 minutes longer. Add the frozen peas and the hot water, beef bouillon or tomato sauce. Cook covered over low heat for about 10 minutes or until the peas are tender but not mushy. Stir in the heavy cream and season with salt and pepper. Simmer without a cover for 5 more minutes, or until the sauce is thoroughly heated through. Stir in the remaining parsley. Pour over freshly cooked *al dente* pasta and serve with freshly grated Parmesan cheese.

ITALIAN PEAS WITH EGGS

4 servings

¼ cup minced bacon or
   pancetta (see page 58)
1 small onion, minced
4 pounds unshelled peas,
   shelled (about 4 cups)
½ cup chicken consommé or
   water

salt
freshly ground pepper
¼ teaspoon ground sage
2 small eggs, beaten
½ cup freshly grated Parmesan

Cook the bacon in a heavy saucepan until it is limp and transparent. Add the onion and cook, stirring constantly, until the onion is soft and golden. Add the peas, the consommé, a little salt (the cheese is salty), pepper and sage. Cover tightly and cook over low heat for 10 minutes or until the peas are tender but not overcooked. Stir frequently. Beat the eggs with ⅓ cup of the Parmesan. Stir the eggs into the peas and remove from the heat. Keep warm but off the heat for 2 or 3 minutes. Sprinkle with the remaining Parmesan before serving.

SOUTHERN BLACK-EYE PEAS

6 servings

The dish should have a little sauce but not be soupy.

1 quart water
½ pound blanched salt pork,*
   cut into ½-inch pieces
1 pound dried black-eye peas,
   soaked and ready to cook
2 onions, chopped

¼ teaspoon hot pepper flakes or
   Tabasco or to taste
salt
freshly ground pepper
4 tablespoons butter

Pour the water into a large heavy saucepan. Add the pork and bring to the boiling point. Lower the heat and simmer covered for 30 to 45 minutes. Add the peas, onions and hot pepper flakes. Simmer covered over low heat for about 1 hour or until the peas are tender. Check for moisture. It may be necessary to add a little more hot water, 2 tablespoons at a time, or to cook without a cover to reduce the pan liquid. Add salt and pepper. Stir in the butter and cook for 5 more minutes.

*To blanch the bacon, cover with boiling water and let stand for 5 minutes. Drain.

PEAS WITH CREAM AND MINT

4 servings

The saffron or turmeric is not strictly necessary, but either has a nice flavor and color.

2 tablespoons butter
4 pounds unshelled peas,
   shelled (about 4 cups)
⅓ cup water
salt

2 sprigs fresh mint or 1
   teaspoon dried mint
⅛ teaspoon saffron or ground
   turmeric
½ cup heavy cream

Heat the butter in a heavy saucepan. Add the peas, water, salt (no pepper is needed) and mint. Simmer covered over low heat for about 10 minutes or until tender. If the peas look soupy, cook without a cover to allow the pan liquid to evaporate. Remove the mint from the cooked peas. While the peas are cooking, stir the saffron or turmeric into the cream. Whip just a little and fold into the cooked peas. Serve immediately.

PEAS AND LETTUCE

4-5 servings

2 tablespoons butter
6 green onions, white and green
   parts, thinly sliced
1 small head Boston or Bibb
   lettuce, shredded fine
4 pounds unshelled peas,
   shelled (about 4 cups)
4 tablespoons water or chicken
   consommé

salt
freshly ground pepper
⅛ teaspoon ground nutmeg
1 teaspoon dried thyme or 1
   sprig of fresh thyme
¼ cup minced parsley

Heat the butter in a heavy saucepan which has a tight cover. Add the green onions and the shredded lettuce. Stir to coat the greens with the butter. Add all the other ingredients except the parsley. Cover tightly and simmer over low heat for 5 to 10 minutes or until the peas are tender. Sprinkle with parsley before serving.

Variation: Sauté ½ pound thinly sliced mushrooms in 2 tablespoons butter for 3 or 4 minutes or until golden but still firm. Add to the cooked peas and heat through. Sprinkle with parsley before serving.

PEANUT
Groundnut, Monkeynut, Goober
Arachis hypogaea

The peanut is a legume, a pea rather than a nut, which ripens underground. It is native to South America, from where it traveled at an early time to the Old World tropics. It was introduced into the American colonies in the 17th century by the slave trade, but its cultivation did not become widespread in the Southern United States until the Civil War when the seeds were carried home by soldiers. Since peanut, like soy, agriculture enriches the soil rather than impoverishing it, it revolutionized the economy of our South which until then had been far too dependent on cotton. George Washington Carver (1864-1943), the distinguished Negro botanist, chemist and educator, pioneered peanut production, developing more than 300 products from peanuts including foods, dyes, plastics, soap, cosmetics and medicinal oils. Yet when Carver came to Tuskegee in 1896 the peanut had not even been recognized as a crop. Now it is a major crop in this country as it is in West Africa, India, and China; Nigeria, Senegal and Gambia depend on it to a very great extent.

Pound for pound, peanuts are more nutritious than meat and dairy products. Western cookery uses peanuts mostly as raw or roasted nut nibbles or in salads, baked goods, candies or as peanut butter or peanut oil. However, Far Eastern and West African cookery has several excellent dishes based upon peanuts which appeal to the Western palate.

3½ ounces, raw with skin—564 calories.

3½ ounces roasted with skin—582 calories.

3½ ounces roasted and salted—585 calories.

3½ ounces boiled—376 calories.

PEANUT SOUP

6-8 servings

Use real peanuts rather than peanut butter. It makes a difference in the flavor.

1 pound shelled dry-roasted peanuts
6 cups chicken or beef consommé
¼ cup grated onion
½ teaspoon dried pepper flakes or to taste or 1 teaspoon curry powder or to taste

1 tablespoon cornstarch
2 cups half and half or 1 cup light cream and 1 cup milk
salt
freshly ground pepper
2 tablespoons minced fresh parsley or mint

Grind the peanuts, a few at a time, in an electric blender. Do not overgrind or the peanuts will be a paste rather than a meal. Heat the consommé in a large saucepan. Stir in the onion, the ground peanuts and the pepper flakes. Bring to the boiling point and lower the heat. Simmer without a cover for about 30 minutes, stirring frequently. Return the soup to the blender and purée. Return the puréed soup to the saucepan and to low heat. In a bowl, stir the cornstarch into the half and half. Stir the mixture gradually into the soup. Cook, stirring constantly, until the soup is thickened. Season with salt and a little pepper. Cook for about 3 minutes longer. Sprinkle with parsley and serve very hot.

PEPPER
Sweet Pepper, Bell Pepper, Green Pepper, Globe Pepper
Capsicum fratescens grossum

The peppers under discussion are varieties of the sweet-fleshed mild garden pepper as contrasted to the hot and pungent garden pepper listed under Chile on page 134. Some peppers are long, tapered, and pointed, others short and wide or heart-shaped. However, most of the popular mild peppers are about four or five inches long and two to four inches across. They usually have three or four lobes and taper only slightly towards the blossom end. Sweet peppers are green when mature, but they turn red as they go on ripening. Both green and red peppers are found in our markets. The general preference is for green peppers, but Italians and other Mediterranean people go for the red ones, as well as for a large, yellow variety found in their stores. Sweet peppers are used as cooked or salad vegetables, for pickling in brine or chopped as a flavoring ingredient.

Garden peppers, both sweet and hot, are in no way related to *Piper nigrum* of the Piperaceae, the family which gives us both black and white peppercorns which either whole, crushed or ground serve us as an indispensable condiment.

The fact that *Capsicum,* the garden pepper, bears the same name as *Piper nigrum,* the condiment pepper, is said to be based on a misunderstanding on the part of Columbus and his men. They brought home the fierce chile peppers grown and used by the Indians and the West Indians and assumed these were a more pungent variety of the black pepper traded from the Oriental countries that grew it.

How to Buy

Available all year, peak season May through October. The majority of sweet garden peppers are sold green, but red and occasionally yellow peppers appear in the markets, especially Italian ones. The standard, chunky, fleshy bell-shaped peppers are the most common, but there are also less commonly found longer, more tapering light green or yellowish varieties liked by people of Latin descent. *Buy* firm, well-shaped, thick-fleshed sweet peppers with glossy sheen on their dark bright green color. *Avoid* shriveled, bruised, flabby sweet peppers and those with cuts or punctures and peppers with soft, watery spots on the walls.

Allow 1 medium or ½ large sweet pepper for each serving.

How to Keep

Refrigerate, unwashed, in the vegetable drawer.
Raw, refrigerator drawer—1 week.
Cooked and covered, refrigerator shelf—1 to 2 days.

Nutritive Values

Green sweet peppers are a moderately good source of vitamin A and C and a poor source of minerals. Mature red peppers are a good source of vitamin A and a fair source of vitamin C.

3½ ounces raw green sweet peppers—22 calories.
3½ ounces cooked green sweet peppers—18 calories.
3½ ounces mature red sweet peppers—31 calories.

How to Use

Cut sweet peppers into halves. Trim off pith, seeds and membranes. Rinse under running cold water. Then cut into slices, strips or chop or grind them. For pepper shells for stuffed peppers, slice off the top, remove pith and seeds and rinse. Or cut peppers in half cross or lengthwise and remove pith and seeds. If peppers are to be stuffed and baked, have ready a large saucepan of boiling water. Prepare pepper shells as above and drop into boiling water. Boil for a minute, remove with a slotted spoon or a fork taking care not to pierce the shell, and turn upside down on a plate to drain.

In Italy, and in French Provençal cooking, where sweet peppers play an important part as a vegetable, they are prepared somewhat differently: they are peeled before being put in a salad or cooked further. This is an enormous improvement because the outer skin is bitter, whereas the flesh is sweet. Peppers may be peeled in two ways. Place the peppers directly over the burners of a gas or electric stove and turn on high heat. Roast the peppers, turning them frequently, until the whole outer skin is black and blistered. This will take 5 to 10 minutes. Do not forget to blister the crevices. Pick up peppers with a pot holder and put them in the sink. Under running cold water (so as not to burn your fingers with the very hot peppers), peel and slip off the blistered skin. Cut peppers open and wash off seeds and membrane. Dry on paper towels and then cut according to recipe direction. This is not at all as complicated as it sounds, and the smell of the roasting peppers is lovely. Or place peppers on a baking sheet. Bake in a hot oven (400° F), turning frequently, until blistered on all sides. Proceed as above. I find this method takes longer.

Though sweet peppers should have mild seeds, occasionally a hot one sneaks in. This is why it is advisable to rinse off all the seeds.

PAPRIKA
Capsicum frutescens

Paprika is a Hungarian word, which, when used by Hungarians and Americans alike, means the condiment produced in Hungary from certain mild or pungent *Capsicum* varieties which are dried and ground into a powder. Paprika also means a garden pepper, distinguished by Hungarians from the condiment by calling it a "green paprika" or, as the case may be, a "tomato paprika" to be used as a fresh, cooked or marinated vegetable. Both are cornerstones of Hungarian cooking.

Throughout the Balkans, paprika is also the name for garden peppers as well as the condiment. I shall never forget the lovely vegetable markets of Southern Yugoslavia, with their infinity of green, red, purple, but mainly yellow, peppers ready to be preserved for winter use as one of the nation's most important vegetables; throughout the year, few meals are without their paprikas.

PIMIENTO
Capsicum frutescens

Pimiento or pimenta is the Spanish word for a variety of mild, sweet garden peppers. However, in the United States, pimiento means only the thick-fleshed, bright red variety we buy in small jars preserved in water or in a light brine. Pimiento is also used to stuff olives, to flavor cheese and to add the single touch of color and beauty to many an otherwise colorless dish.

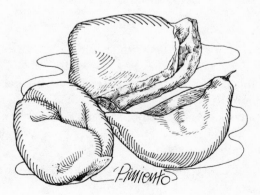

SWEET PEPPER ANTIPASTO OR SALAD

4 servings

This is one of the simplest and best ways with peppers, but it is essential that the peppers for this dish be peeled.

4 large sweet peppers, peeled	8 anchovies
6 tablespoons olive oil	12 capers
salt	parsley sprigs
freshly ground pepper	8 thin tomato wedges

Seed the peppers and remove the membranes. Cut each into 4 pieces. If the peppers were somewhat torn during the peeling, trim them to make even pieces. Turn the pepper pieces into a flat serving dish. Sprinkle with the oil and a little salt (the anchovies will be salty) and pepper. Marinate at room temperature for about 1 hour; then chill. At serving time, lay 4 pepper pieces neatly on an individual salad plate. Top with the anchovies, arranged crosswise. Put 3 capers where the anchovies cross. Decorate with a few parsley sprigs and 2 tomato wedges. Repeat to make 4 servings.

PEPPER SALAD

Cut the peeled, seeded and trimmed peppers into ½-inch strips. Place in a flat serving dish and sprinkle with the oil and the salt and pepper. Marinate for 1 hour at room temperature; then chill. Serve as is.

PEPPER AND POTATO FRITTATA

4 servings

Obviously you can make this frittata without potatoes.

¼ cup olive oil	2 medium potatoes, cooked, peeled and thinly sliced
2 large green or red sweet peppers, unpeeled or peeled, seeded and cut into strips	2 tablespoons water
	8 large eggs, slightly beaten
1 medium onion, sliced very thin	salt
	freshly ground pepper

Heat the olive oil in a large frying pan. Add the peppers. Cook over medium heat, stirring constantly, for 3 or 4 minutes or until the peppers are soft. (Unpeeled peppers will take longer to soften.) Add the onion and the potatoes and mix with a fork. Cook for 5 more minutes or until the onion is soft. Beat the water into the eggs and season with salt and pepper. Pour the eggs over the vegetables and lower the heat. Cook over low heat until the bottom of the frittata is set. Shake the frying pan to prevent sticking. With the fork, pull the eggs that are still liquid over to the side of the pan, lifting the edges of the frittata to allow the eggs to set. When the bottom of the frittata is firm and golden brown put a plate the size of the frying pan over the omelet and slip it out, cooked side up. Slip it back into the frying pan, cooked side up, to let the bottom firm and cook to golden brown, 2 or 3 minutes. Return to the plate and serve hot or lukewarm.

PEPERONI AL FORNO

4-6 servings

4 very large green, red or
    yellow sweet peppers, peeled
    and seeded
2 large ripe tomatoes, peeled
½ cup black olives, pitted and
    coarsely chopped
1 large onion, thinly sliced
2 garlic cloves, chopped
4 anchovies, drained and
    chopped (optional)

salt
freshly ground pepper
1 cup parsley sprigs
½ cup fresh basil leaves
    minced or 2 tablespoons
    dried basil
¼ to ½ cup olive oil
½ cup fine dry bread crumbs

Cut the peppers into wide strips. Cut the tomatoes into wedges the size of the pepper strips. Put the pepper strips, tomatoes, olives, onion, garlic and anchovies into a baking dish. Season lightly with salt (the anchovies are salty) and pepper. Mince together the parsley and the basil and sprinkle the mixture over the vegetables. Then sprinkle them with the olive oil and the bread crumbs. Cook in a preheated moderate oven (350° F) for about 30 minutes. Serve either warm or cold (not chilled) as an appetizer or with plain grilled or roasted meats.

PEPPER SAUCE FOR PASTA

This sauce is best for small pasta, such as mostaccioli, elbow or any of the fancy shell pastas. It should be very well seasoned and on the hot side.

4 large sweet peppers (about 1½ pounds) preferably red, green and yellow, peeled
⅓ cup olive oil
1 large onion, very thinly sliced
3 cups peeled chopped tomatoes (about 2 pounds)
⅔ cup minced fresh basil leaves or 2 or 3 tablespoons dried basil

½ hot red pepper, seeded and minced, or to taste
salt
freshly ground pepper
1 or 2 tablespoons drained capers
1 pound freshly cooked pasta
freshly grated Parmesan cheese

Seed the peppers, remove the membranes and cut them into strips. Heat the olive oil in a deep frying pan. Add the onion and cook until it is soft and golden. Add the peppers. Cook over high heat, stirring constantly, for about 5 minutes. Add the tomatoes, basil, and hot pepper and season with salt and pepper. Reduce the heat to medium and cover the frying pan. Cook, stirring frequently, for about 10 minutes. Stir the capers into the cooked sauce. Cook the pasta while the sauce is cooking, drain it and put it into a heated deep serving dish. Pour the sauce over the pasta and toss. Serve with plenty of freshly grated Parmesan cheese.

PLANTAIN
Musa paradisiaca

First cousin to the dessert banana (see page 46), plantains are vegetables because they must be cooked to be edible. Like bananas, plantains are important food plants because of their high starchy contents; they are an essential part of the diet of the people of Central America, the West Indies, South America, Africa, the tropical Far East and the tropics in general. Plantains are the "potatoes" of the tropics. More than 70 varieties are known but generally speaking, plantains are much larger than bananas, weighing as much as two and more pounds and reaching two to three inches in diameter. They are sold singly rather than in bunches and in a very dark green stage of unripeness. Like bananas, they ripen rapidly in warm surroundings, turning first yellow with brown markings and then a dirty, moldy black. At each stage of skin color they are edible though they will taste different. They are a worthily nutritious rather than an interesting vegetable.

How to Buy

Available the year round in all markets that cater to people of West Indian, Spanish and South American origin.

Buy them green, free of blemishes. *Avoid* spotted, bruised, blackish fruit.

How to Keep

See bananas, page 47.

Nutritive Values

Low in protein and fat, high in carbohydrate and a fair source of vitamins A and B.

3½ ounces raw—119 calories.

How to Use

Plantains can be boiled, baked, fried or added to other ingredients in a dish. Since they are bland and starchy in flavor, they benefit from generous seasoning with lime or lemon juice or hot pepper sauce.

POTATO
Solanum tuberosum

The potato is a perennial herb belonging to the huge Solanaceae or nightshade family, which includes tomatoes and eggplant. The plant has fibrous roots with many underground rhizomes or stems which swell at the tip and become the edible tuber we know as potato, the world's most important single vegetable. The potato plant is handsome with its pretty white to purplish flowers and decorative foliage. It is a cool weather crop, but it does not stand much frost. Potatoes are not propagated by true seeds, but by planting pieces of tubers bearing two or three eyes. With its high carbohydrate content, potatoes also serve as a source of starch, dextrin, alcohol and fodder.

Considering the importance, and the universal appeal of the potato, it seems odd that it is a relatively recent addition to our tables. Different varieties were cultivated centuries before the Spanish Conquest as a leading food crop in the Andean highlands since potatoes can grow at higher altitudes than corn. The highlanders of Peru had even discovered how to preserve potatoes by freezing and drying them. The harvested potatoes were spread on the ground and left overnight to freeze in the biting cold of those high regions. Next, the local population turned out to trample on the potatoes in order to extract their moisture. The process was repeated several times, after which the potatoes, now relieved of much of their water content, were dried in the sun, stored and eaten like bread. These dried potatoes were known as *chuña* and were essential in the diet of the highland people.

Very likely Spanish sailors took the potato with them to Europe around the middle of the 16th century, calling them *batate* from the Indian name *pappas*. And in Europe, it was the Irish who first made great use of the potato as a crop. Unfortunately, they relied almost exclusively on it to feed them. The great potato blight of 1845-46, due to a fungus that attacks potatoes even to this day, brought a dreadful famine as the tubers rotted in the fields. About two-and-one-half million people died from starvation and from the epidemics, such as typhus, that followed.

France was slow in adopting the potato which had been decried as poisonous by doctors and the cause of many illnesses. The acceptance was largely due to Auguste Parmentier, a military pharmacist, who had been a prisoner in Germany during the Seven Years' War, where he had learned to like the potatoes he had to eat. When he returned to France he planted potatoes on a sandy, neglected field where they flourished. He thought of the ruse of having the potato field guarded by fully uniformed armed soldiers during the day only so that people could come and steal the potatoes at night, which they did.

Parmentier had lost his job trying to introduce potatoes into the diet of Army pensioners, but he was determined to make the French realize the importance of the potato. He gave a dinner party for illustrious men, including Ben Franklin, where potatoes, and nothing but potatoes, served twenty different ways made up the menu. The high point of his efforts came, however, on August 25, 1785, when he presented Louis XVI with a bouquet of potato flowers. The next day nobles were fighting for the privilege of wearing the blossoms in their buttonholes.

Today French cuisine glorifies the potato. And Parmentier's countrymen have rewarded him with planting potato blossoms on his grave and giving his name to a soup.

Americans welcomed the vegetable slowly until the middle of the 19th century, when it became very popular. Part of the reason for potatoes' slow acceptance was that until the middle of the century they were usually quite poor in quality. But as they improved, the potato lovers grew firm in their conviction that this was a delicious food. One enthusiast, Eric Janson, a Swedish religious reformer of Illinois in the latter 19th century, was a proponent of strict asceticism. He told his followers that they must drink no liquor and eat a very meager diet. The story is that he was so overcome with love for the potato that he was discovered by a follower secretly eating a casserole of scalloped potatoes.

There are all sorts of superstitions connected with potatoes. The southern Italians and Sicilians used to think the potato evil; they wrote the names of their enemies on a piece of paper, fastened it to a potato, and their victim, hopefully, would die and be laid under the ground.

The potato has the power to do good, however. Toothache, rheumatism, and warts have all been cured by potatoes. These are not all old wives' tales. I know from experience that sliced raw potatoes make very soothing plasters for burns when the skin is still intact.

There are four major potato varieties available in the United States. The long russet Burbank, known as the Idaho potato whether it is grown in Idaho or not, with fairly thick skin and numerous eyes, has a high starch content and is especially suited to baking and to French fries. The roundish, smooth-skined Katahdin is a dark creamy buff and low in starch. The white rose, familiar to us as California long white, is long, eliptical and somewhat flattened in shape with a very thin, sleek fawn-colored skin and barely visible eyes which makes it easy to peel; it is also low in starch and keeps its shape in boiling and pan frying. The red Pontiac has large round to oblong tubers and smooth dark red skin which is occasionally artificially colored. As for distinguishing other potato varieties, even experts have trouble picking them out from a mixed pile.

The cooking quality of the potato depends on its starch content. Starchy potatoes become loose and mealy when boiled or baked; they are excellent for mashing and for French fries. Potatoes low in starch are dry when baked; boiled they lend themselves to pan-fried and scalloped dishes and salads where they keep their shape rather than becoming a soggy mess. Old potatoes (dug mature and stored) are higher in starch than new ones, which are potatoes dug before they reach maturity and shipped immediately after being dug. They are worth every penny of the extra money they cost. Even more delicious are the tiny, marble-sized potatoes called culls found occasionally at roadside stands.

How to Buy

Available the year round since potatoes are stored for nine to twelve months. Peak supply of new potatoes March to August. For general purpose and baking potatoes, *buy* firm potatoes that are well-shaped whatever their size, firm, clean and relatively smooth. *Avoid* bruised, blemished or shriveled potatoes, cut or skinned or frostbitten potatoes, potatoes with signs of decay and potatoes that have sprouted; the sprouts are toxic. For new potatoes, *buy* well-shaped, firm and clean potatoes with a thin, feathery white or red skin that breaks easily. *Avoid* new potatoes with any discolored or skinned areas. In all potatoes, *avoid* cracked potatoes which are hard and wasteful to peel and those with a green color. The greening of a potato is due to exposure to light. The green areas contain solanin, a glycol alkaloid, which, eaten in quantity, is toxic. However, it does not affect the rest of the potato since it is only found in the green parts. Simply scrape and cut away any green (and bitter) areas or spots and treat the potato in the usual manner.

Allow 1 baking potato for each serving.

Allow 2 to 4 new potatoes depending on size for each serving.

1 pound—3 medium-sized potatoes.

1 pound raw, sliced or diced—approximately 3⅓ to 4 cups raw.

1 pound—approximately 2¼ cups cooked or 1¾ cups mashed.

How to Keep

Store in a cool, dry, well-ventilated area away from hot pipes or from places where potatoes can freeze. Keep in dark since light may cause potatoes to green. Do not refrigerate since low temperatures convert potato starch to sugar.

Raw, baking and general use potatoes, in cool, dry, dark area—2 to 3 months.

Raw, new potatoes, cool, dry, dark area—2 weeks.

Potatoes stored at room temperature should be used within a week.

Cooked, covered, refrigerator shelf—3 days.

How to Use

Scrub and wash potatoes. Whenever possible, cook with the skin since a good deal of nutrition is found on and near the skin. If the potato is to be peeled, keep the parings thin. When cooked, peeled potatoes are whiter than those cooked in their jackets. Or cut peeled potatoes into slices, julienne sticks, dice or other shapes. Wash again and drain. If the peeled potatoes are not cooked immediately after peeling keep them in cold water to cover to prevent darkening. If you wish to remove some of the potato starch, soak potatoes in cold water for 1 hour or more; drain and dry or use as directed. This also soaks out some of the nutrients, of course. To boil cook new scrubbed potatoes or older potatoes, peeled and cut into quarters, in boiling salted water to cover until just tender. Check for scorching; if necessary add a little more boiling water. Cooking time depends on the size of the potato pieces. Drain and use any water for soups or stews. Return potatoes to saucepan and shake over low heat until dry.

Season with salt and pepper and serve with butter.

To bake, scrub and wash the skin and dry with paper towels. To keep skins soft rub with a little shortening. Pierce the skin to allow steam to escape while the potato bakes. Place on the oven rack or on a cookie sheet or pie pan. Bake in a preheated hot oven (450° F) for about 40 minutes or until tender, that is, when potatoes feel soft when pressed. Cut an inch cross in the center top of each potato. Hold potato with clean towel and press at the bottom until the potato bursts out at the top. Place a square of butter on the potato top and serve. Potatoes can be baked at any temperature; naturally, at lower temperatures the baking time will be longer. If potatoes bake along with a roast at moderate heat (350° F) they will take about an hour and a half (depending on size) or longer.

To pan roast along with meat, cut peeled large potatoes into halves lengthwise or use whole, small new potatoes, peeled or scraped. Wash and dry. About an hour before the roast is done, roll the potatoes in the pan in the dripping from the roast. Place cut side down along the roast. Turn the potatoes several times to ensure even roasting. Baste frequently with the pan drippings to keep the potatoes soft and moist.

For mashed potatoes, peel potatoes, cut them into even-sized pieces, wash and drain. Cook covered in boiling salted water to cover until tender. Check for scorching; if necessary add a little more boiling water. Drain, reserve water. Shake dry over medium heat to make potatoes mealy. Mash with a fork or potato masher, or put through a ricer or a food mill. Do not use the blender or potatoes will acquire a plastic consistency. Return to saucepan. For each pound of potatoes, add at least 2 tablespoons butter, ½ teaspoon salt, pepper to taste and about 3 tablespoons *hot* milk, light cream or potato water. Over low heat, beat the potatoes until they are fluffy. Serve immediately.

Potatoes vary in consistency and in their ability to absorb fats and liquids. It is therefore impossible to say exactly how much butter or liquid should be beaten in. In case of doubt, start with smaller quantities than those listed above. It is essential that the liquid be *hot* to keep potatoes fluffy. The quantity varies depending on whether stiffer of fluffier potatoes are wanted.

Mashed potatoes should be served at once. They must not be left standing at room temperature since they will spoil and make you ill. If they must be kept for a short time, place the pan in a larger pan of hot water and keep warm. Or else, place the mashed potatoes in a buttered casserole that can go to the table, dot with additional butter or sprinkle with cream. Keep warm in a low oven (275° F) and serve soon.

POTATO SOUP WITH CUCUMBERS

4-6 servings

2 large cucumbers
8 medium potatoes (about 2 pounds), peeled and cut into ½-inch dice
4 cups chicken bouillon or water
salt

freshly ground pepper
1½ cups milk
1 cup heavy cream
1 tablespoon grated onion
2 tablespoons minced fresh dillweed or more to taste

Peel the cucumbers and trim off ends. Cut them first into halves lengthwise, then cut again lengthwise. Scoop out the seeds with a spoon. Cut the cucumbers into ½-inch dice and reserve. Put the potatoes and the chicken bouillon into a large heavy saucepan. Bring to the boiling point. Reduce heat to low and season with salt and pepper. Cook until the potatoes are soft and easy to mash. Drain the potatoes through a sieve or a food mill into a large bowl. With a large spoon, force the potatoes through the sieve or food mill to purée them. Do not use a blender: the mixture will be too slick. Return the potatoes and their cooking liquid to the saucepan. Bring to the boiling point and reduce heat to low. Stir in milk, cream and grated onion. Add the cucumber. Simmer without a cover for about 5 minutes or until the cucumbers are tender but not mushy. Check the seasoning and stir in the dillweed.

QUICK POTATO SOUP

4 servings

2 cups peeled potatoes, cut into
    ¼-inch cubes
2 medium onions, thinly sliced
2 tablespoons butter
6 cups hot water or chicken or
    beef consommé

salt
freshly ground pepper
2 or 3 slices fried crisp bacon,
    crumbled (optional)
2 tablespoons minced parsley or
    chives or dillweed

Combine the potatoes, onions and butter in a casserole. Cook covered over lowest possible heat for about 4 minutes or until the potatoes are almost cooked. Stir frequently. If necessary, add 1 or 2 tablespoons of hot water or consommé to prevent scorching. Add the rest of the hot water or bouillon. Season with salt and pepper. Simmer covered for 5 to 10 minutes or until the potatoes are cooked. Sprinkle with bacon and parsley. For a richer soup, purée in a blender, return to saucepan and add ¼ cup heavy cream. Heat through and sprinkle with bacon and parsley.

POTATOES CREAMED IN A DOUBLE BOILER

4 servings

4 large potatoes, peeled and cut
    into ½-inch cubes
1 or 2 tablespoons grated onion
salt
freshly ground pepper

⅛ teaspoon ground nutmeg
    (optional)
1 cup heavy cream
paprika

Soak the potatoes in a bowl of cold water for 30 minutes. Drain and dry between paper towels. Place the potatoes and the remaining ingredients except paprika into the top of a double boiler. Cook covered over boiling water for about 45 minutes or until the potatoes are tender and the sauce thick. Check the boiling water; it may have to be replenished. Check for moisture. Potatoes absorb liquids differently and it may be necessary to add a little more cream or hot water, 2 tablespoons at a time, to get the desired consistency. Sprinkle with paprika before serving.

SUGAR-BROWNED POTATOES

4 servings

This is a favorite Danish way of cooking potatoes.

12 small new potatoes	2 or 3 tablespoons sugar
2 tablespoons butter	1 teaspoon salt

Cook the potatoes in boiling salted water until just tender. Drain and peel. Heat the butter in a frying pan. Stir in sugar and the salt. Cook over low heat, stirring constantly, until the sugar is melted and has turned golden brown. Do not scorch. Add the potatoes. Cook over lowest possible heat until the potatoes are browned on all sides. Stir with a fork or shake the pan frequently to avoid sticking.

LEMON POTATOES

4-6 servings

These are utterly delicious. I prefer olive oil to butter on my boiled potatoes. Adjust the proportions of olive oil and lemon juice to your liking. The dressing is also suited to cooked seafood, chicken and cooked vegetables.

2 pounds small new potatoes or 2 pounds potatoes	grated rind of ½ lemon
boiling salted water	salt
4 tablespoons olive oil	freshly ground pepper
2 tablespoons fresh lemon juice	1 teaspoon dried oregano (optional)

If the potatoes are small and new, scrub but do not peel them. Or peel the potatoes and cut them into 2-inch pieces. Cook the potatoes in plenty of boiling salted water until barely tender. They must not overcook or they will be watery. Drain and return to the saucepan. Over moderate heat, shake the saucepan with the potatoes to dry them out completely. Put into a heated serving dish and keep warm. While the potatoes are cooking, combine the remaining ingredients and beat until creamy. Pour over the potatoes, toss with two forks and serve warm, lukewarm or chilled.

HUNGARIAN PAPRIKA POTATOES

4-6 servings

Serve with pork or sausages.

3 tablespoons butter
1 medium onion, thinly sliced
2 pounds potatoes, peeled and
    cut into 1½-inch cubes
¾ cup water or beef or chicken
    consommé
salt
2 tablespoons sweet or hot
    paprika

freshly ground pepper
2 bay leaves
1 tablespoon cider vinegar or to
    taste
⅓ cup sour cream
2 tablespoons minced parsley

Heat the butter in a heavy casserole. Cook the onion until soft. Add the potatoes, water, a little salt, the paprika and a little pepper and the bay leaves. Simmer covered over moderate heat for about 10 minutes or until the potatoes are tender but firm. Shake the pan frequently to prevent sticking, and if necessary, add a little more water, 1 tablespoon at a time. Stir in the vinegar to taste. Cook for 1 or 2 more minutes. Remove the bay leaves. Stir in the sour cream and heat through, but do not boil. Sprinkle with parsley and serve very hot.

BRAISED LAUREL POTATOES

4-5 servings

1½ to 2 pounds potatoes,
    peeled and washed
2 tablespoons butter
2 tablespoons olive oil
1 garlic clove, minced
⅓ cup minced parsley

2 or 3 bay leaves, finely
    crumbled
⅔ cup chicken consommé
salt
freshly ground pepper

Cut the potatoes into ¼- or ½-inch dice. Wash, drain and dry thoroughly on paper towels. Heat the butter and oil in a heavy saucepan. Add the potatoes. Cook over medium heat, stirring constantly, for about 3 minutes. Add the garlic, parsley, bay leaves and consommé. Taste and season with salt and pepper; the consommé may be salty. Cover tightly and simmer over low heat for 5 to 8 minutes or until the potatoes are tender and moist but not soupy. Stir frequently.

Note: Different kinds of potatoes absorb liquid differently. You may need more consommé; add it 2 tablespoons at a time.

SWISS FRIED POTATO CAKE *(Roesti)*

4 servings

A famous Swiss recipe and a change from home-fried potatoes. Since the potatoes should be thoroughly cooled and firm, they should be cooked well ahead of time; a day ahead is best.

2 pounds potatoes
4 to 6 tablespoons butter
salt

freshly ground pepper
2 to 4 tablespoons hot water

Cook the potatoes in their skins in boiling salted water and cool thoroughly at room temperature. Peel and shred on a shredder or cut into small julienne strips. Heat 4 tablespoons of the butter in a heavy frying pan. Add the potatoes. Season with salt and pepper. Cook over low heat, turning frequently to coat the potatoes with the butter, until they are soft and yellow. Add the remaining butter to the frying pan. Press the potatoes with the spatula into a flat cake. Sprinkle with 2 tablespoons of the water. Cover and cook over low heat for about 15 to 20 minutes or until the potatoes are golden and crusty at the bottom. Shake the pan frequently to prevent sticking. Check for moisture; if the potatoes look very dry, sprinkle with the remaining water. Turn into a heated serving dish crusty side up and serve immediately.

Variation: Add ½ cup diced Swiss cheese to the potatoes before cooking and mix well.

HEAVEN AND EARTH

4-6 servings

A German specialty from the Rhineland, excellent with all pork dishes and with duck.

4 large potatoes, peeled and cut into pieces
3 tart apples, peeled, cored and cut into quarters or eighths
salt

sugar to taste
⅛ teaspoon ground nutmeg
4 tablespoons butter, at room temperature

Cook the potatoes in water to cover for about 10 minutes or until they are about three-quarters soft. Drain off about half of the water. Add the apples, mix and cook until the apples are tender. Mash or rice the mixture and season with salt and sugar to taste. Stir in the nutmeg and the butter and beat until light.

GERMAN POTATO SALAD

4 servings

2 pounds potatoes (preferably California long white)
¼ cup bacon fat, melted
2 tablespoons cider vinegar
1 cup beef consommé
1 medium onion, minced

salt
freshly ground pepper
⅓ cup minced parsley or ¼ cup minced dillweed
2 or 3 red radishes, sliced

Cook the potatoes in boiling, heavily salted water until tender. (The salted water keeps them firm.) Drain. Cool the potatoes only until it is just possible to handle them. Peel and cut into slices. Place in a shallow bowl and sprinkle with the bacon fat and the vinegar. Add the beef stock and the onion. Season with salt and pepper. Toss gently with 2 forks, coating every potato slice with the dressing. Cover and let stand at room temperature for 2 hours. Do not chill. At serving time, sprinkle with the parsley and decorate with the radish slices.

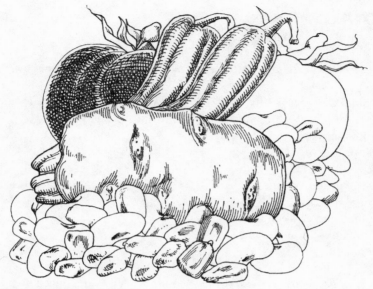

POTATO SOUFFLÉ

4 servings

Serve with cold meats and a tossed green salad.

2 cups fresh hot mashed
   potatoes
½ cup hot light cream or milk
½ cup grated Swiss or
   Parmesan cheese
2 or 3 tablespoons butter, at
   room temperature

3 tablespoons minced parsley
4 eggs, separated
salt
freshly ground pepper

While the mashed potatoes are still hot, beat in the cream, grated cheese, butter and parsley. Beat the egg yolks until thick. Beat the egg whites until stiff. Mix the beaten egg yolks into the potato mixture. Check the seasoning since the cheese is salty; add salt and pepper to taste. Fold in the beaten egg whites. Pile lightly into a generously buttered 1½-quart baking dish. Bake in a preheated hot oven (400° F) for about 15 minutes or until puffed and golden. Serve immediately.

POTATO PIZZA

4-6 servings

A savory, substantial dish. Serve as is or with plain meats.

1 pound potatoes,
approximately, to make 2
cups mashed
¾ cup flour
salt
freshly ground pepper
½ cup olive oil
1 cup canned Italian plum
tomatoes, drained and
chopped

8 ounces mozzarella cheese, cut
into ¼-inch cubes
⅓ cup freshly grated Parmesan
cheese
1 or 2 tablespoons dried
rosemary, crumbled fine

Peel, wash, cook and drain the potatoes. Rice and mash them to a
smooth purée. Beat in the flour, a little salt and pepper and 2 or 3
tablespoons of the olive oil. Work the mixture to a smooth, spread-
able dough. Pat the dough to the thickness of ½ inch into a well oiled
deep 9-inch pie plate. Pat it up to the sides as you would a brittle pie
dough and make no holes or the filling will ooze out during baking.
Sprinkle half of the remaining oil over the potato shell. Top, in this
order, with the tomatoes, the mozzarella and the Parmesan cheese.
Sprinkle with the rosemary and drizzle with the remaining olive oil.
Bake in a preheated hot oven (350° F) for 20 minutes or until the
cheese has melted. Serve hot.

POTHERB

An old fashioned expression for any edible greens whose fleshy leaves and stems are boiled and eaten or used to flavor other foods. All cultures, primitive or advanced, use wild or cultivated greens for their pots. In the United States, the word includes such diverse vegetables as dandelions, beet tops and any wild green that is suited for the pot.

POTHERB SOUP CHEZ MOI

4-6 servings

Use any greens, alone or in combination, such as lettuce, dandelions, kale, beet tops, etc.

4 large potatoes, peeled and
    washed, diced small
8 cups boiling water
2 pounds potherbs, cut into
    very fine strips

4 tablespoons olive oil
½ teaspoon hot pepper flakes or
    to taste (optional)
salt
freshly ground pepper

Cook the potatoes in the boiling water until barely tender. Add the potherbs. Bring to the boiling point and stir in the olive oil, hot pepper flakes and salt and pepper. Lower heat to medium and cook for 3 minutes, stirring frequently. The vegetables should be still crisp. Serve very hot.

For a more substantial soup, add ½ to 1 pound sweet or hot Italian or Polish sausage, thoroughly cooked and thinly sliced, at the same time as the potherbs.

POTHERB PIE

6 servings

Pies of leafy green vegetables turn up in one form or another in the cooking of most countries, especially Southern ones. Basically, they are the food of poor country people, containing what is at hand in the way of greens, rice, eggs, milk, cheese or nuts. Sometimes, they are encased in pastry shells, other times just baked; I prefer this latter version. The cook can combine any greens she wants, provided they are leafy greens. The combination of greens below comes from Lombardy, but it was I who added the dandelion greens; arugala would also have been a nice touch. One word of caution: There is a certain amount of waste in leafy greens, such as wilted leaves, tough stems, etc. To come out with the wanted amount of trimmed greens, buy ½ to 1 pound more, depending on their condition. The amount below makes about 3 cups cooked greens which have been squeezed very dry and chopped. Like all greens, uncooked they will fill the kettle to overflowing but will cook down a great deal.

2 pounds Swiss chard, trimmed
2 pounds spinach, trimmed
1 pound dandelion greens, trimmed
4 tablespoons butter
3 tablespoons bacon fat
2 garlic cloves, minced
½ cup pignoli nuts
3 eggs, lightly beaten
1 cup light cream or milk

1 cup grated Parmesan cheese
½ teaspoon ground nutmeg
salt
freshly ground pepper
⅓ cup currants or seedless raisins, plumped in warm water and drained
butter
fine dry bread crumbs

Wash the greens in at least 3 changes of cold water, or until not a trace of sand or dirt remains in the water. Drain but do not shake dry. Put the greens into a large kettle with the water that clings to them. Cover the kettle. Cook over high heat for about 8 to 10 minutes or until tender. Do not overcook the greens or they will lose their flavor. Drain in a colander over a bowl; save the cooking liquid for soups, stews or sauces—it is full of vitamins. First with the back of a wooden spoon and then with the hands, squeeze as much water as possible out of the greens. Put them on a chopping board and chop medium fine. Drain the chopped greens again, squeezing with the hands. Put the greens into a large bowl. In a large, deep frying pan, heat 2 tablespoons of the butter and bacon fat. Cook over medium heat, stirring constantly, the garlic and pignoli nuts until the latter are golden. Add the chopped greens. Cook, stirring all the time, for about 7 to 10 minutes, or until the greens are thoroughly coated with the fat. Return the cooked greens to the bowl. Beat together the eggs, light cream, ⅔ cup of grated Parmesan and nutmeg. Taste (the cheese is salty) and season with salt and pepper. Stir in the currants. Pour this mixture over the greens and mix well. Butter a 10-inch shallow baking dish or pie plate and coat it with bread crumbs. Turn the vegetable mixture into it and smooth out the top. Sprinkle with the remaining Parmesan and dot with the 2 remaining tablespoons of the butter. Bake in a preheated moderate oven (350° F) for 10 minutes. Turn the oven to low (325° F) and bake for 20 to 30 more minutes or until set and browned. Cut into wedges and serve warm or cold but not chilled.

PUMPKIN
Cucurbita pepo

The pumpkin, also known as pie or field pumpkin, cousin to melons, cucumbers and squash, grows on a low, trailing vine. Technically, it is a berry which we use as a vegetable. The plant's flowers are large, handsome, creamy white to deep yellow and they are edible as well. Pumpkins are oblong to round in shape with a moderately thick ribbed orange skin. The flesh is soft, moist, somewhat coarse and fibrous and sweet in flavor; the color is largely bright orange though some varieties may be a pale to warm buff. Pumpkins are large fruit, measuring an average 10 to 18 by 10 to 14 and more inches, weighing 18 to 25 pounds. The name appears to come from the Greek *pepōn* or large melon via the French conversion, *popon* and *pompon* to *pumpion*.

Pumpkins are as traditionally American as the pie they are largely used for. Early settlers in Massachusetts and Virginia found the Indians boiling and baking pumpkins, making them into soups, drying them and grinding them into a meal for bread. The settlers adopted the pumpkin as their own; an early rhyme says: "For pottage and puddings, and custards and pies, Our pumpkins and parsnips are common supplies. We have pumpkin at morning and pumpkin at noon. If it were not for pumpkins, we should be undoon." The early pumpkin pies were quite different from ours. A slice from the pumpkin was cut out at the top, the seeds were removed and the cavity filled with milk, spices and natural sweeteners such as maple sugar and the whole was baked. Since then pumpkin has become an integral part of American life, from Halloween lanterns to the pie without which Thanksgiving would be incomplete.

Pumpkins also have the faculty of growing immensely large without much trouble on the part of their growers. There are records of specimens weighing 160 and more pounds. One is filled with awe at what nature can do if left unchecked.

How to Buy

Some pumpkins are available in different parts of the country throughout the year, but the main supply is from September through December, peak in October. About 80 per cent are marketed fresh from local sources, mainly roadside stands. Size and shape do not affect the flavor much, though smaller pumpkins have more tender flesh and less waste. *Buy* clean well matured pumpkins with firm rind and a rich orange color. They should be free from scarring, disease or freezing. *Avoid* broken or cracked pumpkins and any with signs of soft rot or wet breakdown.

3 pounds fresh pumpkin—approximately 3 cups cooked and mashed.

How to Keep

Store in a dry, well-ventilated place, or refrigerate.
  Whole raw, kitchen shelf—about 1 month.
  Whole, raw, refrigerator—1 to 3 months.
  Fresh, cooked, refrigerator shelf—3 to 4 days.

Nutritive Values

A good source of vitamin A and a fair source of minerals.
3½ ounces raw—26 calories.
3½ ounces canned—33 calories.

How to Use

To boil, cut the pumpkin into halves and scrape off pulp and seeds.
Cut into quarters and eighths. Place, cut side down, in a baking pan,
for about 10 minutes or until tender. Drain and mash or push through
a food mill. Season with salt and pepper and butter for use as a
vegetable, or use in pies or other desserts.

To bake, cut pumpkin into halves and scrape off pulp and seeds.
Cut into quarters and eighths. Place, cut side down, in a baking pan,
add half an inch of water and bake in a preheated moderate oven
(350° F) for 35 to 45 minutes or until tender. Turn right side up,
season the cavity with salt and pepper, a little scraped onion, brown
sugar or molasses and a pat of butter. Bake 5 to 10 minutes longer.
Or cut into serving pieces and place, cut side up, in a baking pan.
Sprinkle with salt and pepper and brush generously with melted butter or margarine. Bake in a preheated moderate oven (350° F) for 35
minutes or until tender. Brush with melted butter several times. Serve
as a vegetable.

FRENCH PUMPKIN SOUP

4-6 servings

1 quart milk
2 tablespoons butter
⅓ cup flour
2 cups cooked, mashed
  pumpkin

salt
freshly ground pepper
2 tablespoons minced parsley
½ teaspoon ground nutmeg

Heat the milk. Knead together the butter and the flour. Drop this
mixture in pea-sized pieces into the milk, beating well after each
addition. When the milk is thickened and smooth, stir in the pumpkin, salt, pepper, parsley and nutmeg. Cook, stirring constantly, until
the soup has thickened and is very hot. Serve immediately.

PUMPKIN AND TOMATO CASSEROLE

4 servings

The sauce of this dish can be used for other cooked vegetables such as chick peas or green or dried beans. Don't overcook the vegetables since they are already cooked; cook the sauce only briefly for a fuller flavor.

¼ cup olive oil
2 garlic cloves, peeled
1 large tomato, peeled and
   chopped, about 1½ cups
¼ cup minced fresh basil or 2
   tablespoons dried basil

salt
freshly ground pepper
dash Tabasco
3 cups peeled pumpkin cut into
   ½-inch cubes
boiling salted water

Heat the olive oil and add the garlic cloves. Cook over medium heat for 2 or 3 minutes or until the garlic is golden. Add the tomato, basil, salt and pepper and Tabasco. Cook, stirring constantly, for about 5 minutes. Lower heat and simmer for 5 more minutes. While the sauce is cooking, cook the pumpkin in boiling salted water to cover for 3 to 5 minutes or until barely tender. Drain and add to the tomato sauce. Cook over high heat, stirring constantly, for 2 or 3 minutes or until the vegetables are blended. Serve hot.

If the pumpkin is already cooked and cold, heat it in the tomato sauce for 5 minutes over medium heat.

BAKED WHOLE PUMPKIN OR SQUASH

This dish is particularly pretty when made with a many-colored squash like a Turk's turban. If the baked pumpkin or squash is to be filled with a stuffing and baked again, it should only be baked until half tender if the stuffing is uncooked and until three-quarters tender if the stuffing is cooked. Else the pumpkin or squash will be too soft.

There are two ways of baking a pumpkin or squash. The first is best for a large vegetable such as a pumpkin, the second more successful for a smaller one.

1. Cut across the top of the pumpkin, under the stem. Leave the stem on to use as a handle. Scoop out the seeds and the membranes. Replace the top. Place on a dry baking pan. Bake in a preheated moderate oven for about 1 to 1½ hours, or until the pumpkin feels soft; test it with your finger but wrap your finger first in a kitchen towel because the pumpkin is hot. The baking time depends on the size of the pumpkin and it can be longer. Cool. If the pulp is wanted, scoop it out without damaging the shell and mash.

2. Place the squash on a dry baking sheet. Bake in a preheated moderate oven (350° F) for about 1 hour or until the squash feels soft. Cool. Cut across the top of the squash, just under the stem. Scoop out the seeds and membranes.

PURSLANE
Pussle
Portulaca oleracea

Purslane is a wild or cultivated herb with fleshy, jointed, freely forking reddish- or purplish-green stems and very fleshy, narrow, wedge-shaped, reddish-green leaves about one-half to two inches in length. Purslane is used as a potherb and in salads. Its flavor is mildly acid and it has a somewhat mucilaginous quality which thickens dishes much the way okra does. The origin of the plant is not clear; it is said to have originated in India or Persia. In any case, it is distributed throughout the world as a common weed. As is true of many herbs, purslane was used for centuries for medicinal purposes.

Since purslane is a very pretty plant, it is frequently grown as a garden edging. One variety, the tiny *Portulaca oleracea sativa,* is grown in Europe as a salad plant, as a vegetable to serve hot and for pickling. The French particularly make use of it, under the name of *pourpier*. The fresh leaves are plucked, washed and dried and used in salads. They may be steamed or cooked in a little boiling salted water for ten minutes or so and dressed with butter, or cooked with bacon as a potherb. The fleshy stems are good pickled in vinegar, old recipe books tell us.

RADISH
Raphanus sativus

A radish is the crisp root of a hardy annual grown in many varieties throughout the temperate world mainly as a salad vegetable. Radishes vary in shape, size and color. They are round, oblong or long, cylindrical or tapered, in colors ranging from a creamy white through pink, red, white and red, purple to black, and weigh from a fraction of an ounce to several pounds. Their flavor goes from mild to peppery. The radishes favored by us and the Europeans are for the greater part the size of cherries, whereas those of the Orientals, especially the Japanese, range from finger size to more than two feet in length and five to six inches across. China and Middle Asia are believed to be the original homes of the radish. Radishes were common food in Egypt long before the pyramids, and the Greeks seem to have known three varieties. In the Western world, they were first seen in Mexico and Haiti, and by 1629 radishes were cultivated in Massachusetts. A garden catalog mentions ten kinds as early as 1806.

In the United States we munch over 400 million pounds a year of the globular red varieties we prefer, the ones that are topped and sold in plastic bags. But we also grow somewhat oval, turnip-shaped, oblong and long radishes with cherry red, scarlet and crimson skins, radishes which are half red half white, white radishes, and occasionally black radishes, all of which appear at one time or another in our markets. The long, white or the deep rose and winter Chinese varieties grow to seven and eight inches in length and two to three inches across, the long black Spanish radish, with its pungent, crisp, snow-white flesh, is about nine inches long. Among the commercial varieties mentioned here, it is the one found most seldom and then mainly in ethnic markets. Home gardeners, however, grow more varieties because radishes are quick and easy to grow; the so-called spring types take only a little over three weeks to produce edible radishes.

Our use of the radish is far more limited than that of the Orientals since we eat it mainly raw. In China and Japan, where the radish crop is nearly one-third of the tonnage of vegetables grown, most of the radishes are pickled in brine, as we pickle cucumbers, to add some salty pep to a rather monotonous rice diet. Some Oriental varieties are also grown for cooking while another, the rat-tailed radish, *Raphanus caudatus*, is cultivated in Asia for its long pods which are eaten raw or pickled. Yet another variety is grown for the oil from its seeds and in India and the Near East, another variety for its tops, eaten as greens. Even for our tastes, the young and tender leaves of the radish tops, braised for a short time and served with butter, are a pleasantly spicy vegetable as are the radishes themselves, treated in a similar way. The French chill their radishes, and as part of an hors d'oeuvre, eat them with sweet butter and salt; the Germans slice them thinly, dress them with oil and vinegar and consume them as a relish or a salad.

How to Buy

Available the year round. Peak season for round radishes, the most common variety, is May through July. The long tapering white or red-skinned varieties have a mild flavor and their peak season is July through October. The long oval, winter red, white or black radishes, up to nine inches in length, are in season from December through February. Long Oriental radishes (see Daikon, Oriental Radish, page 159) are available in Oriental markets throughout the year.

Buy fresh, smooth, well-formed, crisp, firm radishes with fresh tops, though the condition of the tops is not always an indication of quality. Medium-sized radishes are preferable. Buy bunches of radishes rather than topped radishes in plastic bags. *Avoid* radishes with black spots and pits, cracked radishes, spongy, flabby, wilted radishes or very large radishes which are apt to have pithy centers. Also avoid radishes with yellow or decayed tops.

Allow 4 medium radishes for each serving.

How to Keep

Wash and shake dry.

Refrigerate in vegetable drawer. Cut off any yellowing tops and rootlets.

Raw, whole, refrigerator shelf or vegetable drawer—1 week.

Nutritive Values

If eaten in sufficient quantities, radishes would be a fair source of minerals.

3½ ounces raw, common radishes—17 calories.

3½ ounces raw, Oriental radishes—19 calories.

How to Use

Remove all leaves and rootlets and wash thoroughly. To crisp, refrigerate radishes in a bowl of ice water.

HOT BUTTERED RADISHES

4 servings

Serve as a vegetable or add to a stew at serving time.

3 tablespoons butter	⅓ cup water
⅓ cup minced green onions	salt
3 cups thinly sliced radishes	freshly ground pepper

Heat the butter in a saucepan. Add the green onions and cook, stirring constantly, for 2 or 3 minutes. Add the radishes and the water. Simmer covered for 3 or 4 minutes, shaking the pan frequently to prevent sticking. Season with salt and pepper after the radishes are cooked because cooking in salt drains the color; the radishes should be a pretty pink.

RADISH SALAD

Use red or white radishes or a combination of both. Serve as is or add to potato or vegetable salads for texture and flavor.

Trim, wash and drain the radishes. Cut into thin, transparent slices. Marinate in a simple French dressing. Chill in the refrigerator for 1 hour to crisp. At serving time, drain, and sprinkle with minced parsley.

RAPE
Broccoli di rapa, Cole, Coleseed
Brassica napus

Rape is a member of the cabbage family grown in several varieties as a fodder, as a source of edible oil from the seeds, and as a green summer and fall vegetable. The kinds of rape we eat have green or bluish stalks six to eight inches long and leaves with a very definite strong flavor which appeals mainly to people of Italian descent. In Italy, the vegetable is smaller and less powerful; it is a specialty of Roman cooking, under the name of *broccoletti di rapa*, little rape. There is nothing delicate about the vegetable, which is best treated like any leaf cabbage, such as kale. However, because of its assertiveness, rape goes well with highly spiced dishes or as part of soups or stews.

BROCCOLI DI RAPA ALLA ROMANA
(Rape, Roman style)

4 servings

4 pounds rape
boiling water
¾ cup olive oil
2 or 3 garlic cloves, mashed

¼ teaspoon hot pepper flakes
salt
juice of 1 lemon

Discard the tough outer leaves. Cut off any tough stems. Cut the leaves and stems into 2-inch pieces. Wash in several changes of water and drain. Drop the rape into a large saucepan filled with rapidly boiling water. Bring back to the boiling point and immediately drain the rape. Reserve the drained liquid. Heat the olive oil in a heavy saucepan. Add the garlic and hot pepper and cook for 1 minute. Add the rape and season with salt. Cover tightly and simmer over low heat for about 10 minutes or until tender. Stir frequently and check for moisture; you may have to add a little of the reserved liquid, 2 tablespoons at a time, to prevent scorching. Turn into a serving dish and toss with the lemon juice. Serve hot or cold.

RAPE AND POTATOES

4 servings

This dish can be made with any greens, such as collards, spinach, Swiss chard, dandelion greens, etc.

2 pounds rape
2 large potatoes, peeled and
    very thinly sliced
⅓ cup beef consommé or water
2 garlic cloves, minced

¼ cup olive oil
salt
freshly ground pepper
juice of 1 lemon

Discard the tough outer leaves. Cut off any tough stems. Coarsely shred the leaves and the stems. Wash in several changes of water and drain. Put the potatoes into a saucepan large enough to hold the rape. Add the consommé and the garlic. Simmer covered over low heat for 5 minutes or until half tender. Add the rape and olive oil and season with salt and pepper. Cook over high heat, stirring with a fork, for about 5 minutes or until the vegetables are just tender but still crisp and moist. There should be only a few tablespoons of pan juices. Sprinkle with the lemon juice and serve warm or lukewarm.

RUCOLA
Arugala, Rocket, Roquette
Eruca sativa

This salad green is best known in the United States under its Italian name of arugala. The plant, which belongs to the mustard family, is a low-growing annual native to Southern Europe. Its leaves resemble those of radishes or turnips. The young leaves, which are the edible part of the plant, have a very definite pungent flavor that reminds one of bitter horseradish. Rucola is popular in France and in Italy, where it is used for salads. Rucola has been grown to a very limited extent in the United States for Italian markets, but during the last few years, it has become more popular among people who like a bite to their salads. Rucola can give too much of a bite when the leaves are mature; it is best treated like any salad or potherb green and made part of a tossed green salad rather than used as a salad by itself.

The plant should not be confused with the "sweet rocket," the perennial flower rocket, also spelled roquette.

MIXED ROCKET SALAD

4-6 servings

Serve with roast meats.

2 large potatoes
boiling salted water
1 bunch rucola or arugala
1 bunch watercress
1 small head Boston lettuce or 2
   heads Bibb lettuce

⅔ cup olive oil
3 tablespoons fresh lemon juice
salt
freshly ground pepper

Cook the potatoes in their skins in boiling salted water; the salt in the water keeps them firm. While the potatoes are cooking, trim the arugala and the watercress. Discard any wilted leaves and cut off any tough stems. If the arugala leaves are very large, tear them into two pieces. If the watercress sprigs are very large, separate them but do not make them too small. Trim and tear the lettuce into bite-sized pieces. Wash all the greens in several changes of water. Drain and pat dry on several changes of paper towels. Wrap in a clean kitchen towel and refrigerate to crisp. Beat together the oil and the lemon juice until creamy and add enough salt and pepper to season the whole salad. Drain the cooked potatoes, peel them and cut them into 1-inch cubes. Turn into a salad bowl large enough to hold all the salad and toss with the dressing. Let stand at room temperature until cooled. Add the chilled greens and toss with 2 forks to mix well. Check the seasoning and, if necessary, correct it with a little more lemon juice or salt or pepper. Serve immediately.

RUTABAGA
Swede, Swedish Turnip
Brassica napobrassica

A root vegetable of the cabbage family which resembles the turnip and is often confused with it. The rutabaga is distinguished by an ochre-colored swollen "neck" bearing a number of ridges which are the leaf base scars, and it has smooth bluish leaves. The turnip has little or no neck and thin, hairy green leaves. Rutabagas are also larger than turnips. There are white and yellow varieties but the commercially available ones are yellow.

The origin of the rutabaga or Swede, as most people call it, is not quite clear but Sweden doesn't seem to be the place it developed. It is believed to have hybridized from cabbage and turnip, possibly in the 17th century, probably in Bohemia. Rutabaga is a hardy, long-lasting, easy-to-store, cold weather crop and flourishes in Central and Northern Europe, where they became a staple of the diet of the poor as well as animal fodder. As recently as World War II, many people would have starved to death without the rutabaga, which was vegetable, fruit for preserves and even the material for ersatz coffee.

The rutabaga is not a delicate or particularly interesting vegetable but it is a fresh one, which counts in winter. Cooked with a little imagination and care, it can be turned into surprisingly palatable dishes.

How to Buy

Available all year, peak season July to April. Most rutabagas eaten in the United States are imported from Canada. Storage rutabagas are generally dipped into an edible vegetable wax to prevent loss of moisture. The tops, which are not eaten, are cut off by suppliers and retailers. Their absence does not affect the quality of the root.

Buy roots that are firm, solid and heavy for their size. They should be smooth and well-shaped whether they are round or oblong. *Avoid* cracked, punctured, cut or blemished roots.

Allow ½ pound for each serving.

How to Keep

Store in cool, moist area or refrigerate in a plastic bag.
Raw in good conditions—about 1 month.
Cooked and covered, refrigerator shelf—3 to 4 days.

Nutritive Values

A moderate source of vitamins and minerals.
3½ ounces raw—46 calories.
3½ ounces cooked—35 calories.

How to Use

Rutabagas must be peeled before cooking.
Peel, cut into slices, sticks or dice, wash and drain. Cook covered in an inch of boiling salted water for 5 to 15 minutes, depending on the size of the pieces. Do not overcook. Season with salt and pepper and serve with butter, or mash or cream. A half teaspoon of sugar added to the cooking water improves the flavor.

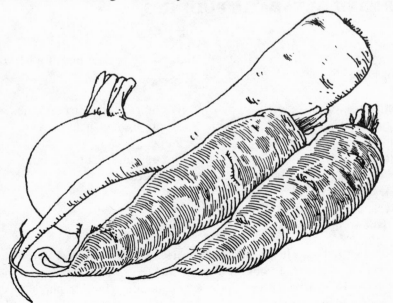

MASHED RUTABAGAS

4 servings

2 pounds rutabagas, peeled and
    cut into 1-inch cubes
boiling salted water
4 to 6 tablespoons butter, at
    room temperature
¼ cup chicken or beef
    consommé

salt
freshly ground pepper
⅛ teaspoon ground mace
¼ cup dry sherry

Cook the rutabagas in 1 inch of boiling salted water for 10 minutes
or until very tender. Drain and put through a ricer. Return to the
saucepan. Over low heat, stir in the butter, beginning with 4 tablespoons. Stir in the consommé and season with salt, pepper and mace.
Beat as you would mashed potatoes; if too dry, beat in the remaining
butter. Beat in the sherry. Cook, beating constantly, for 2 or 3 more
minutes. Serve very hot.

FINNISH RUTABAGA PUDDING

4-6 servings

This recipe, which can be halved, makes a good deal out of a humble
vegetable. Serve with meats.

8 cups peeled and diced
    rutabagas
boiling salted water
salt
freshly ground pepper
⅛ teaspoon ground nutmeg
1 teaspoon sugar or 2 teaspoons
    dark syrup or molasses

¼ cup fine dry bread crumbs
¼ cup light or heavy cream
2 eggs, beaten
¼ cup butter, cut into small
    pieces

Cook the rutabagas in boiling salted water to cover until soft. Drain and
reserve ½ cup of the cooking liquid. Mash as when making mashed
potatoes. Beat in ¼ cup of the reserved cooking liquid, salt, pepper,
nutmeg and the sugar. If too dry, add a little more of the cooking

liquid, 1 tablespoon at a time. Combine the bread crumbs and the cream and stir in the eggs. Stir this mixture into the rutabagas and beat until light. Place the pudding in a generously buttered 2-quart baking dish. Smooth the surface and dot with the butter. Bake in a preheated moderate oven (350° F) for 30 to 45 minutes or until the pudding tests clean and is gently browned on top.

SALAD

The original salads were edible herbs or plants dressed with salt alone. The word itself is derived from the Latin *sal* or salt. From this plain beginning, salads have burst out into some unbelievable creations that are a far cry from the dishes of simple greens that go back to the ancient Romans. Salads are a national American passion and pastime; we assemble diverse elements with surprising success.

One point usually (though not always) agreed upon is that a salad must have a dressing. Controversy has always reigned about the proportions of oil to vinegar in a classic dressing and about what additions are permitted. There is an old saying accredited to the Spanish: "Four persons are wanted to make a good salad, a spend-thrift for oil, a miser for vinegar, a counselor for salt, and a madman to stir all up."

Sydney Smith, a well-known 19th-century English clergyman and man of letters, would put more into his dressing and vary the proportions somewhat. His instructions for a "winter" salad read:

Two large potatoes, passed through kitchen sieve,
Unwonted softness to the salad give.
Of mordant mustard add a single spoon;
Distrust the condiment which bites so soon;
But deem it not, thou man of herbs, a fault
To add a double quantity of salt.
Three times the spoon with oil of Lucca crown.

And once with vinegar procured from town.
True flavor needs it, and the poet beggs,
The pounded yellow of two well-boiled eggs.
Let onion atoms lurk within the bowl,
And (scarce suspected), animate the whole;
And lastly, on the flavored compound toss
A magic teaspoon of anchovy sauce.

Perhaps the classic description of the perfect salad was given by John Evelyn in 1699 in his *Acetaria,* or *Discourse on Salads:* "Every plant should bear its part without being overpower'd by some Herb of stronger taste, so as to endanger the native Savor and Vertue of the rest; but fall into their places like Notes in Music, in which should be nothing harsh or grating and tho admitting some discords (to distinguish and illustrate the next) striking in the more sprightly and sometimes gentler notes reconcile all dissonances and melt them into an agreeable composition."

There is no limit on ingredients that may be brought together in this way. A recipe of 1793 for "A compound Sallett" beloved by George III of England, calls for a simple salad of lettuce, carrots, chives and radish roots dressed with oil, vinegar and sugar with the addition of "a mixture of young buds, and knots of all manner of wholesome herbs at their first springing, mixed with red sage, mint, violets, marigolds, spinage, etc. Blanched almonds, raisins, figs, capers, olives, currants, oranges and lemon, sliced fish, flesh, and fowl may also be added to the grand sallett."

The nature of salads seems to bring out the best in any writer. It was Shakespeare who coined the now common phrase "salad days," to mean those sprightly "green" days of youth. And it was the great dramatist who distinguished between nose herbs and salad herbs. Salad herbs were those plants especially suited for salads, although any salad could be perked up with an addition of common "nose" herbs such as marjoram.

In this country statesmen such as Thomas Jefferson have interested themselves in growing and making salads. With modern methods of refrigeration and shipping, Americans can eat salad all year round, a habit, it has been said, that makes us brothers to the rabbit.

SALSIFY
Oyster Plant, Vegetable Oyster
Tragopogon porrifolius

The fleshy edible root of a herb belonging to the daisy family which raw or cooked, tastes somewhat like an oyster. The tapering root can be ten inches long and two inches across. It is gray-white in color and has milky white, firm, juicy flesh. Another variety, *Scorzonera hispanica,* is black on the outside and white on the inside. Its flesh is similar to that of the salsify, with which it is similar in flavor and interchangeable in cooking. In German, it is called *Schwarzwurzel,* black root, in French *salsifis.*

Salsify and scorzonera are far better known in Europe than here, though occasionally one finds them in our markets, mainly those catering to people of Italian descent, during winter. Salsify is considered a great delicacy, and rightly so. As far as we know, salsify was introduced into America in the early 1800's but it never gained wide acceptance, though immigrants grew and grow the plant in their gardens.

Salsify, like artichokes and celeriac, discolors when cut. Before preparing it, have a bowl of acidulated cold water ready in which to keep the pieces until cooking time. Trim and scrape the roots; cut them in 2-inch slices or into sticks. Wash and drain. Add 1 to 3 teaspoons lemon juice or vinegar (depending on the quantity to be cooked) to an inch of boiling salt water. Cook covered for 5 to 10 minutes, depending on the size of the pieces, or until just tender. Do not overcook. Drain, season and serve with butter and lemon juice. Or rice or mash and treat like potatoes. Or cook in bouillon and serve as is. Or sauté with a touch of dry white wine. Or serve with a light Béchamel or Hollandaise sauce which does not overwhelm the delicate vegetable. Or marinate the cooked, drained vegetable in a light vinaigrette dressing and chill (one of the best ways).

Salsify and scorzonera are sold in bunches. Buy medium, well formed, firm, clean roots. Avoid large roots which are woody, or soft and shriveled roots. Refrigerate in the vegetable drawer for 3 to 4 days.

Allow 1 pound for 3 servings.

Caloric content depends on condition of the root.

3½ ounces freshly harvested raw root—100 calories; cooked—12 calories.

3½ ounces stored raw root—82 calories; cooked—70 calories.

SALSIFY OR OYSTER PLANT IN CREAM

4-6 servings

2 pounds salsify, trimmed, scraped and cut into 2-inch pieces
boiling salted water
3 tablespoons butter
1 tablespoon grated onion

1 cup hot heavy cream
salt
freshly ground pepper
¼ teaspoon ground nutmeg
¼ cup minced parsley

Cook the salsify in 1 inch of boiling water until three-quarters tender. Drain. Heat the butter in a casserole that can go to the table. Add the onion and cook, stirring constantly, for 1 minute. Add the salsify and toss in the butter. Add the cream and season with salt, pepper and nutmeg. Simmer covered over low heat for 5 to 10 minutes or until the salsify is tender. Sprinkle with the parsley before serving.

SALSIFY OR OYSTER PLANT HORS D'OEUVRE

4-6 servings

This dish may be made with cooked, peeled and sliced Jerusalem artichokes.

⅔ cup olive oil
fresh lemon juice to taste
2 teaspoons grated onion
salt
freshly ground pepper

½ teaspoon prepared mustard (optional)
2 pounds cooked oyster plant, sliced thin

Combine all the ingredients except the oyster plant in a bowl. Mix thoroughly. Add the oyster plant and toss gently. Cover and refrigerate for 1 hour or more.

FRIED SALSIFY

4 servings

Zucchini may be fried in the same manner.

2 pounds salsify, trimmed,
    scraped and cut into 2-inch
    pieces
boiling salted water

flour
olive oil for frying
salt

Cook the salsify in 1 inch of boiling water until barely tender. Drain and dry between paper towels. Put the flour into a paper bag, add the salsify and shake to coat. Shake off excess flour. Heat about 2 inches of olive oil in a deep frying pan to the smoking point. Fry a few salsify pieces at a time until they are golden. Drain on paper towels and keep hot in a low oven. When all the pieces are fried, pile them on a hot serving dish, sprinkle with salt and serve hot.

SAMPHIRE
Chicken Claws, Glasswort
Crithmum maritimum

Samphire is a succulent perennial which grows along the Atlantic coasts of the United States and Europe. It is gathered, or in Europe commercially grown, for its leaves, which are crisp and aromatic and which make an excellent salad green. They may also be pickled or cooked as a potherb. The young stems are edible as well and can be similarly prepared. The thin, green, spiky leaves two to three inches long are so arranged as to make the whole plant look like sparse miniature Christmas trees.

Samphire, like parsley, dill, chervil and lovage belong to the umbellifers which are grown for their leaves. It has been long used in Europe and in Shakespeare's *King Lear* there is the following mention: "Half way down hangs one that gathers samphire, dreadful trade."

SCALLION
Allium cepa

Scallions, or green onions, are shoots from white onion varieties that are pulled while the tops are still green and usually before a large bulb has formed. See page 244.

Paring Knives

SEA KALE
Crambe maritima

Sea kale, a native of the coasts of Western Europe, is cultivated for its slender asparaguslike shoots which are bleached in the field much like Belgian endives. Their flavor is nutty, slightly bitter and more acrid than that of Belgian endives. The plant somewhat resembles kale since it has large, heavy, toothed and crisped green or bluish leaves which grow to two feet in height. When young and tender, the leaves may be cooked like kale or collards.

In former years, sea kale was extensively cultivated in England and Ireland, but today it is no longer common. In the United States small (five to seven inches) bleached sea kale shoots appear very occasionally during the winter and spring months in a few fancy markets. They are either boiled or steamed and served like asparagus with butter, a light sauce, or chilled with vinaigrette. The vegetable is known in France as *chou marin*.

SEAWEEDS

Seaweeds include several thousand very different plants of which a number are edible and mainly used in Oriental cooking. Japan, Korea, the Pacific islands and Hawaii all use various kinds of seaweeds as vegetables, as pickles and as flavorings for sauces and soups. Many of these are available in Oriental markets in the United States in a dried form. American health food markets also carry several varieties, such as dulse, *Rhodymenia palmata,* which grows on our Eastern seaboard. The reddish dried fronds are chopped and added to soups and stews, or they are nibbled at as a relish.

Another well-known edible seaweed is Irish moss or carragheen, *Chondrus crispus,* a reddish or purplish plant found in Ireland and on our Eastern shores. When cooked, it becomes gelatinous, thickening and stiffening foods like blanc mange. It also yields industrial sizing. Before the introduction of commercial gelatin, Irish moss served in its stead and it was a household staple.

SHALLOT
Allium ascalonicum

A mildly aromatic bulb, cousin of the onion, used to flavor foods. The shallot grows in clusters of two to six from a common base (somewhat like garlic). The single bulbs are elongated and small, usually less than two inches in length and an inch across. They are greenish at the base and purplish on the upper portion and are covered by a thick outer red-to-gray skin. The edible parts are the green tops, which are harvested in early summer and sometimes sold as scallions, and the dried bulbs which are used like onions or garlic.

Shallots are natives of the Eastern Mediterranean, taking their botanical name from the city of Ascalon. French crusaders are thought to have brought them back to France from the crusades. In the ninth century the shallot was one of the 18 herbs that grew in the kitchen gardens of the great Monastery of St. Gall in Switzerland, then one of the great centers of civilization. Charlemagne, who was also a great expert on edible plants, grew shallots in his gardens near Aix-la-Chapelle, both for demonstrations and for revenue. Shallots were probably brought to America by followers of De Soto who explored Louisiana. There are records that French Huguenots in the Albemarle section of North Carolina grew them in their gardens around 1710.

During the last few years there has been an unprecedented demand for shallots, thanks to the upsurge of interest in French cookery, in which shallots are essential ingredients. Their flavor is complex, neither onion nor garlic yet with traces of both. Their mild yet definite flavor is ideally suited to sophisticated sauces and butters such as Bercy and *beurre blanc*, all the more so since shallots emulsify more easily than onions.

Buy dry, firm, well-filled and rounded shallots. *Avoid* shrunken, shriveled bulbs. Store in a cool, dry, well-ventilated place for 1 to 2 months. Use like onion or garlic. The tiny green shoots sent up by some shallots may be utilized along with the rest of the bulb or snipped into salads.

3½ ounces raw—72 calories.

BERCY BUTTER

about ½ cup

This shallot-white wine butter is served on steaks and broiled meats.

¼ cup dry white wine
1½ tablespoons minced shallots
½ cup beef consommé
½ cup butter, at room
   temperature

1 tablespoon minced parsley
salt
freshly ground white pepper

Combine the wine, shallots and consommé in a small saucepan. Cook over medium heat until all the ingredients have boiled down to about 1½ tablespoons. Cool. Mash the butter with a wooden spoon and beat it until it is light and creamy. Or beat with an electric blender. Beat the butter, 1 tablespoon at a time, into the wine mixture, beating well after each addition. When all the butter has been beaten in, beat in the parsley and salt and pepper to taste.

Shallot

BEURRE BLANC

about 1 cup

This creamy shallot butter comes from Nantes, on the Loire, where it is traditionally served with pike and other poached fish. It has an excellent taste but is somewhat tricky to make; generally, the first attempt is not successful. The trick is to cream the butter with the vinegar-shallot mixture at extremely low heat to prevent the butter from separating and to serve it barely warm. The consistency of *beurre blanc* should be that of a light Hollandaise.

¼ cup white vinegar
¼ cup dry white wine
1½ tablespoons minced shallots
1½ cups (3 sticks) butter, cut
   into small pieces, each about
   1 tablespoon

salt
freshly ground pepper

Combine the vinegar, wine and shallots in a small saucepan. Cook over medium heat until all the ingredients have boiled down to about 1½ tablespoons. Remove from the heat and immediately beat in about 2 tablespoons of the butter until it begins to look creamy. Return the saucepan to the lowest heat possible, preferably over an asbestos plate. Beat in 2 more tablespoons of the butter until the sauce is creamy and the butter is almost assimilated. Repeat until all the butter has been used up. Remove from heat and beat in salt and pepper. Rinse a serving bowl with warm water and dry; it should be barely warm. Spoon the sauce into it and serve.

SORREL
Dock, Sour Grass
genus *Rumex*

Sorrel is a hardy perennial herb belonging to the buckwheat family. Its sour, pungent, arrow-shaped green leaves are used as a salad green, as a potherb and as a flavoring. The edible leaves are three to seven inches in length. The plant is utilized in its wild and cultivated states. All sorrel varieties have acid sap containing varying amounts of citric, malic and oxalic acid which account for their sourness. In large quantities these might be toxic, but they are completely harmless in the limited quantities in which sorrel is eaten.

The best-known sorrel varieties are sour dock, garden sorrel or dock sorrel, *Rumex acetosa;* curled dock, *Rumex crispus;* and bitter dock, *Rumex obtusifolius.* Sheep sorrel, *Rumex acetosella,* is the variety that has refreshed many a thirsty hiker.

The most acid of the sorrels is sour dock or garden sorrel. Diverse varieties are widely cultivated in Europe and to an increasing extent in the United States. Sorrel is part of most European cookery, especially French cookery, where it is called *oseille* and used in one of the best French soups, sorrel soup, steamed, puréed or sautéed like any other flavorful potherb.

Sorrel is available in very limited quantities the year round. Peak seasons are the spring and summer when most of it is grown and sold locally. Sorrel is sold in bunches. *Buy* sorrel as you would any green, choosing young, crisp, bright green leaves. *Avoid* limp, wilted leaves or leaves with woody stems. The smaller and fresher, the more desirable. To store, refrigerate in vegetable drawer for 2 to 3 days. Use as soon as possible. To use, treat like any other salad or potherb. Sorrel is extremely high in vitamin A and has small amounts of vitamin C and minerals.

3½ ounces raw—28 calories.
3½ ounces cooked and drained—19 calories.

SORREL SOUP

4 servings

1 pound sorrel
6 green onions, minced
6 or 7 cups chicken consommé
2 egg yolks

½ cup heavy cream
salt
freshly ground pepper

Remove any wilted leaves and coarse stems from the sorrel. Wash in several changes of water. Shred the vegetable. Combine the sorrel, green onions and consommé. Bring to the boiling point and lower the heat. Simmer covered for 10 minutes. Purée the soup in a blender and return it to saucepan or leave as is. In a bowl, beat together the egg yolks and heavy cream. Gradually stir about ½ cup of the hot soup into the egg mixture, mixing well. Then stir the egg-soup mixture back into the soup. Heat through but do not boil or the soup will curdle. Remove from the heat, taste (the consommé may be salty) and season with salt and pepper. Serve hot or chilled.

CHIFFONADE OF SORREL

4 servings

Serve as a vegetable; it is delicious.

2 to 3 pounds sorrel
6 tablespoons butter
salt

freshly ground pepper
¼ cup heavy cream (optional)

Trim the sorrel and discard wilted leaves and tough stems. Wash in several changes of water and shake as dry as possible. Cut the sorrel into fine julienne strips. Heat 4 tablespoons of the butter in a casserole that can go to the table. Add the sorrel and cook over low heat for 5 minutes. Uncover and cook for 5 more minutes, stirring frequently, to let the pan juices evaporate. Season with salt and pepper and stir in the remaining butter and the cream. Heat through but do not boil. Serve very hot.

SOYBEAN
Soya, Soja
Glycine soja

The edible seeds found in the pods of an erect, bushy annual belonging to the pea family. The soybean is economically the world's most important bean, equally suited for human consumption and for industrial purposes. The proteins furnished by soybeans are the highest quality and most valuable of vegetable proteins; about two pounds of soy flour contain as much protein as five pounds of meat. The beans are also high in vitamins and minerals but low in carbohydrate. Further, soybeans are inexpensive to produce considering the qualities they provide. It is not surprising that they are playing an increasingly important role in the world's food supply. In the United States, the world's largest producer of soybeans in the 1970's, soybeans are principally made into oil and meal. The oil is used as a table oil and as an ingredient in margarine and other foods while the meal is used in animal feeds and for human consumption as well. Different textures of soybean solids play an important part in America's food manufacture. They are used either wholly or in part for scores of products including meat substitutes, sausage binders and breakfast foods. The industrial uses, over 100 of them, range from fire-fighting foam to adhesives and plastics.

Soy is believed to be native to southwestern Asia, where it was grown prior to 200 BC in China. It is the most important food legume in China, Korea, Manchuria, Japan and Malaysia, furnishing essential protein to the protein-poor diets of these countries in the form of sauce, bean curd *(tofu),* bean threads, nuts, candy and even soybean milk.

Soybeans were first grown as a botanical curiosity in France and in England towards the end of the 18th century. The first American mention dates to 1804. Not until after 1890 were soybeans taken as a serious crop with the introduction of many Asiatic varieties by the United States Department of Agriculture. Now the crop is one of our leading cash crops.

Dried soybeans, like mung beans, are used for sprouting. In recent years, fresh green soybeans have appeared in some markets, mainly in California, as a fresh vegetable. Each narrow, hairy pod contains three or four edible seeds. These may be shucked and cooked like peas, or the whole pod may be washed and lightly boiled until soft before the beans are shucked at the table and eaten with soy sauce or any other condiment.

3½ ounces fresh soybeans, cooked and drained—118 calories.
3½ ounces dried soybeans, cooked and drained—130 calories.
3½ ounces sprouted soybeans, raw—46 calories.
3½ ounces sprouted soybeans, cooked and drained—38 calories.
3½ ounces soy sauce—68 calories.

SOYBEAN SALAD

4 servings

Cooked soybeans may be used like any other cooked shelled beans.

⅓ cup olive oil
2 tablespoons fresh lemon juice
2 tablespoons grated onion
1 garlic clove, mashed
1 medium tomato, peeled and
    chopped

¼ cup minced parsley
salt
freshly ground pepper
2 to 3 cups cooked soybeans,
    drained

Combine all the ingredients except the soybeans in a salad bowl and mix well. Add the soybeans and toss with 2 forks. Chill before serving.

CHILI SOYBEANS

4-6 servings

3 tablespoons olive or salad oil
2 medium onions, chopped
2 garlic cloves, minced
1 tablespoon chili powder or to
    taste
4 cups cooked drained soybeans

2 cups peeled chopped tomatoes
1 teaspoon dried oregano
dash of Tabasco (optional)
salt
freshly ground pepper

Heat the olive oil in a heavy saucepan. Add the onions and garlic. Cook, stirring constantly, until the onion is soft and golden. Stir in the chili powder and cook for 2 more minutes. Add all the remaining ingredients. Simmer covered over low heat, stirring frequently, for 15 minutes. Check the consistency and if necessary to prevent scorching, add a little water or consommé 2 tablespoons at a time.

SPINACH
Spinacia oleracea

Spinach is a leafy annual cultivated for its broad, crinkly tender leaves which grow in a heavy rosette and which serve as a salad green or as a vegetable. The leaf stems are also edible, but they grow tough when mature. The dark green leaves may be puckered or smooth; the puckered ones are generally used for marketing and the smooth ones for processing. They are oval in shape, broader at their base; the lower leaves are wider while the higher ones are narrower. Spinach may also be classified according to seed type (prickly or smooth). The latter varieties are easier to plant accurately.

Spinach is a cool weather plant that probably originated in Persia, where it was cultivated at the time of the Greco-Roman civilization. Its introduction into the United States must have been by European immigrants; in 1806, at least three varieties were grown in American gardens.

Spinach has had a colorful history in the United States. As a bodybuilder deluxe it was forced down the throats of countless unwilling children who did not like it any better in spite of Popeye the Sailorman, who started getting his phenomenal strength from it ca. 1929. Its reputation was based less on its prodigious amounts of vitamin A (and to a lesser extent vitamin C), but on its iron content, said to build good red blood. However, during the Sixties, spinach took a fall because of the oxalic acid it contains. Oxalic acid can interfere with the body's ability to absorb calcium. Speaking to this point, Dr. James L. Breeling, A.M.A. Department of Foods and Nutrition, states that "few persons consume spinach in the amount necessary to seriously interfere with calcium absorption.''

Nevertheless, spinach is no longer as popular as it once was. Between 1957 and 1973, the consumption of fresh spinach fell 50 per cent from one pound to one-half pound per capita; canned spinach also declined in popularity but frozen spinach remained steady. Spinach growers have done their best to entice customers by selling fresh cleaned spinach in plastic bags to remove the objection that fresh spinach is so sandy that it is a nuisance to wash. Yet it still has to be washed since dirt will cling to it. The decline in fresh spinach consumption goes on, possibly also because frozen spinach is one of the more successful frozen vegetables. Moreover, it is also already chopped, and what more can a lazy cook ask for?

How to Buy

Available all year, peak season April and May. Since spinach is one of the most perishable vegetables, *buy* fresh, crisp, flat or crinkled dark green leaves. *Avoid* straggly, long-stemmed plants or plants with seedstalks, wilted, decayed or yellowing leaves.

Allow 1 pound fresh spinach for 2 servings.

How to Keep

Refrigerate fresh spinach in the vegetable drawer and use as soon as possible.

Fresh, refrigerator vegetable drawer—2 to 3 days.
Cooked and covered, refrigerator shelf—3 days.

Nutritive Values

An excellent source of vitamin A, a good source of vitamin C and a fair source of minerals.

3½ ounces raw—26 calories.
3½ ounces cooked and drained—23 calories.

How to Use

Trim off roots and cut off tough stems. Cut large leaves into pieces to save on chopping time. Swish the spinach around in a sink full of lukewarm water. The lukewarm water will send the sand to the bottom of the sink. Remove spinach from sink, clean sink of sand, fill with cold water and wash again. Repeat cold water wash until there is no sand left in the water. Drain the spinach. Cook covered for 3 to 5 minutes in the water that clings to the leaves. Do not overcook. Drain in a strainer and squeeze dry by pressing the spinach with a spoon against the sides of the strainer or squeeze dry with your hands. Season with salt and pepper and serve with butter and lemon juice. For salads, use only the smallest, tenderest leaves. Wash as above and dry between paper towels.

Dishes with the word "Florentine" in their title contain spinach.

CHINESE SPINACH
Amaranthus gangeticus

TAMPALA
Amaranthus oleraceus

These two greens and their varieties are used in warm regions especially in China, Japan, India, Burma and the Caribbean as potherbs. The leaves of Chinese spinach are smallish and green, and set on thin smooth stalks which are plucked when about six inches tall. Chinese spinach is sold in bunches in Oriental markets under the Chinese name *yin-choi* and the Japanese one of *hiyu*. Tampala, similar to Chinese spinach, is grown in India for the leaves, which are used as a vegetable, and for its tiny yellow or brown seeds, which are boiled or dried and made into a flour. Both vegetables are used in the West Indies as an ingredient for Callaloo Soup (page 101). Other forms of the amaranths are grown as ornamental garden plants since they have highly colored leaves.

Both vegetables have a pleasant, vaguely spinachy, flavor that has a little bite to it. They must only be cooked for the shortest of times or they become mush. Wash and shake them dry and steam them in their own juice in a covered saucepan for two to three minutes and then dress with butter and season with salt and pepper.

GOOD KING HENRY
Wild Spinach
Chenopodium bonus-henricus

This wild spinach is not a proper spinach, *Spinacea oleracea,* but a native of Europe and West Asia which was formerly cultivated in Great Britain as a green vegetable like spinach. It was introduced into American gardens, from which it escaped to run wild. The plant grows one to two feet high with triangular, arrow-shaped fleshy leaves. They can be used in any way spinach is used.

NEW ZEALAND SPINACH
Tetragonia expansa

This plant is not a proper spinach, *Spinacea oleracea,* but a heat resistant, much branched, spreading plant with small very thick, fleshy pointed leaves on round fleshy stems. The leaves are tougher than spinach, and they have a slightly bitter flavor. They are used in the same way as spinach.

BAKED SPINACH OMELET

4 servings

3 pounds spinach, washed, drained and coarsely shredded
3 tablespoons butter
salt
freshly ground pepper
dash of Tabasco
6 eggs
⅓ cup freshly grated Parmesan cheese
mushroom or tomato sauce (optional)

Cook the spinach for 3 minutes in the water that clings to it. Drain the spinach and squeeze it dry in a strainer. Return the spinach to the saucepan. Add the butter. Cook over high heat, stirring constantly, until the spinach is well coated with the butter. Remove from heat and season lightly with salt (the cheese will be salty), pepper and Tabasco. Beat together the eggs and the Parmesan cheese. Butter a fairly deep 8-inch baking dish or a deep 8-inch pie pan on all sides. Place it for a few moments over direct low heat to heat it up. Pour in half of the egg mixture. Cook like an omelet for 2 minutes or until set. Remove from the heat. Spread the spinach evenly on top of the eggs. Top the spinach evenly with the remaining eggs. Bake in a preheated moderate oven (350° F) for about 15 minutes or until set and golden. Unmold on a plate and serve hot with a mushroom or tomato sauce. Or serve lukewarm with sliced tomatoes.

SPINACH SOUFFLÉ

4 servings

3 tablespoons butter
3 tablespoons flour
1 cup light cream or milk
salt
freshly ground pepper
⅛ teaspoon ground nutmeg

1 cup (¼ pound) grated Swiss
  cheese
1 pound spinach, washed,
  cooked and squeezed dry
4 eggs, separated

Heat the butter in a saucepan large enough to take all the ingredients except the eggs. Stir in the flour and cook, stirring constantly, for about 2 minutes. Stir in the cream, and cook, stirring all the time, until thickened and smooth. Season with salt, pepper and nutmeg. Turn heat to very low and stir in the cheese and the spinach. Cook until the cheese has melted. Remove from the heat and cool. Beat the egg yolks until thick and beat them into the spinach. Beat the egg whites until they are stiff but not dry. Carefully fold the egg whites into the spinach mixture. Turn into a buttered 1½- to 2-quart baking dish. Bake in a preheated slow oven (325° F) for about 30 or 40 minutes or until set. Serve immediately.

WILTED RAW SPINACH SALAD

4 servings

The spinach must be very fresh, young and tender.

2 tablespoons bacon fat
1 small onion, minced
2 tablespoons flour
1 cup water or chicken
    consommé
1 teaspoon powdered mustard

3 tablespoons vinegar
1 pound trimmed, washed,
    drained spinach, in bite-sized
    pieces
salt
freshly ground pepper

Heat the bacon fat in a small casserole. Add the onion. Cook, stirring constantly, until the onion is soft and golden. Stir in the flour and cook 1 more minute. Stir in the water, mustard and vinegar. Cook over low heat, stirring constantly, until thickened and smooth. Put the spinach into a salad bowl. Pour the dressing over the spinach and toss. Season with salt and pepper and serve immediately.

SPINACH WITH YOGHURT

4 servings

3 pounds spinach, trimmed,
    coarsely chopped and washed
1 medium onion, minced
1 garlic clove, minced
2 tablespoons olive oil
salt
freshly ground pepper

4 tablespoons pignoli nuts
1 to 2 cups plain yoghurt,
    depending on taste
2 tablespoons minced fresh
    mint or 2 teaspoons dried
    mint

Combine the spinach, onion and garlic in a saucepan. Cook covered over medium heat, without additional water, for 5 minutes, tossing the pan frequently to prevent sticking. Drain off any moisture. Add the olive oil. Cook, stirring constantly, for 3 more minutes. Season with salt and pepper. Mix in the pignoli nuts. Remove from heat and stir in the yoghurt. Turn into a serving dish and sprinkle with the mint.

ROMAN SPINACH

4 servings

3 pounds spinach, trimmed and
washed
1 tablespoon butter
2 tablespoons olive oil
½ cup pignoli nuts

1 garlic clove, mashed
2 teaspoons vinegar or to taste
salt
freshly ground pepper

Cut any large spinach leaves into pieces. Heat the butter and the olive oil in a deep frying pan. Cook the nuts, stirring constantly, until they are golden. Add the spinach, garlic and vinegar and salt and pepper to taste. Cook covered, shaking the pan to prevent sticking, for about 4 minutes or until barely tender. Serve very hot.

SQUASH
Cucurbita maxima

Squashes are members of the gourd family (Cucurbitaceae) of which there are some 700 different species, many of which are cultivated to be eaten as a cooked vegetable. The squash plant is a trailing or climbing vine or a bush with large leaves and generally large, yellow flowers. The edible part is a pepo, a berrylike structure, filled with seeds. The squash flowers are also edible, see page 164.

Squashes are native to the Americas (probably Peru and Chile) where many varieties were cultivated long before the European conquests. They were, along with corn and beans, a staple Indian food. To this day, squash is associated with American food on both sides of the equator. Few Europeans like it as we do (with the exception of zucchini) though the British go in for the rather insipid vegetable marrows, a summer squash which ambitious gardeners grow to monstrous sizes for gardening competitions.

Squashes are remarkably diversified vegetables as to shape, size and color. Some are outstandingly beautiful in color and form. Their names are confusing since they vary depending on where the squash was grown. Furthermore, the words squash and pumpkin are frequently used interchangeably.

The word squash itself comes from the Massachusetts Indian word *askut-asquash* meaning "eaten raw or uncooked."

For convenience's sake, the main types of squash grown in the United States are defined as summer and winter squash. This is practical but botanically incorrect since the seasons of many of these squashes overlap; some are on the market all year.

SUMMER SQUASH
Cucurbita pepo

Summer squash are quick growing small squash which are harvested while their immature rinds and seeds are still thin and tender. Besides those squash mentioned elsewhere in this book, the best known varieties are:

Caserta: Cylindrical, smooth-skinned, with alternate light and green stripes. Similar to zucchini. Best when six to seven inches long.

Cocozelle: Cylindrical, smooth, widely ribbed skin in alternate dark green and yellow. Similar to zucchini. Best when six to eight inches long.

Chayote: See page 120.

Cymling, Pattypan, Scallop: Disk or bowl-shaped. Prominent ribbing on the edges gives a scalloped effect. Pale green when young, white later. The skin is smooth and slightly bumpy, the flesh greenish. Best when no more than three to four inches across.

Yellow crookneck: Fruit curved at the neck and larger at the tip than at the base. The skin is moderately bumpy, light yellow when young turning to deeper yellow. The flesh is creamy yellow and a little granular. Best when eight to ten inches long. Larger varieties reach up to 20 inches in length and four and one-half inches across.

Yellow straightneck: A relatively straight version of the yellow crookneck.

Zucchini: See page 361.

WINTER SQUASH
Cucurbita maxima

These are larger, mature, hard-shelled squashes with fully-formed seeds and yellow flesh. There are many varieties of which these are the best known:

Acorn: Table Queen, Des Moines: Though considered a winter squash, this variety alone belongs to the species *Cucurbita pepo*. The widely ribbed fruit is acorn-shaped, five to eight inches long and four to five inches across. The shell is smooth, hard and thin, dull dark gray changing to a dull green-orange. The flesh is pale orange, tender, moist and fibrous, and the seed cavity large. There are larger varieties as well as a golden-skinned one.

Acorn Squash

Large banana: The fruit is nearly cylindrical, tapering somewhat at either end, 18 to 24 inches long and five to six inches across. The shell is moderately thick and medium hard, pale olive gray changing to creamy pink, ranging from moderately smooth to somewhat wrinkled and pockmarked. The orange-buff flesh is moderately dry with a fine texture.

Buttercup: Also called a turban squash because of the turbanlike cap at the blossom end. The shape is somewhat drumlike with a protuberant two- to three-inch turban. Buttercup is four to five inches long and six to eight inches across. The shell is moderately hard and thin, dark ivy green to dull blackish green with grayish spots and faintly striped with dull gray; the turban is light or blue-gray. The flesh is orange, fine textured, dry and sweet.

Butternut *(Cucurbita moschata)***:** Nearly cylindrical with a slightly bulbous base nine to 12 inches long and three to five inches across at its widest. The smooth and hard shell is light creamy brown or dark yellow. The flesh is yellow and fine grained.

Delicious: Green Delicious, Golden Delicious. A eight- to 12-inch long top-shaped fruit with the stem at the larger diameter. The hard rind is colored dark green with light green stripes toward the blossom end or bright reddish or tangerine with occasional green splotches or cream stripes toward the blossom end. The flesh is yellow, thick and dry.

Hubbard: A globular squash with a fairly thick tapered neck. Ten to 16 inches long and nine to 12 inches across at its largest. The rind is very hard, warted and ridged, dark bronze green or blue-gray or orange red. The flesh is orange, thick, dry and sweet. It takes its name from Mrs. Elizabeth Hubbard of Marblehead, Mass., who grew it when it was still nameless, but gave seeds to the father of Mr. James Gregory, who called it after her. Mr. James Gregory wrote this in the *Magazine of Horticulture* for December 1857.

Warren turban: A drum-shaped squash, eight to ten inches long and 12 to 15 inches across. The rind very hard, thick and heavily warted is bright reddish orange with scattered striping and a blue turban.

How to Buy

Peak season for summer squash is May to August, though some varieties are available throughout the year. Peak season for winter squash is October to January, though acorn and butternut squash are available the year round.

Buy summer squash that is young, fresh, firm, fairly heavy for its size and free from blemishes. The rind should be tender enough to puncture easily with the fingernail. Seeds should be soft and fully edible. *Avoid* soft, soggy summer squash with a spotty, blemished or scratched rind. *Buy* winter squash that is hard, clean, heavy for its size. *Avoid* winter squash that has soft or decaying spots or that is cracked.

Allow 1 pound summer squash for 2 to 3 servings.
Allow 1 pound winter squash for 2 to 3 servings.

How to Store

Refrigerate summer squash in a plastic bag or in vegetable drawer.
Summer squash, raw, refrigerator shelf or vegetable drawer—3 to 5 days.
Summer squash, cooked and covered—3 to 4 days.

Keep whole winter squash in a dry, well-ventilated place.
Whole winter squash, raw—1 to 4 weeks.
Winter squash, cooked and covered—3 to 4 days.

Nutritive Values

Summer squash provides moderate amounts of vitamins and minerals.

Since it is low in sodium it is suited to low-salt diets.
Summer squash, average caloric content:
3½ ounces raw—19 calories.
3½ ounces cooked and drained—14 calories.
Winter squash is an excellent source of vitamin A and a moderate source of vitamin C and minerals.
Winter squash, average caloric content:
3½ ounces boiled, mashed—38 calories.
3½ ounces baked—63 calories.

How to Use

See recipes below.

OLD-FASHIONED BAKED ACORN SQUASH

4 servings

2 large acorn squash	4 teaspoons grated onion
hot water	4 tablespoons dark brown sugar
salt	4 tablespoons butter
freshly ground pepper	

Wash the squash and cut them into halves lengthwise. Remove the seeds and fibers. Place the squash, cut side down, in a shallow baking dish. Pour in ¼ inch hot water. Bake in a preheated moderate oven (350° F) for 20 to 30 minutes or until the squash is tender to the touch. Drain the water, if any, from the baking dish and turn the squash cut side up. Sprinkle each squash half with salt and pepper. Add to each 1 teaspoon grated onion, 1 tablespoon dark brown sugar and 1 tablespoon butter. Return to the oven and bake for 10 to 15 more minutes.

HONEY GLAZED ACORN SQUASH

6 servings

3 medium acorn squash
hot water
¼ cup butter, melted
½ teaspoon salt

¼ teaspoon freshly ground
  pepper
½ teaspoon ground allspice
¼ cup honey or maple syrup

Prepare and bake squash as for Old-Fashioned Baked Acorn Squash. Drain the water, if any, from the baking dish and turn the squash cut side up. Combine all the remaining ingredients and mix well. Pour equal amounts into the cavity of each squash half and brush the cut surfaces with a pastry brush to glaze. Return to the oven and bake for 10 to 15 more minutes or until the squash is glazed and golden. Baste twice with the honey mixture in each cavity.

BAKED BUTTERNUT SQUASH

4 servings

Serve with ham.

1 large butternut squash
salt
freshly ground pepper
2 teaspoons anise seed, crushed
⅛ teaspoon ground cardamom

2 or 3 tablespoons light or dark
  brown sugar
½ cup melted butter
2 tablespoons fresh lemon juice

Peel and cut the squash open. Remove the seeds and the fibers. Cut into 1-inch cubes. Turn the squash into a buttered 2-quart baking dish. Sprinkle with the salt and pepper, anise seed, cardamom and sugar. Drizzle with the butter and lemon juice. Bake without a cover in a preheated moderate oven (350° F) for about 30 minutes or until tender.

CREAMED BAKED CYMLINGS

4 servings

12 very small cymlings
boiling water
4 tablespoons butter
2 tablespoons grated onion
1 tablespoon flour

1 cup heavy cream
salt
freshly ground pepper
½ teaspoon dried thyme
⅓ cup fine dry bread crumbs

Cook the cymlings in boiling water to cover for 3 minutes. Drain and turn into a buttered 1½-quart baking dish. Heat 2 tablespoons of the butter and stir in the onion and flour. Cook, stirring constantly, for about 1 minute. Stir in the cream. Cook over low heat, stirring constantly, until thickened and smooth. Season with salt and pepper and stir in the thyme. Pour the sauce over the cymlings. Sprinkle with the bread crumbs and dot with the remaining butter. Bake in a preheated moderate oven (350° F) for 15 minutes or until lightly browned. Serve hot.

WINTER SQUASH SOUFFLÉ

4 servings

2 pounds winter squash, any
   kind
boiling salted water
salt
freshly ground pepper
¼ teaspoon dried thyme

2 tablespoons butter, melted
2 tablespoons light or heavy
   cream
4 tablespoons grated Swiss
   cheese
3 eggs, separated

Peel and seed the winter squash. Cook until soft in just enough boiling salted water to cover. Mash as you would potatoes. Mix the squash with the salt, pepper, thyme, butter, cream and cheese. Beat in the egg yolks, one at a time. Beat the egg whites until stiff and fold into the squash. Turn into a buttered 2-quart baking dish. Bake in a preheated moderate oven (350° F) for about 20 or 30 minutes or until set and golden on top.

SAUTÉED SUMMER SQUASH

4-6 servings

3 tablespoons olive oil
2 garlic cloves
1½ pounds summer squash (do
not peel if tender), thinly
sliced
salt

freshly ground pepper
1 tablespoon cider vinegar or to
taste
¼ cup minced fresh basil or
parsley

Heat the olive oil in a deep frying pan. Cook the garlic cloves until they are just beginning to turn golden. Discard the garlic. Add the squash and season with the salt and pepper. Cook over medium heat, stirring with a fork, for 3 to 5 minutes or until the squash is tender but still crisp. Stir in the vinegar and the basil and cook 30 seconds longer.

SUMMER SQUASH IN SOUR CREAM

4-6 servings

2 to 2½ pounds any summer
squash (crookneck,
cymlings, etc.)
boiling salted water
¼ cup butter
1 small onion, thinly sliced
1 teaspoon dill seed, crushed

salt
freshly ground pepper
½ cup sour cream
1 teaspoon cider vinegar
¼ cup minced fresh dillweed or
parsley

Cut the squash into crosswise ¼-inch slices. Cook in boiling salted water to cover in a covered saucepan for 3 minutes and drain thoroughly. Pat dry with paper towels. Heat the butter and cook the onion in it until soft. Add the dill seed, salt and pepper and cook for 1 more minute. Add the squash and cook over medium heat for 3 minutes or until tender but still crisp. Remove from the heat and stir in the remaining ingredients. Toss with 2 forks and serve immediately.

MAPLE-NUT MASHED HUBBARD SQUASH

4-5 servings

3 pounds Hubbard squash	salt
boiling water	freshly ground pepper
½ cup butter, at room	¼ teaspoon ground ginger
temperature	½ cup chopped toasted pecans
⅔ cup maple syrup	or walnuts

Cut the squash into pieces, remove the seeds and the fibers and peel it. Cook the squash in boiling water to cover in a covered saucepan for 15 to 20 minutes or until very tender. Drain and mash as you would potatoes. Return to the saucepan and beat in the butter, maple syrup, salt, pepper and ginger. Turn into a hot serving dish and sprinkle with the nuts.

SWEET POTATO
Ipomoea batatas

The sweet potato is the edible tuberous root of a vine belonging to the morning-glory family. There are many different varieties in many shapes and colors. The flesh is usually golden yellow, though there are white varieties, and it may be moist or dry. Most sweet potatoes taste sweet though some of the tubers are as dry as any Irish potato. The average size is five to ten inches long and two inches across. Two main varieties are grown in the United States: one with a very dry mealy yellow flesh preferred in Northern markets and the other a soft, moist sugary yellow-fleshed one fancied in the South. This latter variety is often called yam by Southerners, but sweet potatoes must not be confused with yams, which belong to another botanical genus (*Dioscorea*). For cooking purposes, however, sweet potatoes and yams are interchangeable.

The sweet potato is a truly American vegetable, grown by the Incas of Peru and the Mayas of Central America long before the conquest. Columbus mentions it in his records, and De Soto found sweet potatoes growing in Indian gardens in 1540 in what is now Louisiana.

The sweet potato has never become popular in Europe, not even in the Mediterranean countries. During the American Revolution and the Civil War the sweet potato is said to have been the single most important food. Though the tuber bears the name of potato, from the Indian *batata,* whenever Indians and Southerners˙speak of batatas or potatoes they mean the sweet potato.

Consumption of fresh sweet potatoes has fallen during the last 40 years. One reason is the enormous choice of food products we now have; another is the greater culinary sophistication we now enjoy. However you gussy up a sweet potato, it always is a sweet potato, a ritual Thanksgiving food.

How to Buy

Available throughout the year, peak season September to March. *Buy* firm well-shaped clean sweet potatoes with evenly colored skins that are free from blemishes. Choose thick, chunky medium-sized potatoes tapering towards the end. *Avoid* potatoes with any sign of bruises or decay since they rapidly go bad.

Allow 1 medium sweet potato for each serving.
Allow ½ to ⅓ pound for each serving.
1 pound—1 to 3 sweet potatoes.

How to Keep

Store in a cool, dry, well-ventilated area. Do not refrigerate since chilling damages sweet potatoes. Store for short time only.

Raw—2 to 3 weeks.
Cooked and covered, refrigerator shelf—4 to 5 days.

Nutritive Values

An excellent source of vitamins A and C.
3½ ounces boiled in skin—114 calories.
3½ ounces baked in skin—141 calories.

How to Use

Scrub and cut off any woody or bruised parts. Sweet potatoes are usually boiled or baked before peeling and then finished. They cook and bake quicker than white potatoes and also reheat better. For cooking methods, see Potatoes, page 275.

5 medium boiled sweet potatoes—approximately 2 cups.

CHICKEN AND SWEET POTATO SOUP

6 servings

Serve with corn bread.

8 cups chicken consommé
½ cup diced carrots
½ cup diced celery
½ cup chopped onion
4 large sweet potatoes, peeled
   and diced
1 or 2 cups chopped cooked
   chicken

1 teaspoon ground thyme
½ teaspoon ground sage
¼ teaspoon dried hot pepper
   flakes
salt
freshly ground pepper

Combine the consommé, carrots, celery and onion in a soup kettle. Bring to the boiling point and lower the heat. Simmer covered for 10 minutes. Add the sweet potatoes and all the other ingredients. Simmer covered for 15 more minutes.

FESTIVE SWEETS

6 servings

6 large sweet potatoes
⅓ cup butter, melted
½ cup firmly packed brown
   sugar
1 teaspoon salt
⅛ teaspoon pepper

½ teaspoon ground mace
½ cup cream
⅓ cup sherry
2 teaspoons grated orange rind
¾ cup dried apricots, cooked
   and chopped

Cook, drain and peel the sweet potatoes. Mash until very smooth. Add all the other ingredients except the apricots. Lightly fold in the apricots. Turn into a buttered shallow 1½-quart baking dish. Bake in a preheated moderate oven (350° F) for 15 to 20 minutes.

SWEET POTATO ORANGE CASSEROLE

6 servings

This dish may be made with yams.

3 pounds (approximately 6 medium) sweet potatoes
boiling salted water
½ cup light brown sugar
½ cup fresh orange juice
2 tablespoons fresh lemon juice

grated rind of ½ orange
grated rind of ½ lemon
¼ teaspoon salt
4 tablespoons butter, cut into pieces

Wash the sweet potatoes and cook in boiling salted water to cover for 15 to 20 minutes or until tender but still firm. Drain and cool. Peel the sweet potatoes and cut them into ¼-inch slices. Place them in a buttered shallow 10-inch baking dish in 1 or 2 layers. Sprinkle with the sugar. Combine the orange and lemon juices, the orange and lemon rinds and the salt and mix well. Sprinkle the mixture over the potatoes. Dot with the butter. Bake in a preheated slow oven (325° F) for 25 minutes or until golden.

SWISS CHARD
Chard
Beta vulgaris

Swiss chard is a type of beet which does not develop the bulbous root of the beet and which is grown for its edible leaves. The plant can grow 24 inches high and has broad, crisp leaves which may be smooth or crinkled. The large white fleshy leaf stems are also edible. The color of the leaves varies from a yellowish to a dark green, but there is also a red variety, rhubarb chard with crimson stems and wine red leaves; it serves as food and as an ornamental garden plant. The flavor of Swiss chard is delicate and not unlike that of spinach. To a certain extent, Swiss chard can be used like spinach. Most spinach recipes are interchangeable with chard recipes.

Swiss chard is probably a native of the eastern Mediterranean. It was used by the Greeks and Romans as "beta" since today's beetroot was unknown in the ancient world. The Chinese speak of the vegetable as early as the seventh century. Different colored varieties were described in 16th century Europe where to this day it is far more popular than it is in the United States. It is especially liked in the warmer parts of the continent where it grows better than spinach. Swiss chard is also one of the easiest and most prolific home garden vegetables. Where the "Swiss" in the name comes from I have not been able to find out.

How to Buy

Local supplies available only in summer. Since it is very perishable, *buy* thick, juicy-looking white or reddish stalks with tender, fresh leaves. *Avoid* wilted stalks and faded leaves.

Allow 1 pound for 3 servings.

How to Keep

Trim, wash and shake dry. Place in a plastic bag and refrigerate.
Raw, refrigerater shelf—1 to 2 days.
Cooked and covered, refrigerator shelf—2 days.

Nutritive Values

Both leaves and stalks are a good source of vitamins A, B and C and a good source of iron.

3½ ounces cooked and drained—18 calories.

How to Use

Trim off root ends. If the vegetable is large and mature, cut off the leaves. Cut the stalks into two- to three-inch pieces. If the leaves are very large, cut them up. Wash thoroughly. Cook the stalks in an inch or two of boiling salted water for five to ten minutes. Cook the leaves in an inch of boiling salted water for five minutes. Cook both in covered saucepans. Drain thoroughly and season with butter, lemon juice or herbs or serve with cheese or Hollandaise sauce. Or leave the stalks whole and cook and serve like asparagus. Or cook and serve the leaves like spinach. Or sauté stalks and leaves in hot melted butter over low heat for two to three minutes; then cover and simmer for five to ten minutes or until tender. Do not overcook.

SWISS CHARD WITH OIL AND LEMON

4 servings

A Roman way of eating this green.

2 pounds Swiss chard, trimmed
   and washed
boiling salted water
4 tablespoons olive oil

2 tablespoons fresh lemon juice
salt
freshly ground pepper

Cut the stalks of the Swiss chard into 2- to 3-inch pieces. If the leaves are large, cut them into bite-sized pieces. Wash both stalks and leaves in several changes of water and drain. Cook covered in 1 inch of boiling salted water for 3 to 5 minutes or until barely tender and still crisp. Drain thoroughly and squeeze dry with the back of a spoon or with the hands. Turn the chard into a deep serving dish. Mix together the oil, lemon juice and salt and pepper. Pour over the chard, toss and serve hot, lukewarm or chilled.

SWISS CHARD WITH TOMATO SAUCE

4 servings

2 pounds Swiss chard,
 trimmed, washed, cooked
 and drained
4 tablespoons olive oil
2 garlic cloves, minced
3 anchovies, drained and
 minced

1½ cups peeled and chopped
 tomatoes
salt
freshly ground pepper
2 tablespoons drained capers

Coarsely chop the chard and set aside. Heat the olive oil in a heavy
saucepan. Add the garlic cloves and cook until they are browned;
discard. Add the anchovies and cook, stirring constantly, for 2 minutes. Add the tomatoes, salt and pepper. Cook covered over medium
heat 5 to 10 minutes. Add the chard, mix well and cook for 10 more
minutes, stirring frequently. Stir in the capers before serving.

TARO
genus *Colocasia*

The name taro covers a group of herbaceous plants which are cultivated in the tropics and subtropics for their edible starchy tuberous
roots. They are called by different names depending on their locality.
The West Indian dasheen is such a name. The taro is probably a
native of southern Asia, but it has been cultivated all over the world,
especially in the Pacific islands and the West Indies. *Colocasia esculenta* is one of the most prominent varieties. It has a rough, brownish
ridged turnip-shaped root and light or purple-tinged flesh. Its flavor is
bland and starchy. It is used as a cooked vegetable and ground into
flour for breads. In the Pacific and Hawaii taro is eaten mostly in the
form of *poi*, a thin sticky paste of boiled taro that has been peeled
and pounded into a paste with a little water before lightly fermenting
for a day or two. *Poi* is highly digestible and also used for invalid food;
Western palates generally consider its flavor insignificant. Like most
plants in the taro group, such as cassava (page 110), taro has to be

thoroughly cooked to destroy a certain natural acridity which can be, depending on the variety, highly toxic.

Different forms of taro have edible leaves, which also must be cooked to remove their toxicity. Taro also produces small greenish-white sprouts largely used in Oriental cooking.

TOMATO
Lycopersicon esculentum

The fruit of a vine that along with potato, tobacco, pepper and egg-plant, belongs to the nightshade family. Botanically speaking, the tomato is a berry as it is pulpy and contains seeds that are not stones. Tomatoes are eaten as a vegetable rather than as a fruit, prized for their flavor, color and high vitamin content. They come in many shapes, sizes and even colors. Tomatoes can be almost totally round or oval, pear, plum or chili shaped or elongated. They range from one-half to more than three inches in diameter and weigh up to two pounds. The skin can be red or yellow or colorless and the flesh may be white, orange, pink or red. The flavor of a tomato depends largely on the ratio of sugar to acid. If there is not enough sugar, the tomato will be sour and flavorless. Those which are watery rather than fleshy will have a poor flavor. Tomatoes are grown for specific purposes such as for the table, for juice and for canning. The solidly-fleshed Italian plum tomato, used mainly for sauces and for canning, is very frequently more flavorful for salad use than the regular table varieties.

Tomatoes are said to be native to the Peruvian and Bolivian Andes, where tomatoes the size of large currants and cherries are still to be found. The Indians cultivated and improved them so long ago that large forms of the tomato have never been found wild. The northward migration of the fruit is also wrapped in antiquity. The Aztecs and Toltecs and other Mexican tribes not only ate tomatoes but also named them since the word is derived from their *tomatl*. Tomatoes were eaten in Italy in 1554, which called them *pomo d'oro* (today's pomodoro) or golden apple, from which we may deduce that they belonged to a golden variety. The French of the time, in a hopeful manner, called the tomato the love apple. By the end of the 16th century tomatoes were grown in England, Germany and Belgium as well, largely as an ornament since they seemed to be too odd to eat. Tomatoes were also considered poisonous in Europe, probably because they belong to the nightshade family, some species of which are poisonous and because their stems and leaves have a certain off-putting smell.

Curiously the tomato, though native to the New World, only came to the United States after it was well known in Europe. However, the Europeans' mistrust carried over to the United States. In 1802 an Italian painter in Salem, Mass., could not persuade people even to taste the fruit. In 1832, in Connecticut, tomatoes were raised as a curiosity because people had heard that the French ate them. The tomato really took off commercially only after 1860; prior to that date no varieties had been developed in the United States. The tomato is now the number-two U.S. crop (the potato is first).

No other vegetable, I think, has suffered as much loss of flavor at the hands of what is now known as "agrobusiness." Any commercial grower will tell you that, with the exception of hot house tomatoes, it is not practical to harvest red-ripe tomatoes; the fruit is too tender to pack and ship. So-called vine-ripe tomatoes are not that at all; they are harvested at the barely pink stage. But most tomatoes that are shipped long distances are harvested at what euphemistically is called the "mature-green" stage, when they have shiny, thick skin that cannot be torn and jellylike inner substance. They are then ripened in storage. These are the horrid, palid, woody tomatoes we pay far too much for. Equal in nastiness are overblown, watery, purplish so-called beefsteak tomatoes. In most parts of the country, only during the summer months is it possible to savor the glorious flavor and color of a naturally ripened locally grown tomato. Even the little red or yellow cherry tomatoes, once nuggets of true tomato flavor, have become insipid during these last years.

How to Buy

Available the year round, peak May to October. Salad varieties include large, meaty red beefsteaks, red or yellow cherry tomatoes and yellow plum tomatoes. The thick fleshed Italian plum tomatoes are usually used for sauces and other cooked dishes but they make excellent eating. Buy as close to serving or cooking as possible. *Buy preferably ripe but not overripe tomatoes only; home ripened tomatoes are never as flavorful.* Buy firm, well formed tomatoes that are heavy for their size. *Avoid* blemished or cracked tomatoes, or tomatoes with torn skin or watery or dark or sunken spots.

Allow ½ pound or 1 tomato for each serving.

1 cup firmly packed fresh—½ cup tomato sauce and ½ cup water.

How to Keep

Tomatoes are hurt by chilling. Keep in a cool dry place, at a temperature around 50° F. Refrigerate for a short time only and only when fully ripe. Ripen green tomatoes at room temperature; then chill.

Fresh ripe, refrigerator shelf—2 to 3 days.

Canned, open and covered, or cooked and covered—4 to 5 days.

Nutritive Values

A good source of vitamins A and C and of minerals.

3½ ounces, fresh, raw—22 calories.

3½ ounces cooked—26 calories.

How to Use

To peel tomatoes, spear on a fork and dip into boiling water for about a minute or two. Then dip into cold water. Slip off skin. Or hold tomato over direct heat until the skin splits; then slip off.

To seed and juice peeled or unpeeled tomatoes, cut into halves crosswise. Squeeze each half gently over a bowl to extract the seeds and the juice.

To slice tomatoes, cut them into vertical rather than horizontal slices. This is the French way and tomato slices stay firmer.

To stew tomatoes, cut into pieces and cook covered without water over low heat for 8 to 10 minutes. Stir frequently. Since the water content of tomatoes varies, check for scorching; if necessary, add a little water. For more flavor, add a little minced onion or celery or a bay leaf. Season with salt and pepper. If tomatoes are sour, add a pinch of sugar. To broil, remove the stem from firm tomatoes. Cut into halves and score the surface of each half. Place on a baking sheet. Season with salt and pepper and dot with butter. Broil under moderate heat for 5 to 10 minutes or until topping is browned. Or bake in a preheated hot oven (425° F) for 10 minutes.

FIRST COURSE TOMATO, MOZZARELLA AND BLACK OLIVE SALAD

4 servings

Have the ingredients ready but prepare this salad just before serving.

4 to 6 large ripe tomatoes, peeled, seeded and cut into 1-inch cubes
8 ounces mozzarella, cut into ½-inch cubes
1 cup black olives, pitted or 1 cup small black Italian olives in oil

salt
freshly ground pepper
4 tablespoons olive oil
1 or 2 tablespoons vinegar
¼ cup minced basil or parsley

Combine the tomatoes, mozzarella and olives in a glass salad bowl. Sprinkle with a little salt (the olives may be salty) and pepper. Stir together the olive oil and the vinegar and pour over the salad. Add the basil and toss carefully with a fork. Serve immediately.

BELGIAN TOMATO SALAD

6 servings

The tomatoes are vastly improved by this dressing which is also very good on cooked vegetables like green beans, carrots, broccoli, etc.

6 large, firm, ripe tomatoes
salt
freshly ground pepper
6 tablespoons olive oil
2 tablespoons mild vinegar or to taste

2 teaspoons Dijon mustard
2 tablespoons grated onion or shallot
¼ cup minced parsley
¼ teaspoon dried thyme

Plunge tomatoes into boiling water for 1 minute. Carefully slip off the peel and cut off the blossom end. Chill the tomatoes before cutting them into thin slices. Arrange the slices in a shallow serving dish in overlapping rows. Combine all the remaining ingredients and blend them thoroughly. Sprinkle over the tomatoes and refrigerate from 1 to 3 hours.

Onion lovers may place a thin slice of onion on each tomato before sprinkling on the dressing.

FRESH TOMATO SOUP

4 servings

Once you've made fresh tomato soup you won't like canned tomato soup.

4 tablespoons butter	1 large bay leaf
1 tablespoon peanut or salad oil	3 parsley sprigs
1 medium onion, minced	2 sprigs fresh thyme or 1
3 tablespoons flour	teaspoon dried thyme
6 large ripe tomatoes, peeled,	salt
seeded and chopped	freshly ground pepper
4 cups boiling water	croutons

Heat 2 tablespoons of butter and the peanut oil in a large, heavy saucepan. Cook the onion, stirring constantly, until it is soft and golden. Stir in the flour and cook, stirring all the time, until golden; do not brown. Add the tomatoes and water. Tie the bay leaf, parsley sprigs and thyme in a triple layer of cheesecloth to make a bouquet garni. Add to the tomatoes. Season with salt and pepper. Simmer covered over low heat for 30 minutes. Remove the bouquet garni and stir in the remaining 2 tablespoons of butter. Serve in a heated tureen with croutons.

FRIED TOMATOES WITH CREAM GRAVY

4 servings

4 large tomatoes	3 tablespoons bacon fat
salt	1 tablespoon flour
freshly ground pepper	1½ cups light cream or milk
flour	

Wash the tomatoes and cut them into halves crosswise. Sprinkle with salt and pepper and dredge with flour; shake off excess flour. Heat the bacon fat in a frying pan. Add the tomato halves, a few at a time, and brown quickly on both sides. Transfer to a heated serving dish and keep hot. Stir the flour into the pan drippings. Gradually stir in the cream. Cook over low heat, stirring constantly, until thickened and smooth. Taste and if necessary add a little more salt and pepper. Pour the sauce over the tomatoes and serve immediately.

SKILLET TOMATOES

4-6 servings

8 large ripe Italian-type plum tomatoes, washed	2 tablespoons minced basil or 2 teaspoons dried basil
salt	2 tablespoons minced parsley
freshly ground pepper	1 tablespoon minced mint or 1 teaspoon dried mint
4 tablespoons olive oil	

Cut the tomatoes lengthwise into halves. Lay them cut side up, side by side in a large frying pan (or use 2 frying pans; the tomatoes *must* be in a single layer). Sprinkle each half with salt and pepper, a little olive oil, basil, parsley and mint. Cook over low heat for 5 to 7 minutes, shaking the pan to prevent sticking. Cover the frying pan and cook for 3 to 5 more minutes; the cooking time depends on the firmness of the tomatoes.

ROMAN STUFFED TOMATOES

4-6 servings

It is impossible to give totally accurate amounts for the rice used since the size of the tomatoes varies. If the tomatoes are very large, about 2 tablespoons of raw rice are needed for each tomato. If any rice stuffing is left over, cook it alongside the tomatoes. The saffron in the rice makes it a pretty color.

8 large ripe but firm tomatoes
½ cup olive oil
⅓ cup minced parsley
2 garlic cloves, minced
1 cup raw long-grain rice

1 teaspoon saffron (optional)
2 cups hot chicken consommé
salt
pepper
⅛ teaspoon ground cinnamon

Cut a slice from the top of each tomato under the stem and scoop out the pulp with a teaspoon. Be careful not to break the shell. Strain the pulp through a sieve and reserve. Place the tomatoes side by side in a shallow baking dish. Sprinkle each tomato with a few drops of olive oil. Heat the remaining oil in a saucepan. Cook the parsley and garlic for 2 minutes. Add the rice and cook, stirring constantly, for 3 more minutes. Stir the saffron into the consommé. Add the hot consommé to the rice and cover the saucepan. Cook over low heat, stirring frequently, for about 10 minutes or until the rice is three-quarters done. Remove from the heat and season the rice with the salt, pepper and cinnamon. Fill the tomato shells with the rice mixture. Pour the strained tomato pulp over the tomatoes; if there is not enough strained pulp to make ½ inch in the pan, add a little water. Bake in a preheated moderate oven (350° F) for about 30 minutes or until the rice is tender and the liquid has been absorbed. Check for scorching; if necessary, add a little more hot water. Baste occasionally with the pan juices. Serve hot or lukewarm or cool but not chilled.

PIZZAIOLA SAUCE

4 servings

Serve with steaks or on thin pastas. The tomatoes in this sauce are cooked just long enough to soften and keep their fresh taste.

¼ cup olive oil
1½ to 2 pounds ripe tomatoes,
   peeled, seeded and chopped
2 garlic cloves, minced

salt
freshly ground pepper
1 teaspoon dried oregano
¼ cup minced parsley

Heat the olive oil in a heavy saucepan. Add all the other ingredients. Cook over high heat, stirring all the time, for about 5 to 7 minutes or until the tomatoes are just soft and hot.

SALSA FRIA

1½ cups

This sauce is found on all Mexican tables; it can be as hot as desired. Serve it on beans and on any dishes that can stand a little livening up.

2 large ripe tomatoes, peeled
   and chopped
1 medium onion, minced
1 jalapeño pepper or more to
   taste, fresh or canned and
   drained, seeded and chopped
   fine

2 tablespoons olive or salad oil
juice of 1 lemon
½ teaspoon dried oregano
salt
freshly ground pepper

Combine all the ingredients and mix well. Refrigerate covered until serving time.

TRUFFLE

Tuber melanosporum, Tuber aestivum, Tuber brumale

A truffle is a fungus which unlike other fungi grows underground in forests. It is an irregularly shaped, roundish lump with a light or dark brown or gray warty skin, and solid flesh. Truffles measure about three to four inches in width. The truffle's odor and flavor are indescribable but most distinctive, delicious to most people but repulsive to some. Their nutritive values are of no importance. There are several varieties, of which the two finest and most prized are the black-fleshed truffles of the Périgord and other regions of France and the white truffle of Piedmont in Northern Italy. A French dish with the words "à la Périgord" or "Périgourdine" in its title contains some truffle. An Italian dish with the word "trifolato," or truffled, in its title does not mean that it contains any truffles but rather that one or more of the ingredients is sliced very fine, like truffles.

Lesser truffles are also found in France, in England, in some parts of Europe and in North Africa. Unfortunately the truffle varieties that grow in the United States are not good so that we must rely on fresh or canned truffles imported from France or Italy. The fresh truffle season in late fall is very short. They are flown in, for fresh truffles must be very fresh to be good and should not be more than a week old.

Truffles have been prized as the height of sophisticated food since the days of the Romans, when Apicius gave recipes on how to cook and sauce them. Truffles never lost this reputation and they are priced accordingly and often astronomically. Raw or cooked, the haute cuisine of France relies on them in numerous ways, such as in pâtés (that small black square in the middle of a foie gras pâté) or whole braised in wine or cream, baked or sautéed, in a salad, minced in stuffings and so on. The Italians, who say their white truffles are tastier than the French black ones, a statement hotly disputed by the French, shave their raw truffles with a special cutter onto pasta or egg dishes; all truffles show a great affinity for eggs. Aphrodisiac qualities have been claimed for raw truffles in a hopeful rather than a proven manner.

The way truffles grow and are harvested adds to their magic aura. Truffles like light, porous limestone soil in oak, beech or birch forests under the trees that nourish them. When ripe, only their odor betrays them. Since the human sense of smell is not sensitive enough to detect them, truffle pigs and truffle hounds scent out the ripe truffles and dig them out of the ground cracked from the swelling of the ripe fungus. Dogs are better for the purpose because they refrain from eating the precious nuggets whereas pigs don't always control themselves. Truffle hunts usually take place at night, with secret maps to keep the blessed spots from becoming common knowledge.

Truffles usually grow wild and unpredictably, but they keep on growing in the same spots. They are also cultivated, after a fashion, by planting tiny oak trees in places where truffles are known to exist. None of the practices for mushroom growing can be used; one must hope and wait, sometimes from six to ten years or in vain. The method has worked but there can never be enough truffles.

Both black and white imported canned truffles can be found in gourmet stores. Personally, I consider canned truffles without perfume and without much flavor, a show of riches that could be better employed; but others do not agree with me.

Fresh truffles have an overpowering scent which penetrates anything close to them. The French frequently put theirs into a basket of eggs to scent the eggs. The Italian way is to store a truffle in a bagful of rice; the rice insulates the truffles and at the same time is flavored for a lovely risotto. But even then, truffles must be wrapped in paper and in plastic bags. I remember that once I was traveling on a train with a number of wrapped truffles from Milan, a headquarters for the white truffles of Piedmont, to Switzerland. Not only the compartment, but practically the whole car, smelled of truffles. The occupants did not mind; they congratulated me instead.

To Use

To clean truffles, check if there is any soil clinging to them. If there is some, wash and brush the truffles rapidly under running cold water and dry them before using. If they are clean, scrape them gently and very lightly or brush them with a soft brush and then wipe them with a damp cloth. Store cleaned or partially used truffles or truffle scraps in a tightly lidded glass container in the refrigerator and use as soon as possible. If you are using canned truffles and have some left over, transfer them to a tightly lidded glass container and cover them with sherry, port, Madeira or brandy. Close the jar well and keep refrigerated for about a week.

Some people advise peeling truffles, a sheer waste for a product that fetches well over $100 a pound and that many producers lock up in safes. Slice them thinly, or dice, chop or mince or cut them into thin strips. Add them to a dish towards the end of the cooking period to avoid overcooking and loss of flavor. Or use raw thinly sliced truffles in salads. Since canned truffles are already cooked, add them to a dish so they will just heat through. Use the canning liquids for flavoring soups, stews and sauces. Truffles used for decoration in aspics, pâtés and other festive dishes may be cut into fancy shapes with little metal truffle cutters.

Whole raw black truffles may be cooked in many ways but white truffles must never be cooked. For anyone lucky enough to own more than one truffle at a time and who wants to cook them I suggest this simple method. Place cleaned black truffles in a heavy cast-iron casserole. Add enough of a good full-bodied dry white wine, such as a Chablis or a Chardonnay to come about three-quarters of the way up the truffles. Add for each truffle about half an inch of lean bacon cut into thin strips. Bring quickly to the boiling point, reduce heat to low, cover tightly and simmer for about 15 or 20 minutes, depending on size. Season with a little salt and pepper. Serve hot as a separate course, with a spoonful or two of the cooking liquid, or as a vegetable. Some recipes call for champagne in this dish but I think it is better with a really good white wine.

White truffles are delicious thinly sliced or grated over a ready-to-serve dish of pasta or rice dressed with butter and grated Parmesan cheese or into an egg dish or salad. Be careful not to expose the white truffles to much heat.

SCRAMBLED EGGS WITH TRUFFLES

3 servings

6 large eggs
salt
freshly ground pepper
1 medium black or white truffle
   or to taste, fresh or canned

butter
4 tablespoons heavy cream
hot buttered toast

Break the eggs into a bowl and beat them. Season lightly with salt and pepper. Chop the truffle and stir it into the eggs. If canned truffles are used, also add the juice to the eggs. Cover and refrigerate for 1 to 2 hours. Melt a generous amount of butter in a small, heavy frying pan. Stir the cream quickly into the eggs. Add the eggs to the butter and scramble lightly over low heat. Do not dry out the eggs. Serve immediately with hot buttered toast.

Fry Pan

SAUTÉED BLACK TRUFFLES

3-4 servings

I had this dish once in France made with fresh truffles and goose fat and served with a little plain boiled rice. It was an unforgettable experience.

1 pound black truffles, ready for cooking, fresh or canned	salt
2 tablespoons butter	freshly ground pepper
1 tablespoon bacon fat	1 cup dry Madeira

Slice or chop the truffles. Heat the butter and bacon fat in a small, heavy casserole. Add the truffles. Season with a little salt and pepper. Cook over medium heat, stirring very gently with a fork, for about 3 to 4 minutes. With a slotted spoon, transfer the truffles to a heated serving dish and keep warm. Stir the Madeira into the pan juices, stirring up all the little brown bits at the bottom. Turn the heat up to high and cook for 2 to 3 minutes or until the sauce is reduced by about one-fourth. Pour over the truffles and serve immediately.

TURNIP

Brassica rapa

The turnip is a root vegetable belonging to the cabbage family; the leaves are also eaten as a potherb. Some coarse turnip varieties are grown as forage plants. The roots measure an average of two to three inches across and are round or conical in shape and have white, green or purplish crowns. The hairy leaves are green and thin. The flesh is crisp, and either white or yellow (most commercial varieties have white flesh). The flavor of the turnip resembles that of all the vegetables whose names end in "nip," but it is milder. Even yellow turnips must not be mistaken for rutabagas, page 298, though sometimes the two botanically different but similar tasting vegetables are called by the name of turnip.

Turnips have long been one of the more popular vegetables of France, Germany, Switzerland, Austria, Northern Europe and of the British Isles. Turnips were cultivated very early in America. In 1540, Carter sowed turnip seed during his third voyage. Virginia grew them in 1609, Massachusetts in 1629 and there were a lot of them around Philadelphia in 1707.

In this country turnips have never achieved the popularity they enjoy in Europe. Turnip greens, however, are especially popular in our southern states, where even canned and frozen versions can be found in the markets. They are boiled with some sort of pork and served with their thin broth, the potlikker.

Turnips and their greens are extensively used in Chinese, Japanese and other Oriental cooking.

How to Buy

Available the year round, peak season October to March. They are sold in bunches with full-length tops or without tops. *Buy* small to medium firm turnips with smooth unblemished skin. The tops should be fresh and green. *Avoid* large, fibrous turnips with too many leaf scars or wilted, yellowing, blemished tops.

Allow ½ pound for each serving.

How to Keep

Turnips like very cool surroundings. Remove tops and store in a well-ventilated cool dry place. Or refrigerate in a plastic bag. Wash greens and shake dry. Wrap in plastic and refrigerate.

Fresh raw roots, refrigerator shelf—3 weeks.

Cooked and covered roots, refrigerator shelf—2 to 3 days.

Fresh green tops, refrigerator shelf—2 to 4 days.

Nutritive Values

The roots are a moderate source of vitamins and minerals. The greens are an excellent source of vitamins A and C and a good source of minerals.

3½ ounces raw root—30 calories.
3½ ounces cooked and drained root—23 calories.
3½ ounces raw greens—28 calories.
3½ ounces cooked and drained greens—20 calories.

How to Use

When turnip roots are used imaginatively, they can be an excellent and interesting vegetable. As with many vegetables, their size when cut up affects their taste. They are at their mildest when cut into thin julienne strips in the French manner, thinly sliced or diced. Even small turnips must be peeled before cooking, though large turnips may be baked in their skins in the usual manner. To cook, place peeled, sliced, diced or matchstick turnip roots in an inch of boiling salted water for 5 or more minutes or until tender. Do not overcook. Season with salt and pepper and serve with butter. Or cook further according to recipe.

TURNIPS, LUCERNE STYLE

4 servings

Serve with boiled beef or sausages.

12 small or 6 medium white
   turnips, trimmed and peeled
boiling salted water
¼ cup diced bacon

1 large onion, minced
salt
freshly ground pepper
2 tablespoons minced parsley

Cut the turnips into julienne strips. Wash and drain. Cook them in about ¾ of an inch of boiling salted water until barely tender. Drain. In a frying pan, cook the bacon until it is limp. Add the onion and cook, stirring constantly, until soft and golden. Add the turnips. Season with salt and pepper. Cook over low heat, stirring occasionally, for about 10 minutes or until the turnips are golden brown.

CURRIED TURNIPS

4-6 servings

Also try parsnips. Serve with ham.

3 tablespoons butter
1 medium onion, minced
1 tablespoon curry powder or to
   taste
½ to 1 cup hot chicken
   consommé or water

2 pounds turnips, peeled and
   cut into 1-inch cubes
salt
freshly ground pepper
½ cup yoghurt

Heat the butter in a heavy saucepan. Cook the onion in it until soft. Stir in the curry powder. Cook, stirring constantly, for 2 or 3 minutes. Stir in ½ cup of the consommé. Add the turnips. Cook covered over very low heat for about 10 or 15 minutes or until the turnips are tender. Check the moisture; if necessary to prevent scorching, add more consommé, 2 tablespoons at a time. The cooked turnips should be dry. Season with salt and pepper. Remove from the heat and stir in the yoghurt. Serve immediately.

WATER CHESTNUT
Chinese Water Chestnut
Eleocharis tuberosa

The edible tuber of a rushlike plant that grows in shallow water at the edges of lakes and in marshes, used widely in Oriental cookery. Water chestnuts are roundish with brown or black skin and firm white flesh. Since their flavor is delicately nutty through rather bland, their main virtue is that of giving crispness to a dish. The Chinese water chestnut must not be confused with the nutlike fruit of another aquatic plant, *Trapa natans,* which is also called water chestnut or Jesuit's nut and used in the same manner. Both plants are natives of the Far East where they have been cultivated as food plants for centuries.

Fresh Chinese water chestnuts are occasionally available on the West Coast and Hawaii from July to September. When buying fresh, choose firm, plump specimens. More generally they are available canned in water, imported from Hong Kong, Taiwan and Japan, and found in supermarkets. Fresh Chinese water chestnuts should be peeled, thinly sliced, quartered or diced and cooked 2 to 4 minutes in boiling salted water, drained and cooled in cold water before further use. The canned chestnuts also profit from a brief immersion in boiling, then cold, water.

Sliced, diced, halved or quartered, Chinese water chestnuts may be added to any salad or cooked dish.

3½ ounces raw—79 calories.

STIR-FRIED PORK AND WATER CHESTNUTS

4 servings

3 tablespoons salad oil
1 garlic clove, mashed
6 green onions, white and green
   parts, minced
¼ pound lean boneless pork,
   cut in small, thin strips
4 tablespoons soy sauce

1 tablespoon sugar
2 tablespoons lemon juice
1½ cups thinly sliced water
   chestnuts
salt
freshly ground pepper
shredded lettuce

Heat the salad oil in a wok or a large frying pan. Cook, stirring constantly, the garlic and the green onions until they are golden brown. Add the pork. Stir-fry until the pork is browned on all sides. Stir in the soy sauce, sugar and lemon juice. Stir-fry for 1 minute. Lower the heat, cover and simmer over low heat for 5 minutes. Add the water chestnuts and salt and pepper. Stir-fry for 2 more minutes. Pile on shredded lettuce and serve immediately.

WATERCRESS
Nasturtium officinale

Watercress is a perennial, succulent leafy plant of the mustard family which is gathered or grown for its peppery green leaves which serve as salad greens and flavorings. The plant grows best in running water and is found wild by or in springs and clear streams in many parts of the country. Commercially, it is grown in shallow pools of flowing clean water with an adequate lime content.

Watercress is believed to be native to the Eastern Mediterranean. Persians, Greeks and Romans all ate it with pleasure and considered it extremely healthful. Xerxes, the Persian king, recommended watercress to his soldiers for the good of their health and the Greeks thought it a brain food and a cure for deranged minds. Watercress was cultivated in Germany in the 16th century, but England, though consuming wild cress, cultivated it as a salad plant only in 1808. How it reached America nobody knows, but it was probably brought by early explorers and quickly became naturalized and widespread.

Although watercress is used largely as a garnish, it is an excellent salad green by itself or combined with other greens. The French combine watercress with potatoes for an excellent soup and the Chinese too have long used it in their soups. Cooked as a green, watercress is a far more flavorful and interesting vegetable than many greens.

How to Buy

Available throughout the year. Sold in small bunches. Only young, fresh watercress is worth buying. *Buy* fresh, bright green watercress with crisp leaves and stems which snap easily. *Avoid* watercress with yellowing or wilted leaves.

Allow 1 average bunch for 3 to 4 salad servings.

How to Keep

Untie each bunch and remove any poor leaves and stems. Wash in several changes of ice water. Dry between paper towels. Place in a container with a tight lid and refrigerate.

Refrigerator shelf—3 to 5 days.

Nutritive Values

A good source of vitamins A and C and a good source of minerals if eaten in large amounts.

How to Use

Remove all wilted stems and leaves. Snap off tough stems. Wash in several changes of cold or ice water and shake dry. Or dry between paper towels. Chop and add to sandwiches, soups, eggs, vegetables, and cottage cheese or add to salad greens. Or use as a salad with a light French dressing. Or cook as a vegetable.

WATERCRESS SOUP

6 servings

7 cups chicken consommé
6 green onions, white and green
    parts, thinly sliced
1 large potato, peeled and diced
2 bunches watercress, trimmed,
    washed, tough stems
    removed (reserve 2 large
    sprigs)

1 cup heavy cream
salt
freshly ground pepper

Put the consommé into a large heavy saucepan and bring to the
boiling point. Lower the heat. Add the green onions, potato and
watercress. Simmer covered for 10 to 15 minutes. Do not overcook
or the soup will lose its fresh flavor. Purée in a blender. Return to
saucepan and add the cream. Heat through but do not boil. Season
with salt and pepper. Garnish with the leaves of the reserved watercress sprigs. Serve hot.

CHILLED WATERCRESS SOUP

Proceed as above but do not add the cream. Chill the soup and the
cream separately and thoroughly. At serving time, stir the cream into
the soup, season and garnish with the watercress leaves.

BRAISED WATERCRESS

4 servings

Serve with rich meats such as duck, pork or ham.

4 bunches watercress
4 tablespoons butter, cut into
    pieces
salt

freshly ground pepper
¼ cup chicken consommé
sour cream (optional)

Trim off the heavy stems. The easiest way to do this is to lay the bunch of watercress on its side and cut off the stems to the height of the leaves. Plunge into a bowl of cold water and agitate to loosen dirt and sand. Remove any wilted leaves. Change the water until no dirt or sand is left in the bowl. Drain. Do not shake dry. Place in a saucepan. Cook covered over medium heat for about 5 minutes, shaking the saucepan frequently to prevent sticking. Stir in the butter and season with salt and pepper. Add the consommé. Return to heat until the pan liquid has evaporated and the watercress has the consistency of chopped spinach. Serve hot with a bowl of sour cream on the side.

WATERCRESS AND MUSHROOM SALAD

4-6 servings

2 bunches watercress, trimmed, washed, tough stems removed
¼ pound mushrooms, thinly sliced

1 tablespoon fresh lemon juice
4 slices crisp cooked bacon, crumbled

DRESSING

4 tablespoons olive oil
2 tablespoons lemon juice
1 garlic clove, mashed
½ teaspoon salt

¼ teaspoon freshly ground pepper
¼ teaspoon dry mustard
1 egg yolk

Dry the watercress between paper towels. Place in a salad bowl. Top with the mushrooms. Sprinkle the lemon juice over the mushrooms. Top with the crumbled bacon. Chill while you make the dressing. Combine the olive oil, lemon juice, garlic, salt, pepper and mustard. Mix well. Beat in the egg yolk and blend thoroughly. Chill until serving time. Then pour the dressing over the salad and toss.

WEST INDIAN GHERKIN
Cucumis anguria

The fruit of a slender vine of African origin grown largely in the West Indies for use as a vegetable. The cucumber shaped West Indian gherkin is one to three inches long. It has flexible quarter-inch spines. The color is pale green maturing to lemon yellow, the flesh greenish. Known also as the gooseberry gourd, the vegetable is boiled and served with butter and seasonings or added to soups and stews. In the United States, it is occasionally found in West Indian markets.

YAM
Ñame, Cush-cush
genus *Dioscorea*

A true yam is a thick edible oblong tuber which develops at the base of the stem of a confusing number of vines with twining or creeping stems and broad leaves. The genus *Dioscorea* to which it belongs numbers hundreds of species with any number of varieties; mostly they grow in warm and tropical countries. Some are grown as ornamentals, others for their tuberous roots and others produce potatolike tubers on their stems and are aptly called air potatoes. *Dioscorea bulbifera,* our commercial yams, resemble sweet potatoes in appearance and flavor though they belong to a botanically different species. The name yam is said to be a corruption of an African word pronounced "nyam" by early Negro slaves who used it for the true yam or any other similar edible tuber in Africa.

The most commonly cultivated true yam is *Dioscorea alata* and its varieties, a native of Southern Asia. The many varieties vary in size, shape, color and weight. The best ones are small and weigh less than one pound. But they may grow to a length of a dozen inches and a weight of dozens of pounds. The rough skin is light to dark brown and flesh may be white to yellow or red or purple. Another variant is the giant or white yam which can weigh a hundred pounds and measure more than eight feet long. Its flavor and texture are inferior to other yams, but it is an important food in the West Indies, the West African coast and India. The Chinese or Oriental yam, *Dioscorea esculenta,* is a flavorful gray or black tuber with an inner purple skin and white moist flesh; it is frequently found in the Chinese markets of our large cities. Other varieties also serve as basic foods in almost all subtropical parts of the world. Since yams contain little but starch, populations living largely on yams in countries with insufficient protein foods often suffer from malnutrition.

Yams are available the year round in Latin markets. Large yams are sold in pieces. *Buy* firm yams with unwrinkled skins. *Avoid* soft yams with skin blemishes or sunken spots. Store whole uncut yams in a cool, dry, well-ventilated place for no more than 1 week. Refrigerate cooked and covered yams for 2 to 3 days. Yams can be cooked in any way potatoes and sweet potatoes are cooked. Peel, wash and slice or cube yams. Cook in boiling salt water to cover until tender. Drain and mash like sweet potatoes. Or use according to recipe.

3½ ounces raw—101 calories.

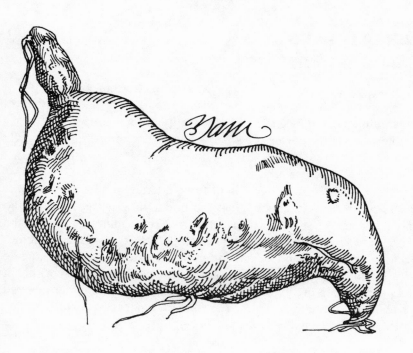

CANDIED YAMS

4 servings

4 large yams
boiling salted water
salt
freshly ground pepper

¾ cup firmly packed dark
   brown sugar
⅓ cup water
4 tablespoons butter

Cook the yams in boiling salted water to cover until barely tender. Cool, peel, and cut into halves lengthwise. Sprinkle with a little salt and pepper. In a frying pan combine the sugar, water and butter. Cook over low heat, stirring constantly, until the sugar has melted; do not scorch. If necessary, add 1 or 2 tablespoons more water. Lay the yam halves side by side in the frying pan. Cook over very low heat, turning over once, until the yams are candied on both sides. This will take about 10 to 12 minutes. Transfer to a heated serving dish and serve hot.

CURRIED YAMS

4-6 servings

2 pounds yams
2 tablespoons butter
1 medium onion, minced
1 tablespoon curry powder or to
   taste

1 cup chicken consommé
salt
freshly ground pepper
juice of ½ lemon

Cook the yams in their skins until three-quarters tender. Drain, peel and slice or cut into cubes. Heat the butter in a saucepan. Add the onion and cook, stirring constantly for 2 or 3 minutes. Stir in the curry powder and cook 2 minutes longer. Stir in the consommé. Bring to the boiling point and lower the heat to low. Cook, stirring occasionally, for 3 minutes. Taste and if necessary, season with salt and pepper. Add the yams and mix well with a fork. Simmer covered for about 10 minutes or until the yams are tender. Remove from the heat and sprinkle with the lemon juice.

ZUCCHINI
Italian Squash
Cucurbita pepo

Zucchini is a variety of narrow summer squash developed in Italy, as is its brother Cocozelle (see page 322). Zucchini is cylindrical in shape and almost straight; the base is wider than the top. The average length is four to nine inches. The color is a moderately dark green over a yellowish ground color which gives the vegetable a striped appearance. The rind is soft, thin and smooth and the flesh crisp, greenish white with tiny soft seeds. The flavor is fresh, delicate and infinitely more subtle than that of other squashes. Zucchini might be called the elegant sophisticate among them.

Until fairly recently, zucchini was known only to people of Mediterranean descent, though the French have also made wide use of it, calling it *courgette,* the name under which it is also known in England. However, during the last few years zucchini has become a fashionable vegetable, prepared in far more diverse ways than regular summer squash.

How to Buy

Available the year round, peak season May to August. Buy firm, well-rounded zucchini, with tender, glossy, unblemished rinds. Preferably buy zucchini from three to six inches in length and about one inch across. Avoid soft zucchini, with torn rinds and dark spots.

Allow 1 pound for 3 servings.

How to Keep

Buy in small amounts and use as soon as possible.

Raw, refrigerator shelf or vegetable drawer—3 to 4 days.

Cooked and covered, refrigerator shelf—2 days.

Nutritive Values

Zucchini contains only a moderate amount of nutrients.

3½ ounces, raw—17 calories.

3½ ounces, cooked and drained—12 calories.

How to Use

Wash and trim off blossom and stem end. Do not peel or scrape if the rind is clean; otherwise, scrape off or cut off any blemished spots. Cut into julienne strips, slices or dice. Cook as quickly as possible with a minimum amount of water since zucchini itself is watery.

MIRIAM UNGERER'S ZUCCHINI SOUP

6-8 servings

This is the best zucchini soup I ever had; it is much admired by all who eat it. It comes from a delightful and practical cookbook, *Good, Cheap Food* (Viking, New York, 1973, paperback $3.95), by the above-named lady, a great cook.

4 young, dark green zucchini (6 to 7 inches long)
1 green bell pepper
3 medium onions
2 large garlic cloves
4 tablespoons butter
salt
freshly ground white pepper
2 tablespoons fresh thyme, chopped (skip this if the fresh herb is unavailable)
6 cups chicken broth
1 cup heavy cream
fresh chives or parsley, minced

Slice 3 zucchini, green pepper and onions. Mince the garlic. Sauté the vegetables in 3 tablespoons of the butter over very low heat in a heavy pot. Cook, stirring often, about 10 minutes or until the vegetables are tender but have not browned. Add salt and pepper to taste and thyme if available. Stir in the chicken broth and simmer, uncovered, for 15 minutes. Meanwhile, thinly slice (do not peel) the remaining zucchini and sauté it briefly in 1 tablespoon butter until barely tender and still bright green. This should take about 3 minutes—stir and watch closely that it doesn't overcook and go mushy. Immediately turn the sliced vegetable out onto a china plate to cool quickly. Reserve. Cool the soup slightly and purée it in a blender (or a food mill). Stir in the cream and the sliced cooked zucchini. Adjust the seasoning—the soup should be rather highly seasoned as chilling vitiates flavors. Chill (covered) for 24 hours and serve with a scattering of fresh herbs (chives or parsley).

BAKED ZUCCHINI AND EGGS
FOR LUNCH OR SUPPER

6-8 servings

The secret of this dish is that the zucchini must be squeezed free of as much of their moisture as possible so that the finished dish won't be watery. It may be served hot or lukewarm but never chilled. Serve with ham and tomato salad.

7 or 8 large zucchini squash
salt
¼ cup olive oil
4 tablespoons butter
1 large onion, thinly sliced
½ cup plain yoghurt or 3 slices white bread, crusts removed, soaked in milk

4 eggs, well beaten
⅓ cup grated Parmesan cheese
½ cup minced parsley sprigs
3 tablespoons minced fresh marjoram or 2 teaspoons dried marjoram
freshly ground pepper
½ cup fine dry bread crumbs

Wash the zucchini and cut off the ends. Cut them into quarters lengthwise. If the quarters are very large, cut them into halves. Scoop out most of the seeds with a knife. Cut the strips into ¾-inch pieces. Spread out a clean kitchen towel and put the zucchini pieces on it. Sprinkle them with salt, but not heavily. Tie the four ends of the kitchen towel together and hang it over the sink or put it into a colander. Let stand for about 30 minutes. The zucchini will start losing their moisture. Squeeze and twist the towel to extract as much moisture as possible; you will be surprised how much there is. In a large deep frying pan, heat the olive oil and 2 tablespoons of the butter. Cook the onion in it until it is barely golden. Add the zucchini and cook uncovered over medium heat, and stirring frequently, for 10 minutes. Cool. Stir in the yoghurt or the bread and mix well. (If you are using bread, mash it but do not squeeze it.) Stir in the eggs, Parmesan cheese, parsley and marjoram. Check the seasoning and, if necessary, add a little salt and pepper. Blend the mixture thoroughly. Lightly grease a 12-inch baking dish with olive oil and coat it with fine dry bread crumbs. Turn the vegetable mixture into the baking dish. Sprinkle more bread crumbs over the top and dot with the remaining 2 tablespoons butter. Bake in a preheated moderate oven (350° F) for about 30 minutes or until set. Serve sliced.

ZUCCHINI OMELET

3 servings

6 eggs
¼ cup minced parsley
2 tablespoons minced fresh
basil or 2 teaspoons dried
basil
salt

freshly ground pepper
2 tablespoons olive oil
3 medium zucchini, trimmed
and thinly sliced (do not peel
if young)

Beat together the eggs, parsley, basil, salt and pepper. Heat the oil in a frying pan. Add the zucchini. Cook over high heat, stirring with a fork, for 2 or 3 minutes or until the zucchini is golden but still crisp. Lower the heat. Add the eggs; cover all the zucchini. Cook over low heat for 5 minutes or until the bottom is set and browned. Turn the omelet over on a plate the size of the frying pan and slip back. Cook for 2 or 3 more minutes or until set and browned. Cut into wedges and serve.

ZUCCHINI AND TOMATO CASSEROLE

6 servings

¼ cup olive oil
1 small onion, minced
1 garlic clove, minced
4 large zucchini, cut into ¼-
inch slices
2 tablespoons minced fresh
basil leaves or 2 teaspoons
dried basil

½ cup freshly grated Parmesan
cheese
4 large tomatoes, peeled and
sliced
salt
freshly ground pepper
½ cup fine dry bread crumbs
2 tablespoons melted butter

Heat the olive oil in a frying pan. Cook the onion and garlic in it, stirring constantly, for about 3 or 4 minutes or until the onion is soft. Add the zucchini. Cook over medium heat, stirring constantly with a fork, for about 3 to 5 minutes, or until the zucchini are turning golden but are still firm. Place a layer of zucchini into a buttered

1½-quart baking dish. Sprinkle each layer with a little of the basil and the Parmesan cheese. Top with a layer of tomatoes and sprinkle these with a little salt and pepper. Repeat the process. Combine the bread crumbs and the melted butter and sprinkle over the vegetables. Bake without a cover in a preheated moderate oven (350° F) for about 20 minutes or until golden brown.

STUFFED ZUCCHINI

6 servings

You need very large zucchini for this. Serve hot or lukewarm.

1 pound ground beef or lamb
1 large onion, grated
¼ cup raw long-grain rice
½ cup tomato juice
¼ cup minced dillweed
salt

freshly ground pepper
6 large zucchini (about 8-9 inches long)
3 tablespoons butter
1½ cups chicken bouillon
lemon wedges

Combine the meat, onion, rice, tomato juice, dillweed, salt and pepper to taste in a bowl. Mix well. Scrape and wash the zucchini. Cut off the stem end, scoop it out a little and reserve. With an apple corer or a sharp knife, scoop out the zucchini leaving an ⅓-inch shell. Throw away the scooped out pulp. Fill each zucchini with a little of the meat mixture, pushing it down with the handle of a spoon. When full, cover with the stem end. Place a rack on the bottom of a heavy saucepan. Arrange the zucchini side by side on the rack. If any filling is left, shape it into small balls and place them on top of the zucchini or between them. Dot with the butter and pour the bouillon around the vegetables. Cover with waxed paper or aluminum foil. Place a plate on top of the zucchini to weigh it down during cooking. Cover and cook over medium heat for about 1 hour or until the zucchini are tender. Check occasionally for moisture; if necessary, add a little more bouillon. Transfer to a serving dish and pour the pan juices over the vegetables. Serve with lemon wedges.

COLD MARINATED ZUCCHINI

6 servings

8 medium zucchini about 5
  inches long
olive oil for frying
1 cup mild vinegar
½ cup olive oil
1 garlic clove, mashed
2 tablespoons minced fresh
  basil or 1 teaspoon dried
  basil

salt
freshly ground pepper
salad greens
4 tablespoons minced parsley

Trim the zucchini and scrape them lightly with a knife to remove any waxy coating. Wash and dry them. Cut the zucchini into ¾-inch slices. Heat about ¼ inch olive oil in a heavy frying pan until the oil is hazy. Carefully fry a few zucchini slices at a time in the oil for about 2 minutes on each side, turning once. The zucchini should be golden but still crisp. Drain on paper towels and cool. In a small saucepan, combine the vinegar, olive oil, garlic, basil, salt and pepper. Simmer over medium heat for 5 minutes. Cool to lukewarm. Meantime, line a salad bowl with salad greens. Pile the fried zucchini in orderly rows on the greens. Pour the marinade over the zucchini and sprinkle with the parsley. Serve immediately.

If this dish is to be refrigerated instead of served at once, put the fried zucchini carefully into a bowl, pour the marinade over them and refrigerate. At serving time, pour off any excess marinade and arrange zucchini on salad greens; sprinkle with parsley.

Further Reading

AMERICAN HERITAGE EDITORS and HELEN MCCULLY ASSOCIATES. *The American Heritage Cookbook*. New York: McGraw-Hill, 1969.

AMERICANA EDITORS. *The Encyclopedia Americana*. New York: Grolier, Inc., 1975.

ARESTY, ESTHER B. *The Delectable Past*. New York: Simon & Schuster, 1964.

BAILEY, LIBERTY H. *The Standard Cyclopedia of Horticulture*. 3 vols. New York: Macmillan, 1935.

BROTHWELL, DON and PATRICIA. *Food in Antiquity*. New York: Praeger, 1969.

CAMP, WENDELL H.; VICTOR R. BOSWELL; and JOHN R. MAGNESS. *The World in Your Garden*. Washington, D.C.: National Geographic Society, 1957.

CLAIR, COLIN. *Kitchen and Table: A Bedside History of Eating in the Western World*. New York: Abelard-Schuman, 1965.

———. *Of Herbs and Spices*. New York: Aberlard-Schuman, 1961.

DRUMMOND, SIR JACK CECIL, and ANNE WILBRAHAM. *Englishman's Food*. London: Jonathan Cape, 1958.

ENCYCLOPÆDIA BRITANNICA EDITORS. *The Encyclopædia Britannica*. 15th ed. Chicago: Encyclopædia Britannica, 1973.

FERNALD, MERRITT; *et al*. *Edible Wild Plants of Eastern North America*. New York: Harper & Row, 1958.

GIBBONS, EUELL. *Stalking Library: Stalking the Wild Asparagus, Stalking the Blue-Eyed Scallop, Stalking the Healthful Herbs.* New York: David McKay, 1975.

GRIMM, WILLIAM. *Indian Harvests.* New York: McGraw-Hill, 1974.

HARRISON, S. G. *The Oxford Book of Food Plants.* New York: Oxford University Press, 1969.

HATFIELD, AUDREY W. *Pleasure of Herbs.* New York: St. Martin's Press, 1964.

HAWKS, ALEX D. *A World of Vegetable Cookery.* New York: Simon & Schuster, 1968.

HILL, ALBERT F. *Economic Botany.* New York: McGraw-Hill, 1952.

HORIZON EDITORS. *Horizon Cookbook.* New York: McGraw-Hill, 1971.

JANICK, JULES, ed. *Plant Agriculture.* Readings from *Scientific American.* San Francisco: W. H. Freeman, 1970.

JENSEN, LLOYD. *Man's Food.* Champaign: Garrard Press, 1953.

LEHNER, ERNST and JOHANNA. *Folk-lore and Odysseys of Food and Medicinal Plants.* New York: Farrar, Straus & Giroux, 1973.

LEYEL, HILDA. *Cinquefoil; Herbs to Quicken the Five Senses.* London: Faber & Faber, 1957.

LOVELOCK, YANN. *The Vegetable Book: An Unnatural History.* New York: St. Martin's Press, 1973.

MONTAGNÉ, PROSPER. *Larousse Gastronomique: The Encyclopedia of Food, Wine & Cookery.* New York: Crown, 1961.

MORISON, SAMUEL ELIOT. *Samuel De Champlain.* Boston: Little, Brown, 1972.

PULLAR, PHILIPPA. *Consuming Passions.* Boston: Little, Brown, 1974.

PYKE, MAGNUS. *Food and Society.* Levittown, New York: Transatlantic, 1970.

RENNER, H.D. *The Origin of Food Habits.* London: Faber & Faber, 1944.

RHIND, WILLIAM. *History of the Vegetable Kingdom.* London: Blackie & Son, 1868.

TANNAHILL, REAY. *Food in History.* New York: Stein & Day, 1974.

TAYLOR, NORMAN. *Encyclopedia of Gardening.* revised ed. Boston: Houghton Mifflin: 1961.

WEATHERWAX, PAUL. *Indian Corn in Old America.* New York: McGraw-Hill, 1954.

WYMAN, DONALD. *Wyman's Gardening Encyclopedia.* New York: Macmillan, 1971.

Index

(Figures in bold-faced type indicate main entry)

O

P

T

V

W

Y

Z